The Subject of Anthropology

The Subject of Anthropology

Gender, Symbolism and Psychoanalysis

Henrietta L. Moore

polity

First published in 2007 by Polity Press
Reprinted in 2008

Polity Press
65 Bridge Street
Cambridge CB2 1UR, UK

Polity Press
350 Main Street
Malden, MA 02148, USA

ISBN-10: 0-7456-0808-6
ISBN-13: 978-07456-0808-2
ISBN-10: 0-7456-0809-4 (pb)
ISBN-13: 978-07456-0809-9 (pb)

A catalogue record for this book is available from the British Library.

Typeset in 10.5 on 12 pt Palatino
by SNP Best-set Typesetter Ltd, Hong Kong
Printed and bound in the United States by Odyssey Press Inc., Gonic, New Hampshire

For further information on Polity, visit our website: www.polity.co.uk

For
Marilyn Strathern

Contents

Acknowledgements

The Economic and Research Council of the UK generously funded the project on which this book is based, 'Gender and Symbolism: New Theoretical Approaches', from 1 January 1998 to 31 December 2000, grant number R000237794. I am very grateful for their support.

This book has been a long time in the making, perhaps because I have always envisioned it as the third and last in a series of works on gender beginning with *Feminism and Anthropology* and continuing with *A Passion for Difference*. In consequence, my intellectual and personal debts are many and of a very profound and deep-seated character. I can only apologize in advance to friends and colleagues who recognize their thoughts in mine and yet feel that I have not traced our mutual genealogies in ways that reflect the depth and length of our exchanges. They know how much I owe them. I would like to thank also Nicholas Casarini and François Gemenne for their help with library research and sources, and Geraldine Miric for the kind of practical support that is itself a gift.

My thinking, as it has evolved over many years, owes a particular debt to the writings of Melford Spiro, Bernard Juillerat and Marilyn Strathern. The influences of their brilliant, measured, yet incisive intellects may not be evinced here as much as they should, but I nonetheless offer my sincere appreciation. They opened the doors through which I have been able to walk.

My understanding of psychoanalytic theory has developed out of long conversations and interactions with two outstanding practitioners of this art, Renata Salecl and Darian Leader. My disagreements with them have always proved tremendously productive and enjoyable. I have been fortunate to have had the friendship and intellectual support of David Held, Kriti Kapila, Nicholas Thomas, Christina Toren, Todd Sanders and Megan Vaughan during the time this book was being conceived and written. They have always set the pace, and I do my best to keep step. It would probably never have been written at all without the encouragement and unstinting support of John Thompson.

1

Body, Mind and World

Symbolism must make its appearance with the earliest appearance of human culture. It is in essence that modification of the human organism which allows it to transform the physiological drive into a cultural value.

Malinowski, 1939: 955

Symbols in fact envelop the life of man in a network so total that they join together, before he comes into the world, those who are going to engender him 'by flesh and blood'; so total that they bring to his birth, along with the gifts of the stars, if not with the gifts of the fairies, the shape of his destiny; so total that they give the words that will make him faithful or renegade, the law of the acts that will follow him right to the very place where he *is* not yet and even beyond his death; and so total that through them his end finds its meaning in the last judgement, where the Word absolves his being or condemns it.

Lacan, 1977: 68

This book is about how we come to be sexed beings, and how in that process we also become makers and users of symbols. The crux of this enquiry is the complex relationship between body, mind and world. Anthropology and psychoanalysis address themselves to the complexity of this relation, and while they have often proceeded in parallel rather than in concert, they share an abiding concern with culture and with symbolism. The puzzle for both is how does the social come about? – how do humans acquire culture? The idea that civilization depends on the control of instincts was an old one even in Freud's day, but he developed it into a theory which linked the psyche to the social, arguing that human social life is only possible if individuals restrict their possibilities of satisfaction, relinquish something (1985a [1929/30]; 1985b [1927]). Freud made extensive use of anthropological data in his writings, and his interest began a process of borrowing and lending that has continued to this day (Wallace, 1983).

Relations between anthropology and psychoanalysis are frequently portrayed as turbulent, but the image of dislike and suspicion that pervades their relations is belied by the huge volume of psychoanalytically inspired work in anthropology,[1] and the great number of psychoanalysts intrigued by anthropological data. What seduced earlier generations of anthropologists was Freud's insight that culture was the product of the repression of incestuous sexuality. In the first decades of the twentieth century, evolutionary thinking was giving way to questions about the relationship between instinct and social rule, between the repressed passions and the forces of law and morality. Freud's view of the relationship between ontogeny and phylogeny via a primal parricide intrigued a generation of anthropologists in Europe and the USA who were fascinated by the origins of culture and of cultural difference. Durkheim's influential work on collective representations found a particular connection with Freud's interpretation of religion as the outcome of oedipal conflict, of the relinquishing of desire and identification with the father. What these two theories shared in their different ways was a concern with the relationship of the individual psyche to the 'collective mind', as well as a question about how to account for continuity in the mental life of successive generations: in other words, how does culture get reproduced?[2] A generation of anthropologists built on these ideas and formulated a view of culture as a collective fantasy projected into the external world in response to each person's need to control their anxieties (e.g. Devereux, 1967; 1978; 1980; La Barre, 1954; 1978; Roheim, 1950a; 1971). In accounts of this kind, myth, ritual, religion, joking, folktales and other aspects of culture are treated as defence mechanisms against anxieties (e.g. Kilborne, 1981; Levine, 1992; Spiro, 1987). Many anthropologists have sought ways to link cultural symbolism to unconscious fantasy, arguing that while culture is the product of individual unconscious fantasy, it is also the means through which individuals organize their own fantasies and internal worlds (e.g. Crapanzano, 1980; Hook, 1979b; Obeyesekere, 1981; Turner, 1967; Spiro, 1982; 1987). The idea that individuals use cultural symbols, myths and rituals to convey and manage their personal symbols and psychic processes is a dominant feature of much contemporary work in psychoanalytic anthropology (e.g. Blum et al. 1988; Hook, 1979b; Kracke, 1987a; Obeyesekere, 1990; Paul, 1982).

While psychoanalytic anthropology has never been a term of great specificity, living in an ill-defined cognate relation with, among other things, cultural psychology, ethnopsychoanalysis, ethnopsychiatry and cross-cultural psychology, it has, as a sub-field within anthropology, treated a number of recurrent subjects and themes. These have included the study of dreams, ego and person-ality formation, child-rearing practices, trauma and cultural sym-bolism, theories of mind, the origins of religion, interpretation and the value of psychoanalysis for fieldwork, sexuality and sexual behaviour, and psychodynamic understandings of social behav-iour.[3] Underlying all this work is a strong and abiding interest in cross-cultural comparison: the perennial question of what it is that all cultures share. This question is most evident in the work on sex-uality and kinship, on how incestuous desires are socialized. The main discussion in this context continues to focus on the signifi-cance of the Oedipus complex, and the broader question that lies behind it of the role of fathers as opposed to mothers, and the sig-nificance of wider kin networks (see chapter 7). Most psychoana-lytically inspired analyses of anthropological data continue to draw directly on Freud, object relations theory and/or ego psychology, and there is curiously still very little work that is inspired by Lacan's re-reading of Freud.[4] In this book, I set out to develop a new model for the relationship between anthropology and psycho-analysis which draws to varying degrees on different aspects of these psychoanalytic traditions. It takes as its starting point the question of how we become sexed beings and the consequence this has for an understanding of self, culture and power. In consequence, I do not embrace one or other psychoanalytic school to the exclu-sion of all others. My aim is to subject their theoretical formulations to a series of 'ethnographic' readings, as a way of driving forward theoretical advancements in the analysis of gender (see below).

In the last ten years, a new trend has emerged of anthropologists and psychoanalysts working closely together on interpreting anthropological materials. This builds on an older tradition of anthropologists, psychoanalysts, psychologists and psychiatrists working together in the field, of which perhaps the work done under the leadership of Henri Collomb at the Fann Hospital in

Dakar, Senegal is the most famous (Collignon, 1978). These new forms of sustained intellectual engagements have produced break-throughs in thinking because they have introduced anthropologists to recent developments in psychoanalytic thinking which have allowed some of the old antinomies in the debate to be disassembled or transcended.[5] This does not, however, mean that anthropologists and psychoanalysts are in agreement; the evidence from these encounters suggest that they are often painfully divided over key issues, and what produces the most difficulty is the tension between the schematizing tendencies of psychoanalytic theorizing and the mass of cultural complexity to which the anthropologists feel deeply committed.

This harks back to older disagreements, since the main difficulty with psychoanalysis for many anthropologists has been the application of a universal model for the relationship between psychosexual structures and social organization, coupled with an insensitivity to cultural variation (Juillerat, 2001: ch. 1).[6] The commitment to cultural variability in a discipline dedicated to studying cultural differences is a very particular one. Interestingly, this debate is reprised in a very similar form in the discussions between feminism and psychoanalysis (see chapters 4, 5 and 6), where critics find it hard to square a universal and invariant model of sexual difference with the lived realities of gendered lives. Feminism has criticized psychoanalysis for providing a theoretical model that describes and reinforces patriarchy and heterosexuality rather than providing alternative accounts of the construction of femininity (e.g. Braidotti, 1997; 2002; Braidotti and Butler, 1984; Butler, 2004; 1995a; Cornell, 1997; Felski, 1997; Frye, 1996). I address this problem in the chapters that follow in two different ways. First, I critique the way psychoanalysis treats mothers and fathers as self-evident, natural entities. This tendency is anyway quite at odds with the insistence in psychoanalytic theorizing on the fact that sexual difference cannot be reduced to biology, and that the relationship of the child to parental figures is one set up in representation, and thus imaginary in some very important aspects. In this process, I suggest the invariant psychosexual structures of psychoanalysis cannot be treated as if they were contentless, and we therefore need to rethink the relationship between culture and the process of how we become sexed beings (see chapter 7). Secondly, I resituate the problem of universalism as one about the more general dilemma of how to handle history – that is, how to explain the development of the individual in the context of an ongoing social/cultural system which itself changes over time and is subject to the workings of power. I suggest that the question 'Is the Oedipus complex universal?' is no longer one to which we should be seeking an answer, but rather we need to ask, 'How do we become sexed beings?' The difference between these questions may not at first sight seem very great, but it produces a seismic shift in thinking that allows new questions to be addressed in anthropology. In addition, psychoanalytic theory has now refigured its understanding of oedipal conflict in such a way (see chapter 4) that we can move outside the straitjacket provided by the older formulation of the Oedipus complex to ask new questions about the relationship between gendered selves and social relationships.

The anthropological commitment to cultural variation takes an additional form in relation to psychoanalysis and that is the worry that psychoanalytic models are culturally specific, and thus interpretation and analysis which use them must be inappropriately applying a western model to other cultures (e.g. Ingham, 1992; Kirschner, 1992; Spain, 1992). Moving away from an invariant oedipal model towards a specific enquiry about how individuals become sexed beings in a particular cultural context answers part of the problem. Once again, feminist theorists have raised a similar set of concerns, arguing that Freud and Lacan employed unexamined pre-theoretical assumptions in their theorizing, particularly in regard to the relationship between sexed identity and object (love) choice, the determination of heterosexuality as normal sexuality, the role of the father, the characterization of the mother as passive and the assumption that femininity is constructed around the lack of the male organ. All of these assumptions have been rigorously challenged and in chapters 4, 5 and 6 I explore how developments in feminist theorizing have cleared the way for a reworking of psychoanalytic theory for anthropological purposes.

The argument in this book does not rest on the validity or non-validity of imposing a universal model onto all the cultures of the world. Rather, it develops a specific ethics of engagement by placing psychoanalytic, anthropological and feminist theories alongside other cultural theories of the origins of society, the nature of sexuality and gender identity, and the relationship between the social and the symbolic. In laying anthropological, psychoanalytic and feminist theories of gender, subjectivity, representation and power alongside ethnographic material I approach the anxiety about applying a western model to other cultures from a different perspective, attempting from the outset to provide an 'ethnographic' reading of anthropological, psychoanalytic and feminist theories alongside readings of specific ethnographic materials. The basis for this 'dual set' of ethnographic readings is that both the so-called 'western' theories and the ethnographic materials I discuss are concerned with particular ways of imagining and delineating a cartography of the relation of self to society. In the process, they work over a series of themes about the nature of representation, the way bodies are marked by sexual difference, the problems and specifics of gender identity and the way individuals are connected to each other and to social laws and institutions. My aim is to treat all these accounts as 'theories', and to view them as a set of ruminations on the interconnected problems of bodies, genders, power and agency. My purpose is to develop a new ethics of engagement for the analysis of cross-cultural material and to use the fruits of that engagement to drive thinking forward with regard to the relationship between culture and gender. Paradoxically, the inspiration for this strategy is derived in part from Lévi-Strauss. He refers to *The Jealous Potter* as 'a book in which I am trying to show that certain notions credited to psychoanalysis . . . were already inherent in mythic thought', arguing in relation to his analysis of North and South American myths that 'they were far ahead of us when it comes to a good many of the notions that did not find expression in the western world until Freud' (Lévi-Strauss, 1988: 131). Lévi-Strauss does not mean that these notions did not exist in the West prior to Freud, but that they did not find systematic expression in the form of a theory.[7] My intention in this book is to read various 'theories' against each other, examining their differences and similarities, tracing the effects of their differing assumptions about the relationships of self to society, and of psyche to culture. My ultimate aim is to develop a theory of how we become sexed beings, and to show how this is at the core of our capacity for representation and symbolism.

The reproduction of culture

In the first stages of its life, an infant lives in close symbiotic relationship with its mother or primary carer, and has no experiential divisions between self and other, self and external reality, subject and object.[8] It is now generally agreed that from their earliest days – prior to the acquisition of language and the cultural conceptions of the world it makes possible – children develop representations, fantasies, as a result of their experiences of their bodies and their needs, as well as their interactions with parents and significant others. In this process, instincts and needs become attached to images and representations, and through this set of dynamic inter-actions the unconscious is formed. Children have an active mental life from birth, but one that has to work in concert with developing neurological competences. These early experiences all happen prior to object constancy, language competence and reality testing, and they are often accompanied by intense affect. Freud's insight was to see that even the unconscious had to be formed out of the child's fantasized relation to its own body, to its parents and significant others, and to the world. The result is that the child actively con-structs objects (including other people) and symbols through engagement with the world, and thereby develops psychological capacities but in relation to a specific social and physical environ-ment. The formation of the unconscious is the condition for sub-jectivity, for consciousness and for social relations through the mechanism of representations. It is through the capacity for repre-sentation that the child becomes anchored in and attached to a social world, and slowly begins to recognize that it is separate from the mother. Separation is a condition of selfhood, but this is a process that takes place in and through social interaction. Over time, the child is able to make a firmer distinction between internal and external worlds, and to engage in social relations with others, but the very young child's fantasies of parents and others are reified, and can be experienced as objects and/or agents. Since the boundary between inner and outer worlds is porous, these objects can be experienced both as internal to the child and/or as external – that is, existing in the world. As the child develops physically and neurologically, it acquires the capacity to recognize objects (includ-ing other people) in a stable way, to link language to representa-tions and to distinguish its internal world from the external world (reality testing). As object constancy, language competence and reality testing develop, the child's earliest fantasies are relin-quished, in the sense that they become repressed and form part of the unconscious. Repression is what opens children to the wider world; without it they would be caught in their own fantasized internal world.

The relationships young children have to their parents and others are set up in representation and in that sense are fantasized. Con-temporary views of psychoanalysis emphasize the importance of both parents in the development of a sense of self: both parents are sources of identification from the earliest stages in life and both provide support and encouragement for differentiation (see chapter 4). Children are born anatomically sexed, but from the time of birth, caregivers encourage development in ways they think appropriate to the child's gender, so that anatomy and social relations, along with physiology and neurological development, provide the matrix for the earliest representations of gender. Clinical data shows that between 18 and 24 months children become aware of the differences between the sexes, but both boys and girls believe at this stage that they and others have both masculine and feminine attributes and capacities. The recognition of differences between the sexes is in tension with this 'over-inclusive position', and entails the child recognizing and accepting the loss of certain masculine and feminine attributes/capacities they had assumed were theirs. These lost aspects of masculinity and femininity are ascribed meanings which become attached to body parts. But the meanings do not follow from the body parts themselves (penis, vagina); they are not based on the physical sex, but rather are meanings that the child attaches to her/his body and that of others. Thus, the body is shaped by ideas about masculinity and femininity and not the other way around (see chapters 4 and 5).

What many theorists now emphasize in different ways – neurologists, psychoanalysts, philosophers – is that for humans the world is a libidinal object, because part of being human is involved in taking an interest in the world, assigning it value, interacting with it and all that it contains.[9] This has consequences for how we develop as biological and as cultural beings. Psychoanalysis develops this perspective in relation to the body ego, the idea that the ego only emerges in the world as embodied. As the child develops, the map the ego forms of the body allows for no distinction between material and representation, between the physical and the psychical body, because there is no lived phenomenological body prior to a psychic investment in the parts and surfaces of the body. The body ego which provides the grounds for an emerging sense of self is produced by, and only grows in relation to, its interactions with the external world, and these take place via the perceptual surface of the body and in the brain. There is an ongoing discussion about whether Freud's body ego is supported by recent developments in neurological science (e.g. Morin and Thibierge, 2004). Obviously, Freud did not have access to what scientists now know, but the available evidence suggests that consciousness is related to the development of an integrated representation of the body.[10] What

Freud and many subsequent psychoanalytic theorists have emphasized is that for any body part to come into psychic experience,
the ego must form a fantasy relation to it, that is one set up in
representation.

The way we develop our capacity for representation, and the fact
that we do so only as a psychosomatic organism, has consequences
for the way we think about the relationship between culture and
individuals. Recent work in anthropology has provided a formida-
ble critique of the old socialization thesis, the idea that culture is
either learned by or somehow imposed on an undifferentiated and
pre-existing biological organism – the idea that cultural meanings
are somehow 'dumped into the minds of children' (Robertson, 1996:
599). The contemporary view is much more in keeping with recent
work in neurobiology, and argues that rather than seeing culture as
something added to a biological entity or viewing that entity as
having pre-given (often neural) modular properties, we should see
culture and biology as ontogenetically related (Ingold, 1991). From
this perspective, humans are not biological entities with the capacity to acquire culture, but biologically cultural beings who develop
as individuals through intersubjective relations with cultural others
in a specific environment (Toren, 1999; Roberston, 1996). Biology
and culture develop as an ensemble. The human mind and body
develop as each new child enters the world, but they do so in the
context of a socially constituted, interactive world.

This is part of the answer to the question of how culture gets
reproduced across the generations. But, it also signals a shift in
the way anthropologists are beginning to think about culture. We
can demonstrate this argument by asking how the subject comes
to know, understand and operate the cultural system he or she is
part of. This is an area in which anthropology has been borrowing
from developmental psychologists and from cognitive scientists
(Bloch, 1989; 1998; Toren, 1983; 1990; 1999). Traditionally, anthropologists have seen cultural systems of cognition as forms of collective representation that precede the individual in historical time
and into which the individual is born. In this sense, they
must be non-individual, and when allied to a series of positions that
see culture as determining, they become all-encompassing. The
result is a kind of merging of the notions of culture, cognition,
symbolism and ideology, and the solidification of the idea that
culture and the ability to think about culture are inherited from
history (Bloch, 1989: ch. 5). Anthropologists drawing on the work
of modern developmental psychology, on the other hand, have

emphasized that the child forms concepts as a consequence of a pre-linguistic interaction with their environment which includes their body, other humans and the physical environment. These concepts later come to be associated with words as the child develops, but the important point is that words are matched to concepts rather than the child acquiring concepts by learning words (ibid.: 114). Culture is built up through engagement with a world of objects (things and people), but this environment is not neutral, it is culturally constructed.

Work of this kind stresses that language is not essential for conceptual thought, at least as far as the developing child is concerned. However, we have to acknowledge that while the acquisition of cultural concepts can be pre-linguistic, they are transformed to a significant extent as they enter language, as they become linguistic (Bloch, 1998: ch. 1). Non-linguistic knowledge is an important part of the acquisition of culture, and anthropologists working on knowledge transmission have argued that 'knowing, thinking and understanding are generated in practice' (Lave, 1990: 310). In addition, much of the knowledge we require to act as competent members of a cultural community is non-conscious and generated within a culturally constructed environment (Bourdieu, 1977; 1990; Moore, 1986; 1994: ch. 4). This knowledge is not organized in a linear form as a set of propositions and ideas, but is organized into highly complex integrated networks, the elements of which are connected to each other in a large number of ways, and they are characterized by simultaneous interconnections operating at many different levels. They are partly linguistic, but also integrate visual imagery, other sensory cognition, memories, evaluations, intentions, things learned. The information in them can be accessed simultaneously from many different parts of the model (Bloch, 1998: 24–5). These models allow for very rapid responses to situations in social life, and provide a mechanism through which individuals continue to develop in and through interaction with their environment in the broadest sense over time.

In this discussion of the development of the young child and the acquisition of culture from a variety of different perspectives, I have tried to show that from the earliest days of its life, and before language, the child enters the world only through the capacity for representation on which the development of the ego depends. This ego is a body ego in which physical and cultural development are an ensemble. The psychoanalytic theories underlying this position are discussed further in chapter 6. The ways in which a child learns lan-

guage and acquires culture follow this early basic pattern of engagement with the world. Culture does not come from without, and we
cannot imagine it as being either simply learned or imposed,
although in specific situations in social life both those things can
and do happen. What anthropological theories ignore – except
of course for those drawn from psychoanalysis – is the role of
fantasy. Because of the biological dependency of the child and
because of their developing neurological and perceptual abilities,
needs and affect become attached to their earliest images and
representations. These representations primarily concern their
body, and the bodies and body parts of their carers. They are therefore bound up from birth with the sensations, experiences and
emotions of interacting with a world peopled by parents and
others who already have a fantasized, intellectualized and practical
relation to their own bodies, and to the bodies of others, including
the child. These representations of bodies and body parts are
not, as the clinical data shows, gendered by the child themselves
at this early stage – that is, in the sense of conforming to an
existing cultural model of gender. But, neither are they a matter
of a straightforward relation to a pre-existing biological sex, because
there is no sexed body outside the representations within which it
emerges. The body is experienced and shaped by masculinity
and femininity, and not the other way round. Gender then is at
the very root of our capacity for representation because it is
inextricably tied to the basis for the emergence of the body ego and
subsequently the self.

Symbolism, fantasy and culture

So what do we do with these very early representations of bodies
and body parts? What role do they play in later life, and how do
they connect with the models of gender that anthropologists habitually study? To answer these questions, we need to return initially
to discussions in anthropology about the relationship between fantasies and cultural symbols, or, as they are sometimes termed,
private and public symbols. Much of the work in anthropology in
this area focuses on myth and religion, and it has long been held
that whatever the public understanding of the symbols involved
might be, individuals invest them with private, often unconscious
meanings (e.g. Hook, 1979b; Spiro, 1982b; Obeyesekere, 1981; 1990).
Thus, we cannot understand symbolism unless we attend to its

affective and motivational properties, both conscious and unconscious. Melford Spiro has argued that dreams, fantasies and other
linked material are of a type where ideas and thoughts are typically
represented by visual signs, whose logic is that of condensation,
substitution, combination, part for whole. This he links to Freud's
primary process, while other realms of life, such as the technologi-
cal and the economic, are characterized by secondary process thinking which employs verbal signs operating under conventional rules
(Spiro, 1982b: 52–3). Spiro's position is one used by many anthropologists. It does not imply that primary process thinking should
be exclusively equated with unconscious mental activity or that
symbolization does not occur in conscious thinking; it clearly does
(Hook, 1979b: 278). What it does imply is that secondary process
thinking draws on and is dependent on primary process. Spiro
argues that prior to the acquisition of language children develop
what he calls 'socially-constituted conceptions' as a result of transactions with parents and carers, and that these images of powerful
beings from the family world are 'highly similar' to the 'culturally-
constituted' images individuals later form of the powerful beings
inhabiting the mythico-religious world (1982b: 59–61). One does not
have to agree with Spiro's claim that 'religious figures' are modelled
on 'family figures' to recognize the deeper import of his argument,
which is that one cannot have culture without a capacity for representation, and that anthropology needs to give an account of how
representation arises.[11]

   Bernard Juillerat clarifies this further by pointing out that as the
child moves into the world his or her fantasies undergo a transformation as a consequence, as noted earlier, of improved reality
testing and repression, but when the child encounters the evolved
symbols, cosmologies and narratives of culture, he or she 'finds
there (like a sort of reminiscence), reworked and multiplied, certain
of his [sic] own unconscious representations which he in turn adds
into the culture as if by a process of sedimentation' (Juillerat, 2001:
68). Citing Guy Rosolato (1992), Juillerat argues that there is an
exchange of representations between the subject and culture, where
cultural images work back to structure our internal worlds. But,
Juillerat thinks this account has limitations because it does not
address those cases, like the Melanesian material he is familiar with,
where cultural systems make evident use of representations concerning sexuality, reproduction, descent and death. In these situations, public symbols are closely linked to private fantasies, but we
cannot understand how this works if we focus at the level of the

individual. Juillerat's point is that the fantasies that are worked over in cultural productions often relate to a kind of 'generic subject', and these fantasies are accepted and well understood by society at large. He cites the case of oedipal conflicts which appear in myth and ritual in a cultural form relating to the emergence of the male subject, and clearly these representations must have an impact on the subject because the primary mechanisms organizing his subjectivity are reflected at the collective level (Juillerat, 2001: 69). But he argues that it is necessary to distinguish between the oedipal conflicts as they are experienced by particular individuals in the context of their own family, and the way in which they are elaborated in cultural symbols and cultural productions, such as myth and ritual (ibid.: 72). These two things should not be collapsed into each other, and in the following chapters I am concerned with the latter rather than the former.

The intellectual position I develop in this book owes much both to Spiro and Juillerat. I agree with Spiro that the very earliest representations within which the body ego emerges are social; that is, they are produced through and in consequence of interaction with a culturally constituted environment inhabited by social actors. These fantasies are thus both individual and social from the beginning. These ideas are in concert with those of relational psychoanalysts, and, drawing on the work of Irene Fast and others, I go on in chapters 5 and 6 to argue that we become sexed beings in a social context and environment which is already gendered. Thus, contrary to the major tenets of psychoanalysis, gender is the ground for the emergence of sexual difference. There may be universal conditions for subjecthood, involving identification and differentiation, but these conditions only have purchase, only become effective in the context of an engagement with a social/cultural world. They cannot be effective if they are contentless. To become a sexed being is to be marked by sexual difference, to recognize the limits of sexual difference, to struggle with the fact that masculinity and femininity do not map easily onto male and female bodies. No one becomes a sexed being in a vacuum.

However, what both Spiro and Juillerat suggest is that we cannot simply see cultural products as a reflection of infantile fantasies, nor can they be simplistically analysed as the return of the repressed. Something far more interesting is going on, because cultures take these earliest images and use them to create through multiplication, elaboration, reflection and analysis the kind of beautiful, awesome and sometimes terrifying cultural products which anthropologists variously label as myth, ritual, cosmology, and symbolism. This process of production is a complex one because, as these images enter language, become subject to rationalization, are enacted and performed in ritual, dance, song and myth, they undergo a profound transformation. Not all this transformation is intended: some of it is unconscious, some of it arises in praxis and does not enter language, some of it is the product of highly developed ratiocination. We cannot predict how this process of transformation will proceed, but as social scientists we can trace it and its effects. One important point to note is that cultures and societies vary with regard to the degree that they engage in cultural elaboration and reflection of this kind, as well as the degree to which they make explicit or non-explicit, conscious or unconscious, use of fantasy material (Obeyesekere, 1990: ch. 3; Bidou et al. 1999: 19–20). What is evident is that these images form part of, and are organized into, the kind of highly complex integrated networks mentioned earlier, where elements are connected to each other simultaneously in a large number of ways, and where fantasy is integrated with visual imagery, language, sensory forms of cognition, comportment, bodily praxis, experience, memories, evaluations, intentions, things learned. Since all this information can be accessed simultaneously from many different parts of the network, it provides a dynamic, highly energetic matrix in which creation and innovation, as well as over-determined sedimentation, can take place.

Juillerat argues that the deployment and sharing of early fantasy material in a cultural context favours the multiplication, development and elaboration of cultural representations (Juillerat, 2001: 108). This is congruent with the arguments made by relational psychoanalytic theorists that the early 'over-inclusive' fantasies of masculinity and femininity provide the basis for creative thinking throughout life. These arguments are discussed further in chapter 4. It is helpful here to make a distinction between imagination and the imaginary. Drawing on Lacan and Castoriadis, I make the case throughout the following chapters that anthropology needs to take the imaginary seriously if it is to provide an account of the relationship of individuals to cultural orders, and if it is to locate that account within the workings of power. Humans have imaginations, they can draw on all their experience, history, sensations, sounds, colours, words and knowledge, etc. to be creative, to produce works of the imagination. Imagination is an ability, a capacity, an orientation in the world. The imaginary, however, is a different notion focusing on fantasy and the workings of the unconscious, and it is connected both to the self's ability to create an internal world and to its capacity for agency. For Lacan, the imaginary is a general term corresponding to a time before the child enters the symbolic order, and becomes marked by sexual difference. A time when the child is in a relationship of symbiotic plenitude with the mother. It also refers to the imaginary relationship the emerging ego/subject has with itself. It is connected to the process whereby the child aged between 6 and 18 months is able to recognize and respond to its image in a mirror. This process provides the child with an illusory sense of wholeness. It is only by identifying and incorporating the image of itself that is already an image of another – either the specular image in the mirror or the image the (m)other has of the child – that the child begins to represent itself to itself. But, the image of a stable subject or 'I' is necessarily illusory because the subject is always other to itself, and identity is ceaselessly disrupted by the workings of the unconscious. This split between the unconscious and the social is, for Lacan, the very condition of subjectivity and of identity. The strengths and weaknesses of this argument for anthropology are discussed further in chapter 3.

The idea that the subject cannot be isomorphic with the social is also central to Castoriadis's account of the imaginary. His concern is to link the unconscious to the self's capacity for agency. He stresses that what he calls the 'radical imaginary' has the capacity to ceaselessly produce images, representations, desires and intentions through its desire for engagement with the world. This originary capacity for figuration, for making representations, is essential to the formation of the psyche, and it is associated with the earliest stages of a child's life. As the individual becomes part of the social world, becomes a social being, they are taken up by the 'social imaginary', that is by the terms and values through which a society represents itself to itself. It is only through acceding to the social imaginary that the subject is brought out of its world of fantasy, but the 'constitution of the social individual does not and cannot abolish the psyche's creativity, its perpetual alteration, the representative flux as the continuous emergence of other representations' (Castoriadis, 1987: 320–1). The continued existence of the radical imaginary, just like the unconscious for Lacan, means that some part of the individual always escapes the dictates of social identity, guarantees that the psyche is never completely captured by the social.

Gender and the post-oedipal

The proposition I am making is that anthropology needs to take account of the imaginary, of the human capacity to produce images, representations and fantasies, if it is to understand how and why culture (as myth, ritual, incantation, symbols, etc.) is produced. Anthropology has for too long assumed that because it has a theory of symbolism, it does not need a theory of the imaginary. Developing a concept of the imaginary requires us to take psychoanalytic theorizing seriously as a way of understanding how the imaginary and the symbolic (culture) are interconnected. Key to this is the issue of gender and its relationship to sexual difference. Both Freud and Lacan saw the Oedipus complex as central to an account of how the psyche is formed, and of how the subject is fashioned through entry into the world of culture. In the traditional model, what the subject has to relinquish is desire for the mother, and through the imposition of the incest taboo, social laws are instituted. This makes the Oedipus complex the defining moment for the imposition of sexual difference and the acquisition of a sexed identity. I discuss the failings of this model, as well as its strengths, in the following chapters, but this very narrow account produces two major difficulties for anthropologists and feminists. First, Freud and Lacan insist that it is the relation to the phallus that determines sexual difference. Lacan goes further, arguing that the phallus is the privileged signifier of the symbolic order. Within this model, the feminine is always configured in terms of the masculine, having or not having the penis (see chapter 5). In response to this, I develop a theory based on my reading of ethnography which argues that while the insertion of the subject into the symbolic order is a necessary one for all subjects, there is no reason to suppose that the process itself is invariant, or that the symbolic order is invariant, or indeed that the process always constitutes sexual difference in a fixed way. In chapters 6 and 8, I provide ethnographic material to demonstrate that the phallus is not always the privileged signifier of the symbolic order, and that even when it is, it is not always the male phallus.[12] I argue that while the processes of representation, separation, identification, differentiation and signification are essential for the emergence and the development of the ego/subject, there are clear reasons to develop a theory that allows for cultural variation both in the formation of the body ego and in the nature of the symbolic order. In short, I argue that while becoming a sexed being is a condition for subjecthood, this is not a culturally invariant process.

Second, I tackle the problem of the impossibility of accounting for the multiple discourses on gender that coexist in all contexts, and the multiple ways in which individuals identify with being a woman or a man, by referring them to an invariant model of sexual difference. Here, I draw on recent work in anthropology to argue that the self is constituted through multiple subject positions. This involves a detailed discussion of the history of the person/ self/subject in anthropology (see chapter 2), and the differences and similarities between these conceptions. Recent discussions of the self have relied on the development of a non-unitary theory of the subject, coupled with a dual focus both on the discursive determination of the self and on the self-styled aspects of subjectivity in any particular context. It is no longer enough to talk loosely about cultural variation in the concept of the self and thereby to imply that the self is somehow simply determined by culture. Following this, I further develop a theory of the subject outlined in my earlier work (Moore, 1994), and argue that anthro- pology needs a theory of the subject rather than a theory of the self because this allows us to focus on the multiple constitution of subjectivity, and on the agency of the subject in that process. Within this framework, a single subject cannot be equated with a single individual. Individuals are multiply constituted subjects who take up multiple subject positions within a range of discourses and social practices. Some of these subject positions will be contradic- tory and conflicting, and individuals constitute their sense of self through several, often mutually contradictory, positions rather than through one singular position (Ewing, 1998; Mahmood, 2005; Moore, 1994).

This opens up the process of subjectification to power and ide- ology which, although they may work to produce these subject positions, cannot determine how individuals will identify with and take up different subject positions at different times. In order to do this, the anthropological subject has to be reunited with the subject of psychoanalysis so as to account for how individuals both iden- tify with and resist subject positions. The key to this problematic is the issue of desire. What a focus on desire does is to draw attention both to what motivates the subject to identify with certain sub- ject positions, and to what escapes discursive formations and hegemonic orders. Ultimately, the self cannot be reduced to a

discursively constituted subject, since desire, fantasy and unconscious motivation cannot be contained completely by discourse.
There is a part of the self that escapes determination by the social.
Thus, we have to recognize that while dominant discourses may
shape a subject's self-perception in a particular context, they do not
determine how the subject will operate in all contexts because of
the workings of desire, fantasy and unconscious motivation (Ewing,
1998: 36).

No one has complete knowledge of themselves or others, thus
fantasy, desire and unconscious motivation are in play alongside
strategy, rationalization and emotion in the process of making and
sustaining a self through identification and/or resistance to multiple subject positions. This process is never one that is complete
or finished; it is never fully realized. The self that emerges is
imaginary, in that it is set up in representations. But, the earliest
representations undergird and interact with later representations.
Contemporary relational psychoanalysis emphasizes this point
through an insistence that both the pre-oedipal and the oedipal are
crucial in the formation of a gendered self, and that the Oedipus
complex cannot be seen as the singular, fixed and defining moment
in the imposition of sexual difference and the acquisition of a gendered identity. Psychoanalytic theory has only recently – primarily
through its engagement with feminism – come to terms with the
contradictory nature of gender identifications and with the idea that
subjects identify with multiple gender positions, some of which
may be contradictory and conflicting. I review these arguments in
chapters 4 and 7, showing how shifts in the way the Oedipus
complex are theorized over time within specific psychoanalytic
traditions have opened up new spaces for anthropological work.
What is evident is that one does not acquire a gender identity by
acquiescing to a single model of masculinity or femininity. Thus
gender identities are not determined by cultural models as some
anthropologists sometimes suggest, nor by a single defining
moment in the acquisition of a sexual identity as psychoanalysts
propose. I use this starting point as the basis to develop a new
theory of gender.

In chapters 6, 7 and 8, I use ethnographic data to show that
multiple models of gender exist within any culture, and that
images and representations from the pre-oedipal period (the
earliest years) of life, which emphasize the relational, fluid and
combinatorial characteristics of masculinity and femininity, coexist
with more rigid, binary understandings of the differences between

the genders characteristic of oedipal resolutions. Following Jessica Benjamin and others, I introduce the notion of the post-oedipal, showing that adult understandings of masculinity and femininity, of what it is to be a gendered individual, make use of both pre-oedipal and oedipal material to develop complex, long-running and highly elaborated ideas about gender. It is important not to lose sight of the fact here, as emphasized earlier, that both pre-oedipal and oedipal representations undergo considerable transformation, both conscious and unconscious, as they are elaborated on in cultural life, but their coexistence in adult life explains why post-oedipal gender identities are able both to recognize and work with the binary and rigid distinctions of gender difference, while at the same time tolerating models of masculinity and femininity that emphasize ambiguity and instability. It also goes a long way in explaining why and how multiple models of gender exist in any context, and why dominant gender models are subverted not just by lived experience, but by culturally expressed and validated alternative discourses on gender. In short, it provides a way of linking sexual difference to gender, and making sense of their relation.

Desire and ideology

To be a gendered individual is to be marked by the effects of power, but not to be wholly determined by them. This means that the self cannot be reduced to a discursively constituted subject, nor simply to one whose resistance to such construction is confined to the conscious and the intentional.[13] The subject does not coincide with herself or with her consciousness, because the subject's relation to itself and to the symbolic order is an imaginary one. Both Freud and Lacan stress that individuals consistently misrepresent and misrecognize themselves as coherent, self-produced and self-identical. Stated baldly in this way, it seems to me that this rather overstates the case, since the individual self's experience of self-continuity, self-awareness and self-identity (see chapter 2) are quite compatible with feelings about non-stability, non-coherence, fragility and unspecified attacks from outside. Nonetheless, their point is that the self is a fictive construction, one that cannot emerge organically, but must be made in the process of becoming a socially sexed being and cannot be conscious of all that makes it. This raises immediate questions about how the self relates to power and to ideology: do certain kinds of societies require certain kinds of subjects? In chapter 3, I discuss the different theories of Žižek and Castoriadis with regard to the production of the subject under determinate historical conditions. What all these theories emphasize in their different ways is that subjects only emerge as a consequence of the way they identify and invest in social values, systems and ideologies.

In chapters 7 and 8, I use ethnographic material to discuss how this process of identification and investment works in specific contexts. I take as my starting point the fact that ritual and myth work over a series of themes that link the origins of human society to the inauguration of sexual difference. Time and again, we see that relations between women and men need to be marked by sexual difference in order for society to be brought into being. The result is an imaginary cartography which links the emergence of the sexed self to the conditions for sociality. At the core of this complex representation is a theme about the desire for a return to the mother, to a time before sexual difference is imposed. This theme is worked over implicitly and explicitly; it is referred to in esoteric interpretations, enacted in performances, and felt as a palpable, but not always articulable orientation to the world. This material has been discussed by a number of anthropologists who refer to 'maternal schemas' and link the desire for the mother to exegesis, both local and anthropological, and to the nature of Melanesian social relations. I re-analyse this material, pointing out that from a psychoanalytic perspective, these societies are not founded on a desire for a return to the mother either in a literal or in a figurative sense, but rather on the structural impossibility of such a return. I show how the cultural materials explicitly work over the idea that the masculine subject emerges as a result of a split from its desired union with the mother, thus the subject depends upon the negation of its own desire for its existence. Consequently, social relations and cultural forms emerge not as something that is built upon a 'maternal schema', but as something that is shaped by the impossibility of desire for the mother. Desire is always socialized in a specific form, but it remains unrealizable; it is not possible to return to the mother, nor, in fact, is it actually desirable to do so, because this would mean non-existence for the subject. Desire is elliptical in its nature, it works by attaching individuals as subjects to its negation or denial, and through that process constitutes both the subject and the social.

In discussing desire, I am not referring to the private desires, sexual or otherwise, of individuals, nor advocating that anthropology should or could have access to them. Instead, I am talking about the way cultures work over the problem of desire, and the way cultural ideologies are built upon the impossibility of the realization of that desire. From a psychoanalytic perspective, desire arises out of the incompleteness of representation, the fact that neither the subject nor the social are ever finished or complete. This makes of desire something that cannot be integrated within the symbolic system, but nonetheless shapes it, in the sense of having a series of structural effects that can be traced and analysed. We can say here, contra Freud, that culture does not repress desire, but rather is the product of its circulations and contradictions. It is the way that the individual is caught up through fantasy in these circulations and contradictions that accounts for their investment in the social, in ideology.

Since the origins of the social are connected to the origins of the gendered subject in the ethnographic material I discuss, sexuality and gender become the terrain of social transformation, they are the location of intense struggles over power, meanings, values and resources. They are the major means through which a society represents itself to itself. It is in thinking about and imaginatively reworking the connections between the origins of the social and the emergence of the sexed subject that these societies reflect and elaborate on the relationship of the imaginary to the symbolic. What is remarkable, particularly with regard to the Melanesian material, is how what we would consider in the West to be part of the unconscious is part of conscious reflection and elaboration. A recurrent theme in this material is the incompleteness and instability of representation itself. In the cases I discuss, social relations are patriarchal and male-dominated, and women are rigorously excluded from male knowledge. Yet, myths, rituals and esoteric knowledge constantly work over the fluid, relational, ambiguous nature of femininity and masculinity, the puzzle of the fact that they do not map easily onto male and female bodies, that body parts do not belong unambiguously to men or women. These images of masculinity and femininity, tied as they are to long-run explanations of the origins of the social, seem to be at odds with the governing principles of patriarchal society. What they draw attention to time and time again is the instability of sexual difference, the fact that representations cannot ultimately be mapped onto the world in a stable and fixed way. Myths, rituals, narratives and cosmologies seem preoccupied with the perplexing problem that cultural representations do not form a single, coherent system, that appearance and being do not match.[14] It is the problem of sexual difference that reveals the failure of signification at the heart of culture, and lets slip why it is that desire for engagement with the world forces us into becoming sexed beings who are driven to become makers and users of symbols.

2

A Genealogy of the Anthropological Subject

[S]ocial thought, owing to the imperative authority that is in it, has an efficacy that individual thoughts never have; by the power which it has over our minds, it can make us see things in whatever light it pleases.

Durkheim, 1971[1912]: 228

Perhaps it is characteristic of man to be always different yet always the same. Perhaps this is what anthropologists have sensed without formulating it, since in moving from one people to another the field-worker always has assumed that there were both psychological and cultural constants to be expected; identifiable emotions such as sorrow and hate, self-awareness and reflective thought, a scheme of moral values, a world view, tools etc.

Hallowell, 1976: 228

This chapter argues that in order to understand the relationship between the individual and society, psyche and culture, anthropology needs a theory of the subject. Such a theory is of paramount importance, as I demonstrate in later chapters, for any attempt to analyse how gendered individuals are marked by the effects of power. One of the key difficulties for a modern anthropology is to find a means to avow and maintain the importance of cultural difference whilst simultaneously acknowledging that culture is not and cannot be wholly determining. This produces awkward and involved epistemological and empirical over-determinations between the limits of negotiation and the limits of determinism. When we talk about the relationship between individuals and their cultures, we face, square on, two tricky questions: what is it that culture determines and how does it determine it? Any anthropologist who works on gender knows full well that gender is performatively and discursively produced, and as such is a cultural product, but understands equally clearly that cultural models are not necessarily a good guide to how individuals live, experience and reflect on being a gendered individual in a specific context. At the root of this difficulty is the way anthropologists have traditionally thought about the relationship between culture and individuals. I show in the course of this chapter and the two chapters that follow how new ways of thinking about this relation make for an original method of reconceptualizing gender.

Anthropological selves and persons

[T]here has never existed a human being who has not been aware, not only of his body, but also at the same time of his individuality, both spiritual and physical. (Mauss, 1985: 3)

Anthropologists have long struggled to develop cross-cultural understandings of the person, self and individual. This exercise in exegesis is complicated by two things. First, the attempt to delineate what might be universal and what might be culturally specific in such notions. Second, the endeavour to distinguish what is meant by the terms person, self and individual in western philosophical and popular cultural understandings, so that these distinctions might be usefully applied cross-culturally. The outcomes have been varied. A number of scholars (e.g. Harris, 1989; La Fontaine, 1985b; Morris, 1994: 10–15) have tried to draw clear-cut distinctions between these terms for the sake of clarity of description and analysis. But, as Anthony Cohen has noted: 'These distinctions are arbitrary, and are often difficult to sustain' (1994: 2). Why should this be? There are basically two kinds of problem. The first is that these terms do not have clear-cut boundaries in western philosophical and popular traditions because they are dynamically interrelated. The kind of person I feel I should be influences how I feel about myself. The notion of the individual carries consequences for ideas of personhood. This fact of dynamic interrelation is also contextually variable not only within an individual's lifetime, but also across different contexts in any given cultural setting.

Thus, for example, the self of intimate relations is connected to, but not necessarily determined by, the person of public engagement. The second problem is that the categories themselves, and the assumptions underlying them – such as the notion that experience of self and the world is always located within an interior self – do not necessarily map easily or unproblematically onto concepts in other cultural contexts (Moore, 1994: 29–35).[1] If these categories are not really separate in western philosophical and cultural understandings, then how can we assume that they are consistently differentiated – or indeed even exist – in other cultures (Sökefeld, 1999: 428)?

Anthropologists have historically treated the uncertainty and slipperiness of these terms by trying to distinguish what is universal from what is culturally specific. Drawing on an intellectual genealogy descending from Irving Hallowell (1971; 1976) and G. H. Mead (1934), there is general consensus that the capacity for self-awareness, self-identity (the ability to distinguish self from other) and self-continuity are essential for basic human and cultural functioning.[2] Hallowell argued strongly that self is intrinsic to human society and to all situations of social interaction, and also, conversely, that social existence is a necessary condition for the development of self. He thus understood self and society as interdependent and mutually defining (Hallowell, 1971). However, he believed that these universal aspects of the self did not necessarily presuppose anything about the local views of the self that would be prevalent in any culture. His notion of 'behavioural environment' was one in which the self was always culturally structured in terms of a world of objects other than the self (ibid.: 84–7). Hallowell's discussion of Ojibwa concepts of the person and self asserted that such categories could not be understood by projecting western categories and concepts onto them, especially since the latter are based on wholly inappropriate dualistic paradigms (Hallowell, 1976: 357–474).

Mead, like Hallowell, claimed that the key to understanding the self is the capacity for self-reflection, which allows the individual to develop a consciousness of being and to develop a sense of self through interaction with others. Culture, and most especially language, provides the means through which the self becomes self-aware as part of a process of taking, internalizing and recognizing the position of the other. The self is thus a product of interaction within a particular environment:

A person is a personality because he belongs to a community, because he takes over the institutions of that community into his own conduct. He takes its languages as a medium by which he gets his personality, and then through a process of taking the different roles that all the others furnish he comes to get the attitudes of the members of the community.... He is putting himself in the place of the generalised other ... it is that which guides conduct controlled by principles. (Mead 1934: 162)[3]

It is clear that in the work of Hallowell and Mead we find a theme first sketched by Durkheim, one that declares the importance of the role of culture in the formation of a sense of self, and insists equally on the necessity of a individual capacity of symbolization for the creation and internalization of social institutions and values:

society ... does not limit itself to moving us from without and affecting us for the moment; it establishes itself within us in a durable manner. It arouses within us a whole world of ideas and sentiments which express it but which, at the same time, form an integral and permanent part of ourselves. (Durkheim, 1971[1912]: 262)

But what might we mean when we claim that individuals internalize cultural discourses as part of themselves? Cultural discourses, institutions and values, if constitutive of our worlds, must by logical extension affect the development and experience of personhood, selfhood and individuality: 'our descriptions of our experience are, in part, constitutive of what we experience.... If people raised in different cultures or sub-cultures come to internalize different ways of describing their experience, this may make what they experience different' (Mischel, 1977: 21). At the core of this is the question of the relationship between language, experience and historical change. If a study of the person, self and individual is largely about the cultural categories and representations of such things, and about the inner states, motivations and actions that connect to such representations, then the question of language becomes crucial. To what degree does language, any language, adequately represent a psychological state, experience or understanding (cf. Gerber, 1985; Lutz, 1988; Lutz and Abu-Lughod, 1990a; White, 1985; 1992)? What is the relationship between language and the development and monitoring of psychological processes and understandings? Words for inner states, emotions, understandings of person and self do change over time. Does this mean that new psychological states and experiences are thus created? Is the focus on language and thought in danger of occluding or obfuscating the way practical and embodied engagement with the world creates, drives and develops inner states, psychological experiences, as well as understandings of person, self and individual? More crucially perhaps, could personal experiences and self-understandings arise *ex nihilo*, outside the available social and cultural discourses? The continuing difficulty is about how cultural representations intersect with personal lived experience, and the degree to which they determine that experience, and by what mechanisms.

In the Durkheimian tradition, the idea that collective representations determine behaviour and thought in 'traditional', 'non-western' societies has been a very powerful theoretical assumption underpinning anthropological understandings of cultural difference and cultural relativism. In an early phase of work on the person/self, anthropological writing tended to make a strong distinction between two types of society/ways of thinking: an ego-centric view of the person/self characteristic of western thought, and a socio-centric view largely said to be defining of non-western cultures (cf. Chang, 1988; Dumont, 1970; Levy, 1983; Rosaldo, 1984; Shweder and Bourne, 1984; White and Kirkpatrick, 1985). The central assumption is that, in socio-centric societies, the person/self is subordinate to and defined by the collectivity, whereas in ego-centric ones, the individual as autonomous and distinctive reigns supreme. This dichotomous view was founded, amongst other things, on a further premise inherited from Durkheim that 'traditional' or 'non-capitalist' societies are bound by moral conformity and cultural convention in a way that modern society is not.[4]

Such assumptions are evidently problematic and the idea that 'traditional' societies are more socio-centric and are without a notion of the individual, bounded, autonomous self has been criticized in anthropology for being overly dualistic and culturally deterministic, and for ethnocentrically denying individuals in other cultures a sense of self (cf. Cohen 1994; Ewing, 1990; 1998; Mines, 1988; 1994; Morris, 1978; 1994; Sökefeld, 1999): for confusing, as Cohen says, individuality with individualism (1994: 12).[5] While this is true in so far as anthropology has tended to over-dichotomize the distinction between socio-centric and ego-centric societies, instead of seeing these orientations as characteristic to varying degrees and in varying combinations of all societies (cf. Mageo, 1998), it would not be correct to say that, historically, anthropologists had always denied the existence of individual selves (cf. Fortes, 1987; James, 1988; Lienhardt, 1985; Riesman, 1977). While earlier writers did emphasize the specificity and peculiarity of western notions of person/self and their non-applicability to non-western cultures, it was rare for them actively to deny the existence of individuality, individual experience and self-awareness.[6] What they did tend to do was to over-emphasize cultural difference and cultural specificity. Individuals were seen as subsumed within culture, over-determined by it, from the perspective of an anthropology predominately focused on the collective and on the socio-cultural aspects of individuals/persons/selves.[7] Anthropologists have usually drawn their models of western selves from philosophical and textual traditions, rather than from ethnographic work on the experience of being a person/self in western contexts (Morris, 1991; Murray, 1993), and this, it has been suggested, is why they are inclined to over-emphasize the ego-centric, autonomous, non-collective aspects of western selves and persons (Spiro, 1993). On the available evidence, it seems more likely that distinctions between western and non-western persons/selves/individuals are often less marked than anthropologists habitually assume (Stephenson, 1989; Holland and Kipnis, 1994; Ouroussoff, 1993).[8] Certainly, the presumption of an a priori cultural distinctiveness undermined the efforts of earlier anthropologists to engage in serious self-reflection on how their own popular discourses of folk models inform their academic models, and how both interpenetrate in determining understandings of western selves/persons and how they are to be distinguished from others (Strathern, 1988; Moore, 1994: 34–5).[9]

The problem, however, is not so easily dismissed, because claiming that the distinctions between western and non-western selves might have been overdrawn by anthropologists does not mean that there are no cultural differences to be considered, that everyone everywhere conceptualizes persons/selves/individuals in the same way. Anthropological data make it all too evident that the opposition between the individual and society on which the discipline's theories depend is not a model that is common to all societies.[10] This is true also of a number of other dualisms that underpin dominant western-derived models of persons/selves in the social sciences: mind/body, subject/object, self/non-self.[11] The challenge then is to take each metaphysical system on its own terms, but not to overdraw distinctions between 'traditional' and 'modern', and/or individual and social selves, in such a way that selves are once more subordinated to cultural conventions, and individuals are denied their agency and individuality (see, for example Mageo, 1998; Stephen, 1995; Epstein, 1999). The line that anthropology still seeks to tread is one that emphasizes the existence of different metaphysics, but simultaneously asseverates the importance of recognizing that an existential sense of an individual self – based on self-identity, self-awareness and self-continuity – however it is made, manifest in terms of subject/object relations, experience, desire, motivation, feeling, agency and emotion, is a human universal.

How much does culture matter?

Anthropologists remain divided, however, on the extent to which locally, culturally constructed models of the self can be thought to be constitutive of psychological processes per se (Moore, 1994: 30). The fundamental question is whether basic psychological processes act as substrata on which cultural variation rests or are themselves altered by their development within a culturally constructed world. Dorothy Lee has argued that indigenous psychologies – specific statements about the nature of the person, individual and/or self and their relation to the world – bear on local understandings of humanness and the relation of the human to the divine and to the natural world, and, in consequence: 'The way a man acts, his feelings of guilt and achievement, and his very personality, are affected by the way he envisions his place within the universe' (Lee, 1959: 170).[12]

This would imply that indigenous psychologies play a key role in developing a sense of self-as-lived – including self-identity, self-awareness and self-continuity – but equally that they are central to constructing and organizing motivations, inner states and schemes for action and perception (cf. d'Andrade, 1992). In other words, that psychological processes themselves are altered by interaction with a culturally constructed environment, and that the two exist in dynamic interrelation. If this is the case, then two kinds of question become pressing: the first has to do with how we draw or understand the boundary between the universal and the cultural; and the second concerns the relationship between language, experience and historical change.

Needham has argued that where aspects of inner states or psychological processes can be 'discriminable as universal natural resemblances', they must be in the realm of physiology. But, since all inner states have to be expressed socially, if they are to be communicated, there is no way of distinguishing, using anthropological methods, between universal psychological processes and the 'ideological inventions' that are the product of culture (Needham, 1981: 76).[13] Thus, strictly speaking, there are no universal psychological processes or functions that all share. Most anthropologists, not to mention psychologists, cognitive scientists and philosophers, would find this position too rigid. They prefer to argue that cognitive capacities are based on neurological and physiological capacities, and that these do provide a dynamic context in which culture operates, but that key psychological processes – memory, for instance – function/operate independently of the way they are conceptualized in any given context. In other words, that we can establish universal psychological processes, and hold universally valid views about how people think (cf. Bloch, 1998).

The key variable here, of course, concerns the pre-theoretical assumptions that underlie differentiated positions. Shweder has demonstrated this point well in his discussion of what differentiates cultural psychology from psychological anthropology and ethnopsychology. He starts by asserting that cultural psychology is the study of how cultural traditions and social practices 'regulate, express and transform the human psyche' (Shweder, 1991: 73). His contention is – and in this he is in a clear tradition of descent from Hallowell and Mead – that no socio-cultural environment exists independently of the way humans seize meaning and resources from it, and that every human's subjectivity and mental life are altered and changed through this process (ibid.: 74). Cultural psychology is thus the study of personal functioning within particular intentional worlds, and one that assumes that subjects and objects, humans and socio-cultural environments interpenetrate and cannot be separated into independent and dependent variables. On this basis, Shweder argues that cultural psychology eschews any notion of the 'psychic unity of mankind' and that this is what differentiates it from psychological anthropology. The latter assumes an 'inherent central processing mechanism' (mind) that stands outside the socio-cultural environment and can be understood as a fixed and universal given, one which is not fundamentally altered by the content of the socio-cultural environment on which it acts or operates (ibid.: 88–90).

Shweder then goes on to discuss what differentiates ethnopsy-chology from cultural psychology, arguing that the former focuses on indigenous representations of mind, self, body and emotion, and is thus cultural psychology without the psyche.[14] Shweder's com-plaint here is that ethnopsychology or indigenous psychology is basically a sub-domain of ethnosemantics, concerned with beliefs, language and representation, whereas cultural psychology is 'the ethnopsychology of a functioning psyche', as it actually functions and malfunctions in different parts of the world (ibid.: 90–1). Cultural psychology, as defined by Shweder, does not presume that the fundamentals of psychic life are fixed and universal, but focuses instead on the processes of an intentional psyche as it responds to an intentional world that is the product of mental representations. Shweder's avowed aim is to break down the dualism of subject/object, psyche/culture and to develop a theory that sees them as interdependent and mutually constituting. This is undoubtedly a breakthrough compared with earlier analyses in anthropology that tended to see selves as subsumed within social and cultural contexts, or even as outside cultural analysis alto-gether. It is also, however, a position that is at odds with various traditions in psychoanalysis which tended to emphasize psychic universals and to treat culture as essentially epiphenomenal in the development of the psyche. A dispute about the limits of cultural variation is at the basis both of the debate on the univer-sality of the Oedipus complex, and of the discussion about how the psychoanalytic notion of sexual difference differs from the anthro-pological concept of gender as I discuss in the two following chapters.

Cultural psychology, as discussed by Shweder, certainly assumes that the human psyche is formed by the culturally constituted par-ticulars of a form of life, and that it changes over time (ibid.: 97). Thus, both the concept of the self and the process of self-making are culturally variable, but how does culture act upon the self? In her discussion of English kinship, Strathern discusses the ways in which individuals take up sets of notions and/or cultural materi-als and use them to make sense of changing circumstances. This process of interpretation and engagement produces new combina-tions of ideas and theories of relatedness. The result is a creative self that speaks in a cultural idiom (Strathern, 1992). This notion of a repertoire or a lexicon has older philosophical roots. Harré

considers how the self as a theoretical concept functions in relation
to the experience of self-consciousness, agency and personal
identity. His argument is that cultural notions of person and self
are drawn on as 'locally validated theories' that enable people
to develop forms of consciousness, and mechanisms for agency
that then constitute a sense of personal identity (Harré, 1983: 167–8).
The first stage in this process is one of learning theories of
personhood (ibid.: 22). Cultural models of person and self thus act
as a 'source model' through which we can organize our experience
and develop a sense of ourselves as conscious beings (ibid.: 193).
Heelas makes the same kind of point when he argues that indigenous psychologies, local understandings of persons/self and psychological processes, 'provide motives *for* the self' (Heelas, 1981: 13;
italics in original).

A focus on cultural 'lexicons', 'idioms' and 'theories' as vehicles
and resources both for meaning-making, and for the development
of orientations, experience, feeling, desires, ideas and motivations,
has the clear advantage of being able to link forms of agency both
to culture and to individual experience, as well as to change over
time. Such a view of the cultural self is in accord with the notion of
the interactive/creative self that has emerged in recent anthropological writing. This model is very critical of analytical frameworks
that portray selves as culturally determined, subsumed and/or
submissive (cf. Cohen, 1994; Ewing, 1998; Mageo, 1998; Rapport,
1997; Sökefeld, 1999). Scholars developing this framework have
emphasized the notion of a self produced in interaction with
others and with cultural categories, but one that is not determined
by either the relations or the categories, and retains a capacity for
creation, refraction and resistance (Ewing, 1998; Mageo, 1998;
Stephen, 1995). This self is also one that is complexly constituted,
bound up with sets of competing and partial discourses, able to
reflect on and combine socio-centric and ego-centric aspects of the
self and to deploy the resulting repertoires in performative and
strategic ways.

Language and the body

This view of the creative and interactive self is fundamentally a self
constructed in and through language, a thinking self that is able to
develop self-identity and self-continuity within social relations.[15]
The emphasis on language and/or on the linguistic aspects of

discourse is often implicit, but is still an important part of the analytical model: 'Through language, individuals become origins of action upon the universe and centres of experience within it' (Rapport, 1993: 152). Consequently, the creative and interactive self tends to be one involved in the performance of strategy and self-construction at the expense of more embodied and phenomenological perspectives. In this regard, it is important to recall, for example, that ethnography from Africa emphasizes the embodied nature of engagement with cultural categories and the practical, as well as linguistic, aspects of discourse.[16] This is discussed at length with regard to masculinity and femininity in chapters 4 and 5. A source of concern here is that a focus on language as the sole medium of symbolic representation and communication risks occluding other forms of embodied discourse that are constitutive of a sense of self, and provide the grounds for emotions, feelings, desire, motivation and agency. The analysis of gender is a useful theoretical starting point for addressing these issues because it deals directly with the relationship between forms of embodiment and cultural categories, as well as individual understandings of gender identities in the context of a lived experience of being gendered (Moore, 1994; 1999a).[17] Bourdieu, in discussing the way embodied habitus – a term he took from Mauss – links social structures and cognitive structures noted in relation to the cultural categories of gender, and women's and men's self-understandings and self-representations as gendered individuals:

> The opposition between the centrifugal, male orientation and the centripetal, female organization, which as we have seen, is the true principle of the organization of domestic space, is doubtless also the basis of the relationship of each of the selves to their 'psyche', that is, to their bodies and more precisely to their sexuality. (Bourdieu, 1977: 92; see also 1990)

Bourdieu's interest here is not so much in phenomenology as in the relationship between the body and knowledge. Bourdieu sees his work on the gendered body as an attempt to transcend the distinction between the individual and the collective, and he is particularly interested in how bodily praxis provides the grounds for the apprehension of gender difference. Thus, praxis is about coming to an understanding of social distinctions through your body, about recognizing that both your intellectual rationalizations and your unconscious motivations and desires arise out of an embodied engagement with the world (Moore, 1994; 1999a). Bourdieu's analysis is useful because he reminds us that symbols do something to our bodies, but he has little interest in psychoanalysis or psychology, and holds a strongly socialized and collective view of the relationship between the body and social representations. Thus, he cannot adequately theorize individual experiences, desires, motivations and self-awareness.[18] While he does raise the question of gendered subjectivity, he confines himself to emphasizing the importance of its materiality, the fact that schemes of perception and cognition are derived from the conditions of existence, and in particular social divisions of labour.[19] Bourdieu has often been criticized for positing too neat a fit between bodily praxis and cognitive structures, such that the former is determined by the latter, but his emphasis on the materiality of subjectivity does allow him to transcend, to a certain degree, the dualism between subject and object: his subjects are always born of a world of objects (Moore, 1994: 78–80).

The materiality of subjectivity, the fact that we are embodied selves and that we only come to have a sense of self through engagement with the world, where objects are both people and things, is of focal concern to psychoanalysis. In object relations theory, acquiring a sense of self involves developing relations with objects that have an existence outside the fantasy world of the child. This relation with objects is at the basis of the human capacity of symbolization, as Hallowell and Mead suggest, yet they differ from object relations theorists because they see the subject–object relation as culturally specific, formed in concrete social environments. From the object relations perspective, the external world is irredeemably social, but it is primarily figured in terms of parent–child relations and is only minimally material, because, while it exists, it remains non-specific with regard to the inequalities of power and resource that characterize any lived world. This leads to a very generalized notion of the social, where mothers and fathers are self-evident categories rather than historically embodied masculine and feminine others.

Bodies are never simply bodies, but are always caught up in forms of representation. The relation between language and the sexed body is a refracted one. As an earlier anthropology showed, gender and sex rarely make an easy match, and the acquisition of gendered identity is never simply a matter of the imposition of cultural categories onto sexed bodies (see Moore, 1988; 1994: ch. 1; Yanagisako and Collier, 1987).[20] Feminism, including feminist anthropology, has struggled with the question of how gender subjectivity relates to the body. In framing gender as a set of embodied potentialities, it has had to bear in mind the historically specific discursive practices within which such potentialities are lived, as well as the potential for dissent from such discourses which, in any event, can never determine gender completely. The relation of language to the body is thus the terrain on which anthropology, feminism and psychoanalysis meet in their attempt to give an account of gendered selves.

I have argued elsewhere that post-structuralist theories of the subject and of positionality are useful because they create a space in which it is possible to talk about the different subject positions proffered by the various discourses on gender that exist in any specific historical context. Gender subjectivity, rather than being conceived of as a fixed and singular identity, can be understood as based on a series of subject positions, some conflicting or mutually contradictory, offered by these different discourses (Moore, 1994: ch. 2). Two further points arise here. One is that gender discourses in any given context are hierarchically organized, some are more powerful and carry greater social sanction than others. Such coexisting discourses are dynamically interrelated and their mutually defining inclusions and exclusions shift over time. This is because their hierarchization is linked to inequalities of power and resource, and to overarching ideological formations such as nationalism, the market and the role of the state, which frequently seek to reformulate identities in categorical and sometimes fixed terms. In consequence, gender is never a neutral category; it is already marked by other forms of difference, including race, class, ethnicity and religion (Moore, 1994: chs 3 and 5).

Specific groups may develop their own discourses that work in contradistinction to dominant ones. This is evident in the New Gender Politics, where activists and theorists want to refuse the terms of dominant categorizations.[21] This connects to the second point which is a question about the degree to which people actively recognize and choose the different subject positions they take up, and to what degree they are actually able to resist the terms of dominant discourses. This is the core of a long-running debate in feminist politics and theory (see chapter 6). What is evident is that, although individuals are able to reflect on the practices and discourses of day-to-day living and to engage in ongoing processes of self-reflection, this alone cannot provide a compelling account of agency. Any such account must afford some understanding of the motivation for individual investment in certain subject positions, why some are preferred over others, but it must also – and perhaps more crucially – create a space for the role of fantasy and desire with regard both to compliance and resistance (Moore, 1994: ch. 3). Gender identities are always embodied forms of engagement with the world, and consequently bodily praxis can provide a form of self-reflection that does not always enter language (ibid.: ch. 4; Jackson, 1996; Csordas, 1990; 1994). Such embodied self-reflection, whilst not articulated in language, may also not enter conscious thought (see chapter 1). What one may know through the body and the status of that knowledge with regard to the experience and understanding of oneself as a gendered self is a contentious issue. But, psychoanalysis shows that language and behaviour are often at odds with one another. What cannot be articulated is sometimes repeated in behaviour (Moore, 1994: ch. 4). It is important, however, not to imagine that practical embodied knowledge somehow reveals a truth that is cut off from or repressed in language. Bourdieu has often been criticized (see above) for positing too neat a fit between bodily praxis and cognitive structures, such that the former is determined by the latter. There are two considerations here. First, culture can never simply determine individual agency, although it certainly sets out the patterns within which that agency becomes intelligible, and is open to consideration and self-reflection by self and others, as Mageo and others suggest. However, secondly, and more importantly, one does not simply reproduce a cultural world by acting in it; one also acquires knowledge of it through material engagement. Such knowledge, like conscious knowledge of the world and of the self, can be both incomplete and misleading (see chapter 1). There is, therefore, no absolute sense in which practical knowledge of the world can be figured as a repressed truth, something that language denies. Bodily praxis, like language, is subject to the circulations and workings of fantasy and desire, and we need to keep this very firmly in mind when discussing the relationship between gender identities and sexed bodies.

Power, discourse and multiplicity

We might be able to accede to the emerging trend in anthropology that takes it as axiomatic that societies or cultures do not determine the selves of their members, including their gendered selves, but where does that leave the theorization of the interrelation between culture and self, and crucially, where does it leave the question of power (cf. Mageo, 2000)?[22] Mageo has tried to address this problem for Samoa. Her analysis interleaves familiar views about cultural categories or cultural lexicons with ideas about the relational and situational construction of the self, whilst recognizing the importance of power and ideology. Her premise is that each culture has ontological premises about the nature of being human, and that these premises give rise to cultural categories or lexicons that privilege certain ways of being over others. She acknowledges that cultural lexicons are an attempt to capture the self in language, and one that is doomed to failure. However, she links aspects of these lexicons to discourses not only on the nature of the self, but more generally on morality and on the nature of social relations, as well as to the emergence of strategic discourses that are attempts to manage the contingencies and ambiguities of lived relations (Mageo, 1998: 7–17). The self in this analysis is thus relational, creative and strategic, but also enmeshed in cultural lexicons on the nature of being human and on person/self that give rise to social and moral discourses. The emphasis on praxis in context is maintained, and Mageo acknowledges that forms of body praxis are part of discursive strategies, particularly situationally defined strategic strategies.

Moral discourses arise when individuals notice that forms of behaviour or experience do not correspond to some aspect of their culture's ontological premise about the nature of being human. Moral discourses allow individuals to assess and judge the behaviour of themselves and others. What such discourses draw attention to, in Mageo's formulation, are those aspects of the person/self that are ideologically suppressed, less valued overtly and/or less culturally acceptable. The result is that formal moral discourses stress cultural values, while the experience of less culturally valued aspects of self and behaviour becomes localized in informal discourses and contexts. Power thus works to produce a hierarchy of discourses, but does not prevent or exclude the experience of emotions, feelings or ideas that are not culturally actively sanctioned. Ultimately, the bounding of formal and informal discourses always breaks down because this binary division is insufficient to allow people to deal with the complexities and ambiguities of life. Thus, people adapt, rework and reposition aspects of discourse, borrowing and mixing them, to make them applicable to lived situations. For Mageo, these are all discourses of the self, in the sense that they are discourses in which and through which the self is realized, and they become progressively more reflective and self-aware as one moves from moral to strategic discourses.

What makes Mageo's analysis engaging is the way she meshes neo-Foucauldian discourse analysis with a notion of the creative and non-determined, but still culturally located self. Her examination of non-sanctioned aspects of the self and the way in which they give rise to multiple discourses on persons/selves and morality allows space both for the workings of ideology and power, and for a creative, individual self involved in social relationships and acting as an agent.[23] Her emphasis on self-making in a specific historical context owes much to Foucault's dual conception of the subject/ self: 'If one wants to analyse the genealogy of subject . . . one has to take into account not only techniques of domination, but also techniques of self. One has to show the interaction between these two types of self' (Foucault, 1985a: 367).[24] In his discussion of techniques of the self, Foucault takes up the theme of the distinction between moral rules and prescriptions, as against the real moral behaviour of individuals – that is, the degree to which they do or do not adhere to imposed rules (Foucault, 1985b: 5–6, 25). His aim is to examine how individuals might resist techniques of subjectification through a creative process of self-stylization (Foucault, 1986).

A concern with self-making is central to the notion of the creative, interactive self emerging in contemporary anthropology, and it focuses on the twin processes of recognition and identification and how these are negotiated in social interactions through time.[25] The discourses on self and identity in anthropology have traditionally overlapped quite minimally (Sökefeld, 1999: 418), but how and why an individual acquires, accedes to or resists aspects of social identities – gender, class, religion, race – is a major aspect of the experience and management of self–other relations.[26] Sökefeld discusses how differences of religion, language, regional affiliation, clan and kinship groupings in northern Pakistan provide plural and contradictory identities that have to be negotiated by acting individuals. These identities are relationally connected and their intersections shift both over time and in different contexts of action. What holds these conflicting identities together for Sökefeld is a superordinate, narrative, self-reflexive self (ibid.: 424–6). This is also the position taken by Mageo and Knauft, who define the self as 'a domain term that includes within it virtually all aspects of personhood and subjectivity'. The self is the product of acts of identification with internal elements of experience, but also with other people, groups and cultural representations. Identity is then the 'sense of self that results from identification'. These identifications may be both subjective and social, in other words they incorporate both individualistic and social aspects of the self (Mageo and Knauft, 2000: 3). The role of the self is thus one of integration, but, as Sökefeld emphasizes, any sense of self must be developed in interaction with an awareness of others. This provides the grounds not only for a relational notion of self, but also for transformation: 'The narrative self, the personal image developed and displayed in such situations, certainly cannot remain the same. It is transformed as the actor relates to other contexts and to other co-actors, integrating him- or herself into other networks' (Sökefeld, 1999: 426).

Although models of the interactive self, like those just discussed, integrate self-understanding with agency and emphasize the importance of social interaction and relations with others, there are few examples of analyses that genuinely focus on the intersubjective aspects of self formation within specific discursive formations. Iris Jean-Klein (2000) demonstrates how identities and subjectivities are intersubjectively created in her work on the Palestinian intifada. Her concern is with reciprocal forms of self-making with significant others, mothers, brothers and sisters, in a determinate historical context where the state and economic and political structures play a decisive role. Jean-Klein shows how multiple subjectivities are produced via familial relationships in ways that are not only reciprocal, but also collaborative.[27] She focuses on the role of women – mothers and sisters – in formulating and constituting young Palestinian men as 'heroic selves'. Young men who are heroes of the struggle are redefined as moral persons in relationship to and in dialogue with their mothers and sisters, who in their turn become 'mothers of heroes' and 'politically active girls'. This process, Jean-Klein terms 'a collaborative, cross-subjective exercise of self' (ibid.: 102–3).

In her analysis, Jean-Klein is insistent that this cross-subjective production of heroic selves is one situated within the context of organized resistance to an oppressive state and contains elements of self-promotion and self-realization. What makes her analysis so powerful is her ethnographic demonstration of the way women's narratives, told in social contexts, of the suffering of their sons and the physical abuses they have endured creates an account of the stoical, resisting son.[28] The discourse of subject formation here is one that deploys the knowledge of suffering and the activities of the state, as well as aspects of resistance activities in a form of cross-subjective narration that involves sons, mothers, sisters and wives in the shared construction of subjects as politico-moral selves (ibid.: 109–14). These moral selves are actively produced discursively by agents in interaction, but are also the product of concrete somatic engagement with the day-to-day perils of lived reality in Palestine. Jean-Klein's analysis is compelling, not just because it demonstrates that male subjectivity is the product of relations with mothers, sisters and wives, but also because it emphasizes both the discursive determination and the self-styled aspects of subjectivity.

The subject of anthropology

The self-made self is crucial to any understanding of agency and individuality, but it could not have emerged in anthropological theory without the development of a non-unitary theory of the subject. The basic premise of post-structuralist thinking on the subject is that discourse and discursive practices provide subject positions, and that individuals take up a variety of subject positions within different discourses. As Ewing argues in her work on sainthood in Pakistan: 'Discourses constitute subject positions, but the experiencing subject is a non-unitary agent' (1998: 5). This notion of a non-unitary agent moved anthropology definitively away from a view of the person or self as wholly determined by culture, and opened up a space in which theorists could reflect on the multiple constitution of subjectivity (Moore, 1994). Dorinne Kondo (1990) provides us with an ethnographically grounded example of this theoretical approach in anthropology. Through her analysis of Japanese workers, she demonstrates how it is possible analytically to de-centre and de-essentialize the notion of self and move away from the notion of a unified, coherent, simply rational subject towards a view of the self as created in discursive fields of power and meaning. Her theoretical focus is on the relationship between multiple discourses and multiple subject positions: 'It is important to realize that conflicts, ambiguities, and multiplicities in interpretation, are not simply associated with different positionings in society – though of course this is a critically important factor – but exist *within* a "single" self' (Kondo, 1990: 45).

Within this theoretical framework, a single subject cannot be equated with a single individual. Individuals are multiply constituted subjects, and they take up multiple subject positions within a range of discourses and social practices. Some of these subject positions will be contradictory and conflicting. Individuals thus constitute their sense of self through several, often mutually contradictory, subject positions rather than through one singular subject position (Moore, 1994: 53–6; Ewing, 1990; 1991; 1998). The process of subjectification, of becoming a subject, is never a finished one or a closed one. Power and ideology may work to produce these subject positions, but they do not determine how individuals will identify with and take up different subject positions at different times, nor do they determine how individuals will be involved in the transformation of discourses of power and difference over time. The value, then, of a theory of the subject is that it provides a way of understanding how a complexly constituted self identifies with and/or resists and transforms various subject positions available within a particular social, cultural, economic and political context. It explicitly links the dual aspect of subjectivity within one theoretical framework, accounting both for the workings of power and difference, and for self-realization, creativity and self-determination. It retains that relationship between cognitive structures and material conditions that underpins aspects of Bourdieu's work, because it does not reduce discourse simply to language, but recognizes the importance of praxis, embodiment and unthought and unconscious engagement with the world. A theory of the creative, interactive self requires a theory of the subject if it is to avoid voluntarism on the one hand and over-determination on the other (Ewing, 1998: 18–19).

However, there is still a theoretical stage further, because what Sökefeld, Jean-Klein and others do not do is to ask what satisfaction, conscious and unconscious, being a subject brings. If ideology and power are not monolithic, if culture is not simply determining and if becoming a self is not simply a matter of socialization, of learning the codes of a particular cultural context, then what makes individuals identify with certain subject positions, and construct a sense of self through them (Moore, 1994; Ewing, 1998; Battaglia, 1995)? Learning and socialization certainly have a role to play, but the picture is much more complicated. No one, not even the most creative and interactive person/self, has complete knowledge of themselves or of others. Fantasy, desire and unconscious motivation are at work, alongside strategy, rationalization and emotional intelligence in the process of making and sustaining a self through identification with multiple subject positions. This process of identification is never complete or finished, and is often ambiguous and painful, but it also provides satisfactions. Some of this process will be available to the conscious mind and some will not. Some will be subconscious, tied up with bodily practices and unthought behaviour, and some will be unconscious (cf. Obeyesekere, 1981). In order to understand persons/selves, we need, in addition to a theory of self, a theory of the subject, and beyond that we need a theory of the acquisition of subjectivity. This will involve, amongst other things, a serious consideration of the role of fantasy, desire and unconscious motivation.

3

Culture, Power and Desire

The case for a new relationship between anthropology and psychoanalysis

In the last chapter I contended that new theories of the subject in anthropology make fresh ways of thinking about gender possible because they enlarge the contexts in which we can imaginatively engage with issues of power and agency. In this chapter, I argue that we need to reunite the subject of anthropology with the subject of psychoanalysis. I make this claim because in many parts of the world subjectivities, and in particular gendered subjectivities, are undergoing rapid and sometimes brutal transformation. In those processes of social transformation that we study which involve the unsettling, often violent, dislocations of neo-liberalism, globalized consumption patterns and state aggression, an enlarged theory of the self and of subjectivity is urgently needed. The making and remaking of selves are everywhere in evidence, but this truism takes on a particular force in the context of many experiences, social movements and changed ways of livelihood and belief that are actively premised on transforming the self. I discuss radical Christianity in this context in chapter 9, pointing out the specific demands involved in trying to analyse people's desire for a change in the very nature of who they are and of how they represent themselves to themselves. It is a desire that takes shape in conditions of poverty, and racial and ethnic discrimination, and within the shadow of new forms of aspiration.

In such contexts, to claim or presume straightforwardly that selves and subjectivities are culturally determined must be an ethical failure. It is equally problematic in my view to swing aggressively away from this position to embrace voluntarism and forms of hyper-agency. Both positions occlude, as many writers have suggested, the complex interrelations and over-determinations of power and agency. In anthropology, much of the theoretical writing on these matters draws inspiration from Foucault and is powerful and persuasive. However, what gets left out is the importance of understanding and analysing fantasy, desire and unconscious motivation. We simply cannot understand people's strenuous and determined efforts to expand their opportunities, defend the livelihoods of themselves and their families, and transform the communities they live in, as well as the other social, economic and political structures that shape their worlds without engaging with fantasy, desire and unconscious motivation. In this book, I argue that this neglect is no longer tolerable, and that furthermore it undermines our ability to theorize gender effectively.

As I argued in chapter 1, the relationship of anthropology to psychoanalysis has been an uneven one, with many enthusiastic supporters and extremely vehement detractors. One of the many assumptions expressed by the latter is that psychoanalytic interpretations are abstract, that it is over-generalized, structurally deterministic and timeless. My aim in this chapter and the ones that follow is to make the opposite argument, pointing out that psychoanalysis is a theory grounded in the materialism of being. Its starting point is the complex relation between body, mind and world, of how we come to understand ourselves as embodied social selves. At the core of this theory is the question of sexual difference and of how each of us comes to be marked by that difference. Psychoanalysis begins where anthropology stops: with desire. It explicitly links sexuality to the nature of social being and, in the process, produces a theory of the origins of culture and of symbolism. At the core of *this* theory is the idea that it is through their capacity for representation that human individuals become anchored in social worlds. One cannot become a self without becoming a social self, but since there can be no question of social structures simply determining the psychic life of individuals, psychoanalytic and psychoanalytically inspired theorists still need to account for the ways in which the regulation of sexuality and desire link the psyche to power, and to social and cultural institutions. Fundamentally, they seek to understand the entrance of the human subject into the existing networks and discourses of social and cultural relations. This is a process that needs to be accounted for over time and in historically specific ways, and this is something I attempt through the analysis of ethnographic material in later chapters.

In this book, I argue that nothing in human social life or in the human psyche is wholly determined by power. The logical corollary of this position for anthropology, as mentioned earlier, is that there are limits to cultural determinism. But what are those limits? In the anthropology of gender, we know very well that the question of how gender subjectivity and the experience of being gendered relates to cultural models of gender is hugely problematic and yet we have frequently determinedly cut ourselves off from any attempt to understand how fantasy, desire and unconscious motivation are involved here and how they can be theorized.[1] As part of an attempt to push theorizing forward in this field, and to trace out a path for the future, I make two propositions. The first is that we balance neo-Foucauldian models in the discipline with an alternative perspective that claims that human social and psychic life are shaped not just by the potentialities and positive effects of power and its circulations, but also by what escapes the determinations of power. This position has particular consequences for the analysis of gender and social transformation, which are discussed in the context of Melanesian material in chapters 8 and 9. The second proposition is that anthropology needs, as I suggested in chapter 1, to develop a theory of the imaginary to complement its various theories of the symbolic. This necessity arises quite simply because in anthropology, while we have theories of the relations of individuals to symbolic systems, we have not adequately theorized how the experiences of body and self and relations with others get caught up in representation and in systems of signification. This question is a hugely important one and bears on the question of how and to what extent individuals come to embody the social, why we make investments in it and how far we resist it or dissent from it. These are not issues that can simply be addressed, as I discuss in chapters 4 and 5, with reference to a theory of socialization or learning. In this chapter, I outline some of the theoretical positions drawn from psychoanalysis and psychoanalytically inspired theory that provide some of the background to these propositions. I begin by exploring why both Freud and Lacan argued that the individual psyche cannot be wholly determined by culture and why they saw this as being intimately connected to the acquisition of gender identity and the self's earliest engagement with forms of representation. Such an account involves a consideration of the way they conceptualize the relationship between desire and social regulations and institutions.

Freud and culture

Freud argued that unconscious desire is the organizing principle of human life, thought, action and social relations. However, Freud saw a certain antagonism between 'man and civilization', between the self and society. He took the view that in order to live a social life, the self must renounce something, individuals must restrict their possibilities for satisfaction.[2] This restriction was, for Freud, bound up with the fundamental opposition between the pleasure principle and the reality principle, between the primary processes of the unconscious and the secondary processes of consciousness. In his view, the self develops out of unconscious pleasure and is differentiated from it only as a result of contact with external reality. The idea that humans have to be brought within the control of society and learn to relinquish their pleasures has a history much older than that of psychoanalysis. However, what Freud brought to this understanding was, first, that 'reality' itself is not something given, but something created; second, that the process of repression is never finished or complete; and, third, that social relations and their laws are the origin of the desiring subject, but can also be actively transformed through the creative nature of desire itself. Thus self and society, psyche and culture are mutually constitutive.

The instincts which concerned Freud most, and which he felt society most needed to control, were the sexual instincts and the aggressive instincts. Repression, the relinquishing of pleasure to reality, is based on substitution, on the giving up of one pleasure in return for another satisfaction.[3] Underlying this idea was the connection between sexuality and knowledge. Freud argued that properly channelled sexual instincts placed large amounts of energy at the disposal of culture and civilized activity, and that this was in virtue of the capacity of the sexual instinct to 'displace its aim without materially diminishing in intensity': 'This capacity to exchange its original sexual aim for another one, which is no longer sexual but which is psychically related to the first aim, is called the capacity for sublimation' (Freud, 1985c[1908]: 39). Freud's notion of sublimation incorporates the idea of a substitution that is a workable, but not an exact, substitution for what has been relinquished. In this sense, repression is never a final or compete process, and never one that is simply a question of the determination of the psyche by the social.

In *Totem and Taboo*, Freud's stated aim was to show that 'the beginnings of religion, morals and society, and art converge in the Oedipus complex' (Freud, 1985d[1913]: 219).[4] At the core of the restrictions that culture places on the individual is the prohibition on incest. For civilization to flourish, individuals must move outside the family unit and enter into relations with others. For individuals to develop, they must give up their love for their mother and identify in some way with the father, and with cultural values and ideals. Incest is prohibited because it represents a turning inwards for both the individual and society. For Freud, respect for the prohibition on incest 'is essentially a cultural demand made by society. Society must defend itself against the danger that the interests which it needs for the establishment of higher social units may be swallowed up by the family' (Freud, 1977b[1905]: 148).

This view of incest and the Oedipus complex underpins Freud's strong belief that the development of the individual is intimately linked to the development of civilization/culture. He establishes further links through the relationship between the unconscious, the needs of the human body and social representations. Freud argues that the psyche is able to invest representations with unconscious desire. He gives as an example the fact that the infant is dependent upon the mother (or caretaker) for sustenance, but when the child has finished feeding from the breast, the desire for the pleasure of sucking continues. A fantasy of pleasure independent of physical need is born. This oral pleasure establishes a libidinal relation to the fantasy-image of the breast, and one which Freud terms sexual. Freud suggests that through the development of oral, anal and phallic forms of sexual pleasure, the infant gradually establishes an emotional fantasy relation to its own body, to other people and to the social world.

For Freud, unconscious desire arises through the sifting out or differentiation of bodily needs from fantasies of pleasure. In this process, libidinal impulses or drives become attached to images or representations. It is the linking of this process to that of repression that gives Freudian theory its distinctive cast, because libidinal impulses or drives can only be represented in the unconscious by an image or idea: 'An instinct can never become an object of consciousness – only the idea that represents the instinct can. Even in the unconscious, moreover, an instinct cannot be represented otherwise than by an idea' (Freud, 1984a[1915]: 179).

The Freudian unconscious is dynamic and transformative. Through the processes of representation at work in the unconscious – displacement, distortion and condensation – the libidinal drives become attached to certain representations associated with the human infant's earliest experiences. This is what Freud termed 'primal repression'. His view was that aspects of culture, such as myth and ritual, engage with and work over the material formed through 'primal repression'. This repressed material forms an unconscious core which attracts/draws to it further connected associations, images and representations, forming the basis for 'repression proper', in which new material becomes associated with or attached to originally repressed material. In consequence, material available to the conscious mind will be subject to repression if it forms links, connections and associations to what is repressed in the unconscious.

Freud establishes a theory where the unconscious is formed as a result of the tying of a libidinal drive/bodily need to a psychic representation. But this is not merely a contingent link, because the instinct in the form of a need actually requires an image as part of its satisfaction, and the process of creating representations linked to libidinal drives not only forms the unconscious, but provides the grounds for the emergence of a conscious self. Thus, the formation of the unconscious is the condition for subjectivity, and for consciousness and social relations through the mechanisms of representation. Indeed, it is through its capacity for representation that the individual subject becomes anchored in a social world. In the very early stages of its life, the infant lives in a close relationship to the mother's body and has no experiential divisions between self and other, self and external reality, subject and object. Consciousness – a notion of self – has to emerge out of this unconscious realm of libidinal plenitude. Freud argued that a recognition of self–other relations, of external reality and social relations cannot take place without a break in the dyadic relation of mother and child. Separation is a condition of self-hood.

In his early writings, Freud saw the ego (self) as having an existence from the beginning of life and as slowly being precipitated out of the unconscious as a consequence of its increasing links to the external world.[5] In his later work, he refigured the ego as essentially a structure that emerges through multiple identifications with others. The individual's separation from the mother sets in motion a process whereby the ego seeks, through introjection and identification, to substitute for the original relation of libidinal plenitude, by investing both in itself (self-love) and in the outside world. The process of constituting a self involves a separation from the mother's body and the assumption of a gendered identity. The latter occurs through the intervention of the father in the Oedipus conflict, specifically through the threat of symbolic castration, which severs the child from the imaginary plenitude of the maternal body. Freud's work on the Oedipus complex and on the acquisition of male and female sexuality, like his work on repression, has been extensively criticized both inside and outside psychoanalysis. However, the important kernel of the argument is the idea that the prohibition on incest, which inaugurates a ban on certain forms of sexual satisfaction, ensures an enduring link between desire, sexual difference and social laws.

Within this scheme, it is the prohibition of the law that creates desire, and the two are bound together in such a way that there can be no simple idea of an external law working on or coercing the individual, of an external authority being imprinted on and enforced upon the individual. Social laws are themselves both resisted and desired. In this sense, subjects are the effects of the workings of the law, not their realization. This was the core of Freud's insight and is most clearly revealed in his work on the superego. The superego is the internalized figure of the father, the internal voice of authority derived from identification with external authority. It is a compromise reached by the psyche with castration where, in response to the threat from the father, the child acquiesces to the law and identifies with the father. As the social law – in the shape of the figure of the father – prohibits the child's libidinal desire for the mother, it introduces the child to wider familial and social structures. The superego comprises ego ideals, and these arise, as Freud says, in consequence of 'an individual's first and most important identification, his identification with the father in his own personal prehistory' (1984b[1923]: 370).[6] Thus, the law works through the desire for identification, but only partly so because the superego is not simply an internal conscience, the inevitable product of schooling or socialization. It is much more contradictory in its nature, being both linked to, and precipitated out of, the id.

How can this be so and why does it matter? The typology of the psyche put forward by Freud in *The Ego and the Id* (Freud, 1984b[1923]) involves three agencies: the id (the home of the unconscious), the ego (the self) and the superego (the ego ideal).[7] Here, the superego arises out of the earliest object choices of the id, because it is as a consequence of the relation of imaginary plenitude with the maternal body that the threat of castration results in identification with the father. The original identification with the mother is also retained, but is now set within a complex of social relations and laws. This is what Freud means when he says that the ego ideal is the heir to the Oedipus complex.[8] From this perspective, the superego cannot be a mechanism for the straightforward determination of the psyche by culture. Social institutions and social significations are bound up with and developed out of the desiring subject's relation to authority, but that relation is an ambiguous one. The complexity here is not just that culture has a need for social order, and for particular kinds of individuals, nor indeed that humans need law and culture to become subjects, but that human subjectivity is founded both on a desire for and a resistance to the law. Freud's account is important because it draws our attention to the fact that the psyche cannot be wholly determined by culture. More crucially, culture, morality and ideology are not simply at war with the id, repressing the unconscious as it is sometimes mistakenly assumed, opposing the workings of desire, but they are also precipitated out of the id, originating within a capacity for representation where images and ideas are linked to libidinal drives, to the very movement of desire.

Language and desire

What we draw from Freud's complex account of the relation between self and world is that social systems – cultures, ideologies – engage with and are founded on the desires of human beings. In his major re-reading of Freud, Lacan develops a notion of the desiring subject based on the idea that the subject can only come into being, and know itself, through its relation to, and recognition by, the other. Lacan thus places distinct emphasis on the relations between intersubjectivity and desire in contradistinction to Freud's view of the monadic subject. However, Lacan, like Freud, starts with the idea that the relationship between the psychic and the social is one of ambivalence, and possible conflict. His basic postulate is that the development and constitution of the human subject is refracted through language and the social world, and that this process is principally one of alienation by and through signification.

Using structural linguistics, Lacan develops a link between the structure of the unconscious and the nature of the social. He identifies three orders of human existence, the real, the imaginary and the symbolic, and the effects of these three orders are need, demand and desire. The child's development from need to demand and desire corresponds to its movement out of the real and its passage into the imaginary and the symbolic. Need for Lacan is as close to instinct as it is possible to come in human existence; it is the experiential correlate of nature. Need requires real objects – warmth, milk – for its satisfaction. It is a pre-representational state, one of unspeakable plenitude. However, this state is very short-lived, and as the infant matures, need is rapidly inserted into a web of significance and meaning that transform it through imaginary and symbolic relations. As the child begins to represent to itself the presence and absences of the mother, it transforms its relation to need into demand. Demand is a state in which the thing demanded – food, warmth, etc. – is no longer simply a demand for the thing itself, but is also a demand addressed to another. It is a demand for a relation to the mother – or primary caregiver – for a love that would represent the reunion with the other, for the imaginary identification with the other where all needs find satisfaction. This demand is an impossible one because even if the object demanded is given, it cannot provide the satisfaction being sought.[9] Demand is the consequence of submitting need to the laws of language and of inserting it into an interpersonal or intersubjective register: the relationship between mother and child.

Demand may represent the child's first point of entry into the social, but it is desire that inaugurates a new relation to language and to the law or symbolic order. What each subject desires is the desire of the other, and, like demand, desire is oriented towards the other: 'man's desire finds its meaning in the desire of the other, not so much because the other holds the key to the object desired, as because the first object of desire is to be recognised by the other' (Lacan, 1977: 58).[10] Desire constitutes the subject through the demand for the recognition of subjectivity, but is itself unconscious and is not concerned with reward or with social approval. As Lacan says: 'Relations between human beings are really established before one gets to the domain of consciousness. It is desire which achieves the primitive structuration of the human world, desire as unconscious' (Lacan, 1988b: 224).

Desire marks the child's entry into the domain of the Other, but this Other is not a person, but a position, the place of language, law and the symbolic order, the world of culture and of wider social and family networks. As the infant matures and begins to recognize the absence of the mother, and registers that her/his body is separate from hers, signification and representation begin to enter into the apprehension of the child's world. This process begins at 6–18 months with the mirror stage, when the child starts to recognize its own image in a mirror and/or its separateness from others. The child internalizes this image of itself and identifies with it. Internalizing this image or imago, the child has a sense of completeness or wholeness that is at odds with its actual experience of bodily fragmentation – a fragmentation that comes about because different parts of the body mature physiologically at different rates. It is by identifying and internalizing this image of itself, which is already an image of another – either the specular image in the mirror or the image the (m)other has of the child – that the child represents itself to itself and begins to develop a sense of self.

Lacan views the mirror stage and the associated imaginary order as sexually undifferentiated, and the child's acquisition of a sexual identity only occurs with its entry into the symbolic. Re-reading Freud, Lacan argues that the break-up of the imaginary mother–child dyad comes about through the intrusion of the symbolic order representing wider social and cultural processes. His focus is not just on sexual prohibition in the Oedipus conflict, but on the role of the father in symbolizing the 'Otherness' of language. Without the transition to the symbolic and the accession to language, the child would be permanently imprisoned in a set of mother–child dyad imaginary identifications and unable to engage in social relations.[11] The transition is enforced by the intrusion of a third term, the symbolic father, representing the law prohibiting incest. The child must submit to the Law-of-the-Father, the paternal metaphor that represents the social. 'It is in the name of the father that we must recognise the support of the symbolic function which, from the dawn of history, has identified his person with the figure of the law' (Lacan, 1977: 67). In this process, the child loses the plenitude of the relation to the mother; what she/he gains is culture, a sexual identity and a speaking position within discourse. Thereafter, significations stand in for desire, and unconscious desire is organized within the symbolic order; through language, desire is cast in the shape of the social.

It is this relationship between language and desire that links the individual to the social world. Signifiers come to stand in for the loss of imaginary desires and loves, and the child seeks to use language to overcome this loss. In place of a Freudian notion of language that provides the child with mastery over the unconscious,

Lacan posits language as constitutive of the unconscious, and it is the entry into language that provides the means for intersubjectivity, individuation and identity. The underlying symbolic structure of the unconscious means that the human subject must always be the product of the symbolic order and not its producer. Language permits desires to come into being, but it also complicates those desires. The unconscious is a chain of signifiers where relations of metaphor and metonymy allow for substitution, condensation and transformation. The meaning of a signifier is thus never fixed, but slips and slides within the overall system of signifiers according to the logic or rules of the system. The ego has no control over this process or over the logic that establishes it. Lacan's use of Saussurian linguistics entails the view that the relationship between the signifier and the signified is an arbitrary one set up in convention, and therefore signs cannot designate objects in any natural sense. Furthermore, the workings of desire within the unconscious necessitates that meaning can never be fixed or pinned down, but continually circulates and thus undercuts any conventional relation of the signifier to the signified. The subject, therefore, is not tied down and fixed, but slips from signifier to signifier. This means, amongst other things, that language fails to fix desire; in fact, it does exactly the opposite, and provides for its malleability and transformation of form. As a result, our knowledge of our desires is imperfect and sometimes contradictory: we can both want and not want something; we can find satisfaction in not getting what we desire; we can remain unsatisfied when we get what we want.

Humans come into a world already made, and yet for each individual the social must be made anew each time or rather each must be inaugurated into the social.[12] So, how does the individual become part of the social? Lacan's response is that it's a matter of analysing 'the effects in the nature of man of his relations to the symbolic order and the tracing of their meaning right back to the most radical agencies of symbolisation in being' (Lacan, 1977: 64). For Lacan, 'a general theory of the symbol' must be the basis for the study of subjectivity, for the study of how an individual becomes a social subject (ibid.: 73). The experiences of the body and of self and of others get caught up in symbols or rather in the system of signification, and that is why there can be no radical disjuncture between the social and the psychic. However, they can never be isomorphic, since one's desires are never entirely one's own.

Language involves alienation because every child is born into a linguistic universe not of its making, and if it is to be able to express needs, wishes and desires to its primary caregivers, it must use language to do so. A child's wants get distorted or approximated, since language contains and/or is constituted out of the desire of others. The child internalizes these desires as it acquires language, but these desires are never completely the child's own; they remain foreign, both part of the child and not part, permanently other. The desires of others may enter us with language, but this process begins before we can properly speak, since it starts with signification.[13] A child is positioned within its parents' desires. Even before it is born, it occupies a space within cultural preoccupations, such as the desire for social standing and the desire for grandchildren. Our own desires are moulded within the structures of language which are the stuff within which these cultural preoccupations are expressed. Aspects of our own desires are therefore already aspects of others' desires. Our goals, aspirations, expectations and fantasies are ours and yet other to us. We internalize these desires as we internalize language, and yet like language they never become completely ours, they remain foreign to us and thus our unconscious is constituted in and through the discourse of the other (ibid.: 55, 312).

The problem of desire bears directly on the question of subjectivity, and on the relationship between the social and the psychic. Children try to be the object of their mothers', parents', carers' desires. They try to fill the lack that makes those individuals desiring beings with themselves. The child wants to be everything to them, and thus the child develops his or her desires in relation to the desires of another.[14] The desire of this Other functions as the cause of the child's desire. The child would like to be the only object of the mother's desire and to exist in a unity with her, but much of the mother's desire has nothing to do with her/him. Unity cannot be maintained, and the non-commensurability of the mother's desires and those of the child creates a gap or a space between them in which desire circulates and operates. When the desired or imaginary unity between mother and child breaks down, as it must for the child to enter the symbolic order, Lacan posits something left over, a remainder of that unity which he terms '*objet a*' (the cause of desire).[15]

The *objet a* is connected in fantasy to what is pleasurable for the subject or rather to an excitation or enjoyment that can be both pain and pleasure, and this excitation is referred to by the term *jouissance*.[16] *Objet a* is what assists the subject in sustaining herself/himself in the world because as the residue of a hypothetical mother–child unity it helps the subject to achieve a sense of wholeness, a sense of their place as the Other's desire. Strictly speaking, however, the *objet a* remains outside symbolization, it is a part of the pre-oedipal real that exists after and despite separation from the mother, entry into the symbolic and submission to the law. Consequently, it retains the capacity to interrupt the functioning of the signifying chain and to disrupt the social laws. And yet, the effects of its displacements on the symbolic can be seen in the way signification works around it, tracing the shape of this absent thing.

The Lacanian subject, like the Freudian one, is a split subject: split between an ego and the unconscious. The ego and the unconscious are two forms of otherness. The ego is formed out of imaginary identifications with others; images of parents and primary caregivers, images deriving from them and the infant's own mirror image. Thus, this other is made up of other people, and is inaugurated by the mirror stage. But, the unconscious is also other, an Other that comes from outside the ego. This Other is language, the symbolic order, the name of the father, that which intervenes in the mother–child dyad and brings about the entry into social relations and social exchange. For Lacan, the formation of the ego is a kind of mirage or misrecognition, based on the difference or the gap between the actuality of the fragmented subject and its unified image of itself.[17] This misrecognition means that the subject is continually threatened by otherness, by an otherness that is internal to it. However, what Lacan never loses sight of here is the role of the other in the constitution of the desiring subject because the path of desire traces and retraces a subject–other encounter based on the need for recognition. Thus, the imaginary misrecognition of self, and of the otherness inherent in self, is continually played out with others.

The power of the imaginary

Both Freud and Lacan emphasize the materiality of consciousness, the fact that we develop an internal world and a capacity to relate to others and the wider world through representations. The formation of the unconscious is a condition for subjectivity and consciousness, but it is also a guarantee that the psychic cannot be wholly determined by the social. The unconscious is formed out of the child's fantasized relation to its own body, to its parents and significant others, and to larger social and cultural networks. These relations are fantasized in the sense that they are set up in representations, and our very capacity for relationality and for agency are crucially dependent upon fantasy, desire and identification. We can have no relation to ourselves, to our gender and to society without a capacity to imagine these relations and represent them to ourselves and to others. Reading Freud and Lacan ethnographically, we can see that their work depends on imagining the relation of self to society in a particular way, tracing a cartography of representations. One of their major tenets is that individuals consistently misrepresent and misrecognize themselves as coherent, self-produced and self-identical, failing to recognize the otherness that is at the core of identity and self–other relations. Their claim, in its simplest form, is that we are shaped by desire and imaginary identifications in ways that we cannot wholly know. This position certainly provides the basis for the assertion that the social and the psychic are not isomorphic, that the self can never be wholly determined by culture, but without further elaboration it cannot explain how and why individuals invest in certain social meanings, narratives and ideologies. In other words, it cannot account for the ways in which individuals are shaped by and identify with power. This is of evident importance to anthropological explanation more broadly, but is crucial in trying to explain the relationship between gender ideologies and the lived experience of gender (see chapter 2). At the crux of this issue is a broader question of how to understand and theorize the relationship between the imaginary processes of psychic life (fantasy, identification) and dominant discourses and ideologies. In short, what kind of account can be provided of the relationship between the imaginary and the symbolic?

Slavoj Žižek uses Lacanian theory to try to develop a theory of ideology that both includes an account of the nature of the subject's identifications with ideological meanings, and also has regard for the dynamic nature of the unconscious (Žižek, 1989: 44). What makes Žižek's work innovative is his insistence on the unstable relations between the social and the subject. This instability is not just the result of the fragmentation of the subject and its dispersal in language, but is also, and more crucially, the consequence of the movement of desire itself. He begins with the Lacanian premise that it is impossible for everything to be symbolized within the symbolic order, and thus language can never encompass all of the real. There is always something left over, some residue(s) that resists symbolization. These residues, which Lacan termed *objet a*, provide 'stumbling blocks' for the subject because they are associated with the trauma of the initial entry into the symbolic, the moment when the subject relinquishes the plenitude of the maternal–child dyad and, by submitting to castration, agrees not only to the law of social relations but also to the twin processes of identification and substitution. What is relinquished at this moment is foundational for the subject, but is paradoxically excluded from the chain of significations that make up the symbolic order. This exclusion functions as a present absence because signification works around what is excluded, and so the symbolic order is shaped by the residues it does not contain.[18]

These residues (*objet a*), as noted above, function as unconscious objects of desire: 'it is this surplus of the Real over every symbolization that functions as the object-cause of desire' (Žižek, 1989: 3). Enjoyment (*jouissance*) is connected to the subject's fantasized relation to these leftovers, these residues of an earlier enjoyment that have escaped or resisted symbolization. The child's original desire for the mother is embodied in these residues, and continues to act for the subject as the cause or motor for desire. Fantasy plays a key role here because, by allowing the subject to maintain a fiction of wholeness, of completeness, it covers over the thing relinquished (the lack) on which the subject is founded and provides the basis for the creation of an internal world. This fiction is crucial since it is only through fantasy that the subject is able to construct a degree of consistency and substance outside of the alienation of the symbolic order (ibid.: 46). For Žižek, fantasy connects the symbolic and the imaginary, and thus provides the link between the subject's capacity for identification with certain subject-positions and the movement of desire (ibid.: 111).

But, how exactly does the subject's identification with certain subject-positions link to ideology? In essence, Žižek proposes that ideology as a form of social fantasy exists to suture or cover over lack. The fact that subjects are incomplete and founded on lack means that they need to fantasize a society that works for them, and with which they can identify. The mechanism for this is the enjoyment gained from the movement of desire.[19] Desire constitutes the subject through the demand for the recognition of subjectivity, because what each subject desires is to be desired by an(other), or, as Lacan says, each subject desires the desire of the other as its object.[20] However, the other is also a subject founded on lack, and what the image of society sustained in ideological discourse seeks to do is to suture or cover over the lack on which both subject and other are founded.

Drawing on Lacan, Žižek argues that the lack at the core of the individual subject finds its counterpart in the symbolic order which is also founded on something that cannot be symbolized but which nonetheless erupts as enjoyment into language and signification. The ordering of the symbolic around this lack or kernel of traumatic residues is what prevents it from becoming complete and closed, from overwhelming, subsuming and determining the subject. The inconsistency and incompleteness of the symbolic order has to be covered over by fantasy, by a world created as worthy and meaningful, by a fantasy of reality which is none other than ideology.[21] Here, we encounter Žižek's definition of ideology as 'an "illusion" which structures our effective, real social relations and thereby masks some insupportable, real, impossible kernel. . . . The function of ideology is not to offer us a point of escape from our reality but to offer us the social reality itself as an escape from some traumatic real kernel' (Žižek, 1989: 45). Ideology is figured as a social fantasy that engages with the fantasies of the subject to structure desire and enjoyment and this accounts for why subjects take up certain subject-positions. The fundamental instability of the social is the product of the fact that it is always inconsistent and incomplete – founded as it is on a lack, an impossibility – and thus socio-symbolic identification for the subject can never be complete or finished. It is ideology that covers over this instability, creates a world that makes sense, hides the fact that the subject can never be completely penetrated by the social. Yet, desire ensures that the relationship between the subject and the social is always unstable, a matter of continuous circulation, rather than of straightforward determination.

Žižek's notion of fantasy as that which propels subjects into the world through the binding of the imaginary and the symbolic is provocative, resting, as it does, on the idea that fantasy is never just internal to the subject but connects to relations with others and thus contaminates the social in unstable and non-determinate ways. He certainly provides part of the answer to a question about how and why social representations, cultural values and ideologies come to be invested with unconscious desire. His basic contention is that desire arises out of the incompleteness of representation, and in chapter 8 I discuss ethnographic material that addresses the link between gendered subjectivity and cultural representations as a means to consider how cultures and selves might be profitably analysed as shaped by what they exclude. However, Žižek's focus on exclusion and on how this shapes subjectivity and culture raises the question of how change comes about. What room is there for agency and its historical relations to power in this formulation? How can new forms of representation, new fantasies, new identifications, new images arise?

These questions are taken up by Cornelius Castoriadis in an explicit critique of Lacanian theory in which he focuses on the role of the imaginary in social life. Castoriadis develops two notions, the radical imaginary and the social imaginary, and they are intended to show how both self and society are the products of the creative imagination. Castoriadis draws on Freud's work to sketch out the imaginary as being characterized by what he calls a 'representational flux', a constant stream of images, significations, passions and desires: 'The imaginary of which I am speaking . . . is the unceasing and essentially *undetermined* (social-historical and psychical) creation of figures/forms/images, on the basis of which alone there can ever be a question *of* something' (Castoriadis, 1987: 3).

Castoriadis is very critical of what he terms Lacan's specular view of the imaginary; that is, of his notion that the ego/self is born out of a process of objectified reflection.[22] Castoriadis poses the question of how the self can be constituted out of a recognition of itself in the 'mirror', if it does not already possess the imaginary capacities necessary for identification and representation: 'The imaginary does not come from the image in the mirror or from the gaze of the other. Instead, the "mirror" itself and its possibility, and the other as mirror, are the works of the imaginary, which is creation *ex nihilo*' (ibid.: 3). The crux for Castoriadis here is Lacan's insistence that the self is the product of misrecognition. He asserts instead that it is only the capacity of the radical imaginary to create continuously images, forms etc. that accounts for the self's ability to create an internal world: 'radical imagination (as source of the perceptual *quale* and of logical forms) is what makes it possible for any being-for-itself (including humans) to *create for* itself an own world (*eine Eigenwelt*) "within" which it also posits itself' (Castoriadis, 1994: 143).

The key here is that Castoriadis is concerned to link the unconscious to the self's capacity for agency, hence his stress on the capacity of the radical imaginary to produce images, representations, intentions, desires, etc. *ex nihilo*, out of itself, and to do so in an absolutely spontaneous way. What he seeks, as David Fel argues, is to distinguish between 'the individual as a real agent and the status of the unconscious as an agent of the real' (Fel, 1993: 188). In other words, he wants to assert, contra the Lacanian notion of the split subject founded on a lack, a belief in the individual's capacity to be actively creative, to be critically self-reflective, to have an alternative future, as opposed to being over-determined by their position within the symbolic order: 'It is one thing to say that we cannot choose a language with absolute freedom, and that every language encroaches on what "is to be said". It is something else again to believe that we are fatally subject to language and that we can never say anything except what language makes us say' (Castoriadis, 1987: 126).

For Castoriadis, the psyche and the social inhere in, but cannot be reduced to, each other, and thus the radical imaginary finds a structural homology in the social imaginary. Castoriadis develops the concept of the social imaginary as a way of refining Lacan's account of the interrelations between the imaginary and the symbolic. The notion of inherence would seem here to imply mutual realization, in contrast to the Lacanian notion of the introjection of law as prohibition. Thus, for Castoriadis, although the social imaginary encompasses the symbolic order, the former is fundamentally a socio-centric rather than a linguistic concept. It is the field within which signification and ideology are conjoined and is characterized by what Castoriadis terms the 'instituting-instituted'. The key to understanding Castoriadis here is the centrality of symbolism to social life, and much of what he says about the social imaginary, as opposed to the unconscious, is more than faintly reminiscent of both Durkheim and Bourdieu (see chapter 2).

For Castoriadis, society is the product of instituting human praxis, but social institutions themselves as instituted have a determining impact on human activity. Existing social relations are necessarily 'instituted' because they have been symbolized, meaning has been attributed to them. Castoriadis has to be careful here to keep the symbolic separate from the social imaginary, to avoid the latter being subsumed by the former. He thus argues that while the social imaginary must pass through the symbolic in order to be expressed, the symbolic cannot exist without the social imaginary, without the capacity to 'see in a thing what it is not, to see it other than it is' (Castoriadis, 1987: 127). Thus, in his account, the social imaginary exceeds the symbolic. This must be so for Castoriadis because the creative capacity of the social imaginary, its ability to create new meanings, is the product not of an abstract system of differences, but of an engagement with a particular social and historical world. The instability of signification cannot therefore be reduced to the internal workings of a system of differences, but is the consequence of expansion into a social world inhabited by creative individuals: 'None of the traits specific to symbolism ineluctably imposes the domination of an autonomous institutional symbolism on social life; nothing, in institutional symbolism itself, excludes its lucid use by society' (ibid.: 126).

Castoriadis reworks aspects of Freud to argue that the psyche is the origin of representation:

> The psyche is the capacity to produce an 'initial' representation, the capacity of putting into image or making image. . . . This may appear self-evident. But this image-making must at the same time relate to a drive, at a time when nothing ensures this relation. This may well be the point of condensation and accumulation for all the mysteries of the 'bonding' between the soul and the body. (Ibid.: 282)

The capacity for representation is a unique mode of being (ibid.: 282). The question of how that capacity for representation links the psyche to the social and intersects with ideology and power is never really made clear by Castoriadis:

> The social individual, as society produces him, is inconceivable without the unconscious; the institution of society, which is indisso- ciable from the institution of the social individual, is the imposition on the psyche of an organization which is essentially heterogeneous with it – but it too, in its turn, *'leans on'* the being of the psyche . . . and must, unavoidably, 'take it into account'. (Ibid.: 298)

In essence, Castoriadis takes a very straightforward psychoana- lytic view of how the subject comes into the social world through the Oedipus complex and he shares the standard view that if a rela- tion to social signification is not established, then psychosis is the result (ibid.: 309). Sublimation is key here, because sublimation is the process through which the self relinquishes its own objects of desire in exchange for those that have social value. However, for Castoriadis, it is not a matter of drives being replaced by objects, so much as the creation of an interstitial space between the psyche and a public world which conforms to the requirements of social institutions (ibid.: 318). Castoriadis's account of how this space is formed is unclear. What does seem more evident is the notion that the psyche retains its creative capacity, its radical imaginary, but as it opens itself up to a specific socio-historical world it is created by society as a unique social individual (ibid.: 300; 311). One cannot become a self without becoming a social self, and there are no social selves who do not have psyches. Where Castoriadis sees both the work of history and of self-creation and autonomy is in the specific way in which the psyche opens up to particular socio-historical meanings and values. He thus distinguishes his position from what he views as the fixed, determining and ahistorical nature of the Lacanian symbolic order, and its impact on the subject.

The commitment to understanding how the psyche interacts with the specificity of particular socio-historical worlds is an important antidote to the often-made criticism that psychoanalysis posits an ahistorical subject, with an invariant relation to social forms. Castoriadis is clear that the child's relation to the mother, for example, has always to be understood as a relation to a specific culturally and socially valorized mother, and not just to a general, generic mother, and in chapters 4 and 5 I discuss ethnographic material to support this position. Thus, while psychic processes may be invariant, the content of the psyche and the way in which it opens into a social world are variable. This is the force of the concepts of the radical and the social imaginary. Castoriadis is typically forthright: 'The psychogenetic perspective, by itself, is therefore radically incapable of accounting for the formation of the social individual, of the psyche's process of socialization. This is a truism which the vast majority of psychoanalysts – beginning with Freud himself – persist in ignoring' (ibid.: 316).

However, Castoriadis cannot provide detailed examples of how this process of becoming a social self takes place. Ultimately, his account of the process of subjectivization does little more than suggest that individuals have to find personal satisfaction in the way they take up positions in the social world.

> The social individual cannot be constituted 'objectively' except through the reference to things and to other social individuals, which he is ontologically incapable of creating himself for these can exist only in and through the institution. And he is constituted 'subjectively' in so far as he has managed to make them things and individuals *for himself* – that is to say, to invest positively the results of institution of society. (Ibid.: 315)

Thus, while Castoriadis focuses on the creative nature of the radical and social imaginary, he does so without providing a clear model for understanding the effects of power and difference on the psyche. In order to develop a more robust theory of these relationships, we need to turn to a different tradition within psychoanalytic thought and to the writings of feminist philosophers.

4

Objects and Relations with (M)others

Gender identity, born in the space of difference between masculinity and femininity, always retains the marks of its birth.

Dimen, 1991: 350

The selves of psychoanalysis have not stayed constant. Like the anthropological persons/selves/subjects discussed earlier, they have evolved over time, their character and shape being determined by broader intellectual, social and cultural shifts within which their theorists have been located. It is sometimes assumed that psychoanalytic theorizing is based on a unified notion of the unconscious, whereas in fact the definition of this fundamental concept, and the characterization of the associated processes of the development of mental structures, vary depending on the kind of pre-theoretical assumptions the theorist holds about the kinds of selves we imagine ourselves to be. The starting point is often, as in anthropology, a set of assumptions about what constitutes the defining characteristics of being human. Are we fundamentally alienated in language, are we basically object-seeking, are we propelled by instincts? The answers to these questions result in changes in the topography of mind, in reconceptualizations of the relationship between social and self-styled aspects of subjectivity, and in reworkings of the relationship between subjects and objects. In this chapter, I begin by discussing some aspects of object relations theory in order to explore how recent developments in psychoanalytic theorizing offer the potential to develop a new theory of gender in anthropology and beyond.

One consistent feature of all psychoanalytic theories is their insistence on the importance of fantasy as a manifestation of a basic capacity for representation and symbolism. The symbolic nature of human beings is strongly reinforced in all accounts, whether in the more formal and determining Lacanian view of the symbolic order or in the object relations and intersubjective theoretical vision as something that draws the self into the world, and into relations with others. Fundamentally, all psychoanalytic theories link desire and fantasy to external worlds and social relations, but they do so in rather different ways. The corollary of this is that different theoretical traditions make different assumptions about how a child's earliest fantasies link to what happens later in life, and they hold diverse views as to how we should envisage the relationship of fantasy and identification to dominant social and cultural representations. In other words, they provide differing accounts of the relationship of the imaginary to the symbolic.

One thing that is shared by the various traditions is the view that the entrance of the human subject/self into existing social networks and cultural discourses always involves negotiating relations with parents and significant others. Within this broad framework, however, different theories place different emphasis on the role of mothers as compared to fathers, and on the significance of oedipal as opposed to pre-oedipal relations. What holds these various positions together is the idea that sexuality resides at the base of both psyche and culture, as well as their relations. Separation from the mother and identification with oneself, with others and with the world is a condition of subjecthood. Psychoanalytic theorizing stresses that this process of separation always necessitates becoming a sexed being because one cannot be a social being without taking up a position with regard to the difference between the male and the female. In other words, to enter into social life is always to be marked by sexual difference. Psychoanalytic theorists consistently argue that sexual difference is not the same thing as gender. It is not something that is socially contingent, but operates rather at the level of the symbolic, functioning as an invariant psychosexual structure, and is contentless from an historical and cultural point of view (e.g. Mitchell, 1991; Shepherdson, 2000). Anthropologists and feminists want to know whether this means that psychosexual structures will always be invariant, whether there is any room at all for cultural and social change? If these structures are invariant, if identity is ceaselessly a product of the acceptance of the paternal law, if women are doomed to be constantly re-inscribed as castrated men, as the sex that marks the difference from the norm, then what potential can there be for a feminist politics, for changing the relations between the sexes? Feminist philosophers have been bitterly divided over the issue of whether it is possible to re-envisage the symbolic order as anything other than coextensive with the phallic law. Many have argued that it is, but that to do so successfully would involve rethinking the nature of the maternal and of feminine subjectivity which would only be possible in the context of a re-evaluation of the relationship between the imaginary and the symbolic. I give an ethnographic reading of some of these arguments below, tracing the effects of their imaginative engagement with the relationship between the psyche and the social, sex and the law. I use these arguments to form the basis for a new theory of gender in anthropology, one which is premised on the claim – contra established thinking in psychoanalysis and feminism – that becoming a sexed being is a condition for subjecthood, but that it cannot be a culturally and/or historically invariant process.

The impetus for this theoretical reworking arises from a concern that a pre-theoretical commitment to the idea that gender discourses and practices are culturally determined does not provide much analytical purchase when confronted with the multiple models of gender, gender identifications, and gender practices in any particular historical context. What a close reading of the ethnographic material reveals is that one does not acquire a gender identity by acquiescing to a single model of gender. This makes it impossible, amongst other things, to find the psychoanalytic argument that the resolution of the Oedipus complex is the defining moment in the attainment of a sexual identity entirely satisfactory. If sexual difference were so straightforward – and in all fairness neither Freud nor Lacan claimed that it was – then why does gender need to be so reiterative, so ceaselessly performed? I take up this question again in chapter 7, but here I explore how we can develop a theory of gender that takes account of multiple models of gender and gender identifications by rethinking the relationship between the pre-oedipal and the oedipal, between the imaginary and the symbolic. I have been guided in my analysis by the way the ethnographic material refuses the tidy categorizations of psychoanalytic and feminist theory.

Subjects and objects

In psychoanalysis, as in anthropology, contemporary selves are more creative, more autonomous, more self-reflexive and generally more resistant to the predations of power. The most striking development in psychoanalysis in recent decades has been the turn towards intersubjectivity, towards an understanding of how selves are formed in and through relations with others.[1] This has been paralleled by a concern with agency, with how individuals can bring about change if their internal worlds are simply determined either by culture or by fixed psychosexual structures. Castoriadis's work on the imaginary as ceaselessly creative is part of this move. However, what gets reintroduced with intersubjectivity are questions of agency and questions of history, and thus the key issue becomes whether we can provide an account of the way the psyche is formed in a specific society. To achieve this end, there must be a means to understand how social structures and cultural values become internalized in such a way as to produce a dynamic unconscious.

Object relations theory has provided a series of interlinked accounts of how the psyche is formed through social relations.[2] Object relations theorists challenge the traditional Freudian understanding of the structures of the mind, and they focus on the influence of external objects (parents, significant others, part objects) in building an internal psychic organization. The starting point for their dissent from Freud begins with the problem of biology, with the instincts or the drives and the idea that they are pleasure-seeking. In Freudian theory, the self develops out of unconscious pleasure and is only differentiated from it as a result of contact with external reality, through the intervention of the reality principle. In object relations theory, the emphasis is on a self that is object-seeking rather than pleasure-seeking. The root of the difference is thus between a psyche that emerges out of the sexual and aggressive drives, aka Freud, and one that emerges out of forming relationships. In object relations theory, it is the ability to form relationships that provides pleasure and not the search for pleasure that forces a drive towards relationships: 'It is not the libidinal attitude which determines the object relationship, but the object relationship which determines the libidinal attitude' (Fairbairn, 1952: 34).

In rejecting the idea that the human psyche is driven by instincts, the sexual and the aggressive drives, object relations theory does two things. First, it replaces the notion that the defining characteristic of human existence is sexual and aggressive desire with the idea that what is innate in humans (presumably biological) is their desire to seek relationships. This replaces the Freudian notion of the monadic subject who must be brought into the world with the notion of a social self who can only develop through interaction with others in a social context. This is a theme that we have already seen as present in the work of Castoriadis.[3] Second, object relations theory challenges the Freudian topography of mind. Freud's view of the id as providing the driving energy of the psyche and as mediated by the ego is disputed because object relations theorists see interpersonal relations as structuring and transforming unconscious desire: 'Instincts can only operate satisfactorily when they belong to a stable ego, and therefore cannot be the source of the ego's energy for object-relating. It seems more conceivable that the energy of the ego for object-relating is the primary energy' (Guntrip, 1968: 422).

The consequences of this position are far reaching, because it suggests that there is no distinction to be made between the id and the ego, and thus no radical conflict between the pleasure principle and the reality principle. Fairbairn suggests, for example, that it makes no sense to talk of the ego as precipitated out of a pre-existing part of the psyche constituted by impulse. He argues instead that from the very beginning of life, instincts or impulses are part of a relationship-seeking ego. Crucially, the fact that from the start the ego is oriented towards relationships with others means that it is to a significant extent determined by the reality principle from the very beginning (Fairbairn, 1952: 88). This view of the ego sees it as a unity which contains its own energy, an energy that drives it towards relationships, and as such it has the potential within itself to develop into a coherent and integrated self: 'The only escape from a dualism of radically opposed structures is to banish the term "id", and reserve "ego" to denote the whole basically unitary psyche with its innate potential for developing into a true self, a whole person' (Guntrip, 1973: 41). This notion has something in common with Castoriadis's idea of the radical imaginary, of a psyche that is perennially and innately 'self-starting' and therefore in important respects autonomous. This is because in object relations theory, ego development is synonymous with the creation of a true self. This self is, by definition, well adapted to its environment and surroundings.

The emphasis in object relations on relationships, significant others, the innate propensity to seek and form relationships and the development of the ego as the basis for the true self results in a focus on the pre-oedipal relationship rather than the oedipal conflict in the formation of the psyche. Fairbairn provides an account of how the originally unified individual becomes split as a result of frustrations in the mother–child relationship. In object relations theory, the ego is bound up with objects (other people) from birth, and difficulties with object relations are thus intersubjective or interpersonal problems. In a perfect world, the relationship with the mother would provide the grounds for a movement towards a whole ego involved in satisfying relationships with others. In reality, society imposes constraints, restrictions and separations (Fairbairn, 1952: 109). As a result, the infant can experience objects as unsatisfying and, in an effort to gain control, internalizes the object. Thus, internal objects become compensations for the frustrating nature of external ones. In this process, the ego is split. Faced with an internal object that is both pleasurable and aggressive, the infant splits the object into a 'good' object and a 'bad' object. The ego is attached to both these objects and thus, as they are split, so is the ego. This process of splitting is painful, but for object relations theorists it is early relations with the mother, pre-oedipal relations, that structure the psyche, causing splitting and repression, and not the Oedipus complex itself. This insistence underpins the contention in object relations theory that the internal world of fantasy, as well as mental structures themselves, are the result of the impact of external social events and others.

The view of the unconscious that emerges in object relations theory is thus quite different from that in Freudian or Lacanian theory. First, because the focus is on the ego as an entity, and, second, because unconscious processes are the consequence of problems in relations with others which then have an impact on psychic development in general. In this view, the unconscious is an epiphenomenon of distorted development, the result of failures in object relations. It is thus precipitated out of, the product of, the ego rather than the ego being precipitated out of the id as in Freud. This view of the unconscious as the precipitate of failure, specifically maternal failure, is a consequence of the way object relations theorists focus on the emergence of a stable self, on how the well-adjusted person is formed. However, not all object relations theorists handle the unconscious and the formation of mental structures in exactly the same way.

Winnicott, Klein and (m)others

Mothering and separation from the mother, rather than a focus on the father and the father's relation to the law, is the primary focus of concern in object relations theory. This can be seen most clearly in the work of Donald Winnicott. He emphasizes that the newborn infant has to contend with a state of 'unintegration', unable to put together its fragmentary experiences.[4] It is the job of the mother to provide a 'holding' environment in which the child can develop a sense of trust and a sense of self through the mother's 'primary maternal preoccupation' (Winnicott, 1965: 85). This 'preoccupation' allows the child to develop a sense of omnipotence as the mother responds to her/his desires. Over time, the child's omnipotence becomes strong enough for a sense of self to emerge, and for the child to cope with her/his experience of being a separate individual in the world (ibid.: 163). It is crucial here, according to Winnicott, that the mother provide a 'non-intrusive presence' that allows the child to freely create an internal world of fantasy, imagination and desire. This is the process Winnicott refers to as 'good enough mothering', and it is through this process that the mother acts as a kind of 'mirror' for the child, mediating between reality and the child's ego. If successful, the process of 'good enough mothering' leads to the development of a 'true' self (ibid.: 83–99, 230–41).

Winnicott argues that the infant moves from a relationship with a subjective object to one that is objectively perceived, and it is good enough mothering that allows the child to move from fusion and merger with the mother to being capable of being separate from her and entering into object relations (ibid.: 45, 224). Object relations in this context means external relations with objects that have an existence outside the fantasy world of the child. This developmental process is essential if the child is to elaborate a self that feels alive and real in the world. If the mothering is not good enough, if the environment is not right and the mother does not respond appropriately to the child, then the child will develop a 'false' self, one that is unable to establish proper relations with others. The 'false' self is one that is too compliant with external demands. If the mother fails to respond to the child appropriately, then the child will strive to connect emotionally with the mother by abandoning its own desires and wishes and incorporating her desires and demands. Thus the child's self becomes defined by desires that are not its own.

Winnicott's theory of the development of the 'true' self incorporates several pre-theoretical assumptions about dependency, autonomy and creativity. The 'true' self is formed when the mother
provides sufficient support – a 'non-intrusive presence' – for the
child both to freely create and desire, and yet to identify with her
sufficiently to learn how to enter into relations with others. The
'true' self emerges out of an interplay of dependence and creativity. Hence, Winnicott emphasizes the importance of the relation to
the mother not just as a means to mediate the self's relation to the
world, but also as the process through which the psychic processes
are developed through creativity, imagination and fantasy. What the
'false' self always lacks is creativity (Phillips, 1988: 133). Here, Winnicott's views have something in common with Castoriadis's insistence on the role of creativity in the radical imaginary. What they
share is a conviction that the self must be a source of creativity in
itself; what they differ about is where that creativity comes from.
Castoriadis insists that the psyche has this capacity to create de
nouveau and is in that sense autonomous. Winnicott sees the capacity for creativity as arising out of the self in relation to the mother:
in a sense symbolism is the product of 'good enough mothering'.

Winnicott thus maintains an understanding of the formation of
mental structures in social terms, through the way ego–object links
are set up as a result of external social relations. However, his
account lays enormous emphasis on the influence of mother–child
relations and on the importance of developing a 'true' self in an
appropriate environment. In this sense, the disruptive nature of
desire and the unconscious, so evident in Freud's and Lacan's work,
is sanitized: the unconscious is the result of environmental failure.[5]
Melanie Klein takes a different view, and starts from Freud's notion
of the aggressive drives and the death instinct. Klein assumes a
primitive ego to be in existence from birth, but this does not constitute the whole of the infant's mind, since there are also instincts
from the start that are represented by fantasies through which the
infant seeks their satisfaction. Where Klein differs from Freud on
the question of instincts is that she assumes that objects exist from
the start and that instincts are always directed towards objects:
'there is no instinctual urge, no anxiety situation, no mental process
which does not involve objects' (Klein, 1997a[1952a]: 53). In other
words, Klein provides a view of the instinct which is both biological and social (Greenberg and Mitchell, 1983: 136–7).

The infant's inner world revolves around fantasy – 'phantasy' in
Klein's usage – which acts as an imaginative representation of

instincts and feelings. The first part object for the infant is the mother's breast (Klein, 1997b[1952b]: 58), which both gives and denies gratification and is thus split into a good and a bad breast (Klein, 1997c[1946]: 2). Klein emphasizes that all children experience anxiety and fear, as well as aggressive and destructive emotions: representatives of the death instinct. These are the starting point of psychological development, just as the sexual instincts are for Freud. In contrast to other object relations theorists, who emphasize the need for a perfect state of support from the mother, Klein focuses on the problem of aggression and destructiveness and how something positive is made out of them. She emphasizes how infants project anxiety outwards in the form of fantasies and thus lessen their anxiety, but then become fearful that the object on which they have displaced their rage will attack and annihilate them (Klein, 1997d[1948]: 31–2). This is what Klein calls the 'paranoid-schizoid' position, which, through splitting the ego, is able to keep good and persecutory objects separate. In this stage, the infant projects positive and negative fantasies outwards (projection), and takes in what it perceives of others and the outside world (introjection) (Klein, 1997e[1959]: 253–5). What is crucial here is that Klein sees fantasy and splitting as the main propulsion both for emotional development and for symbolization.

As long as positive images and experiences predominate over bad ones, the ego will grow in strength and develop (ibid.: 251).[6] Although the development of the ego is towards integration, splitting is fundamental and is part of the development of ordinary thought and discrimination (cf. Ogden, 1986; Aron, 1995). However, over time splitting becomes less characteristic and more effective defence mechanisms, such as repression, are invoked. As the infant develops she or he forms a perception of the mother as a person, and as made up of good and bad qualities. The emergence of the sense of others as independent persons is crucial for the further development of the self. However, the recognition that the infant both loves and hates the mother leads to intense feelings of guilt and sorrow, termed by Klein the 'depressive position' (Klein, 1997e[1959]: 255). Such depression is linked with the ability for integration and thus the child is able to make a firmer distinction between internal and external worlds, and to engage in social relations with others.

For Klein, the Oedipus complex has its origins in the depressive position because it depends on the recognition of whole external objects that can form relations with one another. But she sees the superego as having its origins in the paranoid-schizoid position and in the earliest projections and introjections of the ego whereby aspects of others, particularly the mother, are taken into the self and form the basis for identifications. She thus revises important aspects of Freud's topography of mind (Klein, 1997b[1952b]: 57–60). For the superego cannot be radically distinguished from the ego and precedes the Oedipus complex: 'the formation of the superego precedes the Oedipus complex and is initiated by the introjection of the primal object. The superego maintains its connection with the other parts of the ego through having internalised different aspects of the same good object' (Klein, 1997e[1959]: 245). In addition, the ego cannot be fundamentally distinguished from the id: 'The conscious and unconscious parts of the ego are . . . not separated by a rigid barrier . . . in speaking of the different areas of the mind, they are shaded off into each other' (Klein, 1997g[1958]: 244). Klein does not view the id as a separate structure, and sees fantasy as drawing on a manifestation of combined ego and id functioning within the same entity: ego is all. Klein, like Winnicott and other object relations theorists, sees the ego as creative, as primary (there from the start), and as structured through processes that connect to objects and the external world.

The relationship of subjects to objects is the means by which object relations theory discusses the impact of external events on internal worlds. However, a more radical view of intersubjectivity has been advanced by intersubjective and relational theorists. Jessica Benjamin, for example, seeks to elaborate on the notions of identification and recognition to move psychoanalysis from a 'subject–object' oriented project to a 'subject–subject' one. The key issue here is not so much how we form a sense of self through identification with others and parts of others, but how we come to recognize others as independent subjects, as loci of perception, experience and subjectivity, with whom it is possible to have a dialogue based on mutual recognition. The issue of recognition hinges on 'the problem of how we relate to the fact of the other's independent consciousness, a mind that is fundamentally like our own but unfathomably different and outside our control' (Benjamin, 1998: xii).

Benjamin's concern here, as in much feminist writing, is with the dialectic of sameness and difference, with the ability to recognize the other as both 'like' and 'other than' the self, and her main argument is that identification, when tied to recognition, forms the basis for an ongoing relationship. Benjamin uses the idea of ongoing relationships to rethink the connections between the pre-oedipal and the oedipal, as well as the role of the father in the pre-oedipal phase. Her contention is that the child wishes to become a 'subject of desire' as part of the process of individuation. A subject of desire is a subject who desires, who exhibits agency and intentionality, and who makes desire their own as a way of denying helplessness and confirming independence (Benjamin, 1995: 120–3). However, the sense of being a subject of desire, which is a primary sense of subjectivity, is not informed merely by lack or entry into the symbolic order, as Lacan would have it, but by a prior symbolized relation. The child represents her/himself as a subject who desires by forming a representation of another subject with whom she or he can identify and who will support her/his access to the external world. This relation is usually with the pre-oedipal father (or comparable figure) and is based on what Benjamin terms identificatory love.[7] Identificatory love is a love that wants to recognize the other as like, but it is not just a matter of incorporating the other as an ideal (as in theories of the formation of the superego), but of loving and having a relationship with the person who embodies this ideal (Benjamin, 1998: 61).[8]

Identificatory love is the first step towards recognizing the other as subject. However, it is premised on a notion of 'authorship' or ownership of one's own desire (Benjamin, 1986; 1988). This involves the conviction that one's acts originate inside and reflect one's own intention, and it entails taking and managing responsibility for one's own desire in such a way as to be able to form loving relations with others (Benjamin, 1988: 42). The Oedipus complex does mark the child's entry into the wider world, but it is not about splitting or lack, but about the ability to own one's own desire and through forms of identificatory love to 'learn' how to form ongoing relations with others.[9] In this sense, the boy becomes linked to his father via a relationship rather than being his oedipal rival. Pleasure and enjoyment are linked to being with the other, to shared feelings, in contrast to monadic views of desire (ibid.: 31). The self is thus formed out of recognizing the authorship and agency of the loved other and identifying with it. In addition to the mother, the person the child identifies with in the pre-oedipal phase is the father or comparable figure who represents the kind of 'authorship' the child is beginning to formulate (Benjamin, 1998: 61–2). More crucially, the identification with this figure serves symbolically to represent contact with the outside world, with freedom and agency; it allows the child to imaginatively represent its desire for the outside world (Benjamin, 1995: 58). The key focus here is on a gendered self that is characterized by agency and intentionality, where the other plays an active part in the 'struggle of the individual to creatively discover and accept reality' (Benjamin, 1988: 45).[10]

The oedipal, the pre-oedipal and the post-oedipal

Contemporary theories in psychoanalysis emphasize the importance of both parents in the development of a sense of self. This is in contrast to the Freudian view, which portrayed the father as the key figure in establishing a child's sense of their gendered self, and is also to be differentiated from earlier object relations theory which depicted relations with the mother as determining the capacity to develop an autonomous sense of self. As processes, both identification and differentiation are integral to the development of a gendered self, and both parents are sources of identification from the earliest stages of life, as well as providing encouragement and support in the process of differentiation (Benjamin, 1988; 1995; 1998; Fast, 1984; 1990). From this perspective, both the pre-oedipal and the oedipal are crucial, and mothers and fathers are central to both phases. Consequently, the oedipal can no longer be considered the singular, determining and final moment of the imposition of sexual difference and the acquisition of a gendered identity.

Irene Fast argues that children are born anatomically sexed, but from the time of sex ascription at birth their caregivers encourage development in ways they believe appropriate to the child's gender. In consequence, anatomical structures, physiology and social relations provide the matrix for the earliest representations of gender. These representations will in due course contribute to a gender-differentiated sense of self and other, but in this period prior to the recognition of gender difference, children themselves do not categorize their experience of masculinity and femininity in gender terms (Fast, 1990: 108). On the basis of clinical observation, Fast demonstrates that at about 18–24 months old, children begin to become aware of the differences between the sexes, but this occurs in the context of 'over-inclusive' ideas of sex and gender, where both boys and girls believe that they and others have both masculine and feminine attributes and capacities. The recognition of differences between the sexes is in some tension with the over-inclusive position, and entails an acceptance of loss, the realization by the child that they do not have some of the masculine and feminine attributes/capacities they assumed were theirs.

These lost aspects of masculinity and femininity are ascribed meanings which become attached to body parts and characteristics. But the meanings are not determined by these body parts (penis, vagina), as Freud would have it, but rather are meanings which the child ascribes to his or her body and that of others. Ideas about masculinity and femininity shape the experience and understanding of the body rather than the other way around. Denial of the loss entailed, demands for restitution and envy of the opposite sex are all observable responses to the recognition of the limits of sexual difference. Thus, children think that fathers can give birth and that women have penises, but this does not mean that they think that men are women or vice versa, or that they are confused about males and females. It does mean that they assume that other-sex persons have what they lack, that others are 'bisexually' complete (ibid.: 108–10). This process of the recognition of sex difference is accompanied by other developments, including the distinction between self and other, and between thought (self) and the objects of thought (non-self). At the same time, children redefine their parents in gender terms and use them to help constitute ideas about their own gender and the gender of others (ibid.: 113–14).

Fast contends that children have ultimately to renounce their pre-oedipal over-inclusiveness and establish a firm and definite binary gender identity (Fast, 1984). However, a number of theorists have argued that inclusive bisexuality continues after the oedipal phase, that it persists as a pre-conscious or unconscious capacity, and forms the basis both for imaginative creativity in adult life and the ability to relate to others of the opposite sex, particularly in sexual relations with them (Aron, 1995; Bassin, 2002; Benjamin, 1995; 1998; 2004; Goldner, 1991). From this perspective, the fixed, singular, oppositional gender identity of the oedipal phase is an ideology, an unattainable ideal. There is always a tension between gender ideals and the experience of being a gendered individual. Gender representations and self-representations are constantly being challenged and destabilized by conflicting experiences, ideas and images in everyday life (Goldner, 1991; May 1986). Gender identities are not singular or fixed, but are made up of a series of subject positions proffered by the multiple discourses on gender which exist in any given historical context (Moore, 1994). Psychoanalysis has only recently come to terms with the contradictory nature of gender identifications and with the idea that subjects can identify with multiple gender positions, some of which may be conflicting and contradictory (Dimen, 1991; 1995; Harris, 1991; Rivera, 1989).[11] One does not acquire a gender identity by acquiescing to a single model of masculinity and femininity, but rather by living the contrasts between them, including the spaces occupied by their differences and their similarities (Dimen, 1991).

As Thomas Domenici has suggested, rethinking the relationship between identification and differentiation helps us to see that the gendered self emerges in the context of a set of processes where the child recognizes him- or herself as simultaneously 'like' and 'not like' both parents. The resulting identifications provide the basis for the tolerance of multiple gender and cross-gender identifications. Oedipal resolution, for Domenici, occurs not with the assumption of a singular and fixed gender identity, but when the tensions between masculinity and femininity are tolerated and managed, rather than resolved (Domenici, 1995: 55). Post-oedipal gender identities are about the ability to tolerate the ambiguity and instability of masculinity and femininity, and to found an ongoing sense of self based on that tolerance (Harris, 1991: 83). Benjamin develops this view and argues that although the oedipal resolution splits and reworks gender identifications as oppositional, binary and complimentary, the multiple gender and cross-gender identifications of 'over-inclusiveness' persist, and along with the oedipal resolutions form the basis for a post-oedipal gender identity (Benjamin, 1991; 1995; 1998). Her contention is that the development of a gendered self is not about repudiating over-inclusiveness in favour of singular and fixed gendered identities, but about the ability to return to those representations without losing the knowledge of difference. In other words, that sexual difference, to be workable, requires access to the 'flexible identificatory capacities of pre-oedipal life' (Benjamin, 1995: 75).

Benjamin explicitly states that in formulating this theory she is attempting to take into account the feminist critiques of the non-unitary subject, as well as the debates about multiple subject positions based on gender. I apply a model based on these recent developments in psychoanalytic thinking in chapters 7 and 8, where I demonstrate anthropology's contribution to a reworking of the arguments concerning the relationship between the pre-oedipal, oedipal and post-oedipal. Benjamin's approach to what she calls post-conventional or post-oedipal thinking on gender opens the way for new developments in anthropological analysis because it provides a way of dealing with the hierarchical nature of gendered subject positions, and the perennial problem of the fact that dominant gender discourses are subverted not just by lived experience, but by the existence of culturally expressed and validated alternative discourses on gender. Benjamin contends that the mutual exclusivity of gender identity is instituted in the oedipal complex, but that oedipal identifications, while pervasive at the level of sanctioned gender ideals, do not and cannot seal off other gender identifications. They do not represent a seamless, consistent, hegemonic structure that organizes the psyche to the exclusion of all else. 'They are, after all, only an organized and powerful set of fantasies' (Benjamin, 1995: 77). Benjamin argues that we must recognize equally that we cannot transcend the oedipal, that the limits of sexual difference it institutes frame a boundary within which symbolic acts achieve their meaning. It is the dynamic interplay between pre-oedipal identifications and oedipal complementarity that provides the background for the symbolic transgressions of fantasy (ibid.: 78). In the ethnographic material that follows, we see how complex cultural products, such as myth and ritual, draw on and maintain a dynamic relationship between the pre-oedipal and the oedipal.

Feminist revisions of the imaginary

The idea that the imaginary and the symbolic, the pre-oedipal and the oedipal cannot be sealed off from each other has been developed in specific ways by feminist philosophers seeking to rethink the exclusionary nature of the symbolic order and the way in which 'woman' is represented as other. According to Lacan, the symbolic defines what it is to be sexed; there is no sexual identity prior to entry into the symbolic. All speaking beings must align themselves with that order whatever their physical attributes, but those who lack the phallus and hence the world of culture and language are called 'woman' (Flax, 1990: 99).[12] A number of feminist theorists, including Hélène Cixous and Luce Irigaray, have challenged the Lacanian view that female sexuality has no content other than to be defined as the other of the masculine. They explicitly challenge the representation of the symbolic order as phallic law, and contest the idea that what castration effects is the primacy of the symbolic over the imaginary. Their critique of Lacan focuses on questions of language, the body and the pre-oedipal/imaginary. In this sense, their work finds some resonances with object relations theory and its return to the maternal because they also seek to revalorize and retheorize the maternal, albeit in a distinctive mode.

Cixous and Irigaray both seek to move beyond the definition of female sexuality within the phallocentric order, where woman is associated with passivity and dependence: 'Female sex has always been theorized within masculine parameters' (Irigaray, 1985: 99; cf. Cixous, 1980a). Irigaray is clear that the Freudian notion of woman as visibly castrated renders her body and her desire unrepresentable within the phallic economy: 'she has no "proper" name. And her sex organ, which is not *a* sex organ, is counted as *no* sex organ. It is the negative, opposite, reverse, the counterpart, of the only visible and morphologically designatable sex organ . . . : the penis' (Irigaray, 1985: 101). From this perspective, women are alienated from their desire: ' there is so little place in society for her desire that she ends up by dint of not knowing what to do with it, no longer knowing where to put it, or if she has any, conceals the most immediate and the most urgent question: "How do I experience sexual pleasure?" ' (Cixous, 1980a: 95). Cixous and Irigaray suggest that female sexuality and desire are never simply phallic, centred in a single organ, but are plural and located in the *jouissance* of the female body, in various and multiple sexual organs: clitoris, vagina, cervix, lips, breasts (Irigaray, 1985: 102–3). While representation is organized within a phallocentric order, female sexuality is repressed since there is no way in which it could find expression within the terms of this order: an order 'where woman has never *her* turn to speak' (Cixous, 1980b: 249; emphasis in the original).

Cixous and Irigaray have been accused by many critics of wanting to return to an idealized, pre-given female body and to find forms of feminine representation (such as female writing) within which female sexuality and desire could be represented. However, neither theorist argues that a female libidinal economy should be celebrated in its own right, or that it can exist outside of the symbolic. Irigaray is explicit that the female body she speaks of is one that is within representation, socially and historically constituted. There is no notion of a 'natural', pre-social female body, but only of one that is already socially inscribed and psychically constituted. This is why Irigaray writes of the morphology rather than the anatomy of the body: 'We must go back to the question not of the anatomy but of the morphology of the female sex (Irigaray, cited in Grosz, 1989: 111). Cixous likewise emphasizes that her concern is with sexual difference, and that both women and men can take up feminine and masculine positions (1994a: 132).[13] She stresses that '*écriture féminine*' – that is, forms of representation that allow for the expression of female sexuality and desire – offer potential 'liberation', but liberation is only possible by reforming and recasting the symbolic, not by retreating from it (1980b: 250–1). The aim is to seek the grounds for a new framework of language and culture.[14] For both theorists this is part of a radical politics, because while changes in economic, social, interpersonal and sexual relationships will be required for women's autonomy, such changes will not be possible unless language and representational forms are also transformed.

What both Cixous and Irigaray share is an interest in the maternal, in the links, connections and rhythms of a relation to the mother that continue to have an impact on the adult self. In other words, they are interested in the way in which the imaginary/pre-oedipal is linked to the symbolic, and do not understand that relation as one of irrevocable alienation for the split subject. Cixous sees the question of subjectivity as a site of political struggle: 'insofar as it harbors and secures the lure of unicity, totalization . . . of conservatism and totalitarianism. It is not a question of making the subject disappear, but of giving it back its divisibility: attacking the "chez-soi" (self-presence) and the "pour-soi" (for itself) . . . to show the fragility of the centre and of the ego's barriers' (Cixous, 1994b: 29).

At the core of this problem with the subject for feminist philosophy is the fact that there must be room for a feminine subject and not just a form of femininity that is subservient to male oedipal needs. Irigaray argues that what is absent in the phallocentric symbolic order is a maternal genealogy, and that the relationship between mother and daughter cannot be represented within the symbolic order as it stands. This is linked to a broader argument that women, and specifically the mother, are the repressed of psychoanalysis. Irigaray's view is an interesting one because in the ethnographic material presented in this and later chapters, we can see that there is relatively little symbolic, mythical or religious material that represents the mother–daughter relationship, although mothers are omnipotently present where they are linked to the construction of male subjectivity and sexuality. For Irigaray, the unsymbolized nature of the mother–daughter relation makes it impossible for women to have an identity in the symbolic order that is distinct from the maternal function.

The problematic relationship of femininity to the symbolic and to signification is taken up by Kristeva: 'The desire to give voice to sexual difference, and particularly the position of the woman-subject within meaning and signification, leads to a veritable insurrection against the homogenizing *signifier*. However, it is all too easy to pass from the search for *difference* to the denegation of the symbolic' (Kristeva, cited in Moi, 1986: 11; emphasis in the original). Kristeva is here taking a passing shot at the *écriture féminine* school, but she is also defending the importance of the symbolic. Kristeva casts the subject's relation to the symbolic as being both structured and potentially subversive. The potential for subversion arises because of the eruption of pre-oedipal drives and sexuality into the symbolic, where they continue to exert influence on the foundations of subjectivity (Kristeva, 1986: 93). This is in contrast to Freudian and Lacanian ideas that posit the oedipal transition as one of discontinuity between the pre-oedipal mother and the symbolic law. Kristeva's subject is one that is within the symbolic and fully structured, but also open to change, and with the potential to subvert the determinism of the Lacanian notion of the symbolic order through a continuing connection to the imaginary/pre-oedipal.

Kristeva reworks the Lacanian imaginary and symbolic orders to develop a notion of the semiotic and of its relationship to signification (Kristeva, 1986: 92–9). The semiotic is associated with the pre-oedipal and centred around the mother and her body, but for Kristeva it is prior to sexual difference and therefore acts on both male and female subjects, and is not to be associated with the feminine: 'woman' has no privileged access to the semiotic.[15] Where Kristeva makes a contribution is in seeing elements of the pre-oedipal within language and the law, in imagining a productive tension between the semiotic elements of the maternal body linked to the pre-symbolic imaginary and the structure of signification within the symbolic order. These ideas owe a debt to Freud's notion that the superego is precipitated out of the id and remains in relation to it (see chapter 3), but provide further insight by directly challenging a notion of an invariant paternal law that defines the symbolic order. The symbolic cannot be decoupled from the imaginary, and cannot simply be said to supersede or repress it.

Kristeva's aim is to develop an understanding of the 'subject-in-process' which would take account of semiotic drives, symbolic meanings and socio-cultural contexts (Kristeva, 1986: 95). Her insistence on the creativity of imaginary significations in the semiotic and their eruption into the symbolic order finds resonances with Castoriadis's notion of the imaginary, and the notion of the creative, self-constructed self, discussed in chapter 3. These notions differ in the role they envisage for the unconscious and desire, but what they share is a concern to account for the potential for social change through the creative capacity of individuals for signification and representation. Kristeva takes the semiotic (the pre-symbolic) as the source of an original libidinal multiplicity associated with the maternal body. Critics have questioned whether the notion of the semiotic depends on a concept of the maternal body that is natural, pre-discursive, and pre-linguistic (Butler, 1990; Grosz, 1989; Jones, 1984; Stanton, 1989). Such a claim – were it to be made – would in any event be an impossible one since the very notion of the maternal in psychoanalytic theory is socially and historically constructed, and, perhaps more importantly – as with object relations theory – any representations of a pre-oedipal maternal that could erupt into the symbolic or disrupt language in any way would already be socially, culturally and psychically constituted. As Freud argued, what is present in the unconscious is not the drive or the instinct, but its representation. Kristeva seeks to address the question of the social, symbolic and psychic value of the maternal in her discussion of how the maternal is repressed in psychoanalysis and in western culture in general. However, what she perhaps fails to address, despite her insistence on the possibility of change arising in the symbolic order, is whether the maternal as signification/representation is open to cultural variability: 'What cultural configuration of language, indeed, of discourse, generates the trope of a pre-discursive libidinal multiplicity, and for what purposes?' (Butler, 1990: 91).[16] The ethnographic material that follows demonstrates quite conclusively that both the feminine and the masculine, the maternal and the paternal are open to cultural and historical variation precisely because of the way they are always set up in representation, and because our relation to them is always an imaginary one.

Kristeva draws a provocative set of analogies between the heterogeneity of drives in the semiotic and the multiple meanings of poetic language (Kristeva, 1974). What she seems to suggest is that the multiple meanings of poetic language disrupt the univocal coherence of signification, just as the multiplicity of the semiotic libidinal economy disrupts the symbolic order and the autonomy of the subject (Kristeva, 1980: 124–5). The subject is split precisely because it is founded across the semiotic and the symbolic. What the semiotic represents is the *jouissance* that precedes desire, the emergence of subject/object distinctions and the imposition of the law. The symbolic is predicated on the rejection of the mother, and yet the semiotic retains a link to the maternal body in sound, rhythm, repetition and poetic speech (Butler, 1990: 82). The foundation of the subject/ego is thus based on a continuing somatic and representational link to the body of the mother. Poetic language in

its materiality, its sounds and resonances, carries the trace of this
relation to the maternal body (Kristeva, 1980: 134–6). Language
mimics the materiality of bodily relations and connections, and is a
psychic attempt to recover them through the materiality of sound.
Kristeva suggests that metaphor is the means by and through which
the drives, the pre-symbolic imaginary, a passion for the body, and
sensations and somatic modes of attention find expression in language and burst forth or erupt into the symbolic (Oliver, 1993: 74).
Metaphor links the semiotic and the symbolic, and in the ethnographic material which follows, we can see the consequences of this
for symbolism, imagination and sexuality in the myths and rituals
of different societies.

What Kristeva does is to provide one account of how to rethink
the maternal in relation to the paternal, and suggests that they
should be viewed not as polar opposites, but as aspects of each
other. This perspective finds specific resonance in the ethnographic
material presented in this and later chapters. What becomes evident
is how, in different cultures, the pre-oedipal imaginary is positioned
within the symbolic order, and thus we can trace the relational configurations of the feminine and the masculine, the maternal and the
paternal.

Bodies and objects

The way humans symbolize the world of objects is intimately connected with their capacity for self-reflection and with consciousness
of being.[17] Indigenous psychologies – specific statements, ideas and
images about the nature of person, individual and/or self and their
relation to the world – connect in concrete terms to cultural ideas
about how humans relate to the natural and the divine worlds. This
concrete relation to the world of objects plays a key role not only in
a sense of a gendered self-as-lived, but in constructing and organizing motivations, inner states and schemes for action. It also
reveals the materiality of consciousness, the way in which the acquisition of gender identity is never singular or fixed, but is concretely
linked to work, politics and power. In the following example, I show
how pre-oedipal and oedipal versions of masculinity and femininity are maintained in a dynamic relation to each other and to the
material world in which they are powerful and persuasive.

The Ngulu are a matrilineal agricultural people living in east-
central Tanzania. In the past, when an Ngulu girl had her first men-

struation she was deemed ready to go through the Guluwe initiation ceremony. The purpose of this ceremony was said to be to teach a girl how to manage and ensure her fertility, how to act in sexual intercourse and how to behave as a proper adult woman. The Guluwe ceremony was preceded by a private ritual involving circumcision and some instruction on the sexual differences between women and men. The main ceremony took place in a local house, and was attended by members of the girl's own matrilineage and that of her father.

At one point the ceremony involves a ritual where four women leave the hut: one acts as a hunter and carries a bow and arrow, another is the hunter's wife and carries a calabash of beer plugged with a piece of cooked meat in a basket on her head. They declare that they are going to kill a wild pig (*guluwe*). They are accompanied by two other women, each of whom carries four seeds, and who, when they arrive at a secluded place, crawl on their stomachs to retrieve the seeds from the surrounding grass with their mouths. They then transmit these seeds into the hands of the hunter and wife with their mouths. During this the women sing: 'Ngulu man, foraging man! Forage for your children during the famine!' They also sing: 'The woman with a tumescent vagina opens her legs wide to admit men.' The hunter and wife then pretend to hunt a wild pig. The hunter shoots an arrow and misses three times and each time this happens the other three women knock the hunter down. On the fourth attempt the hunter is successful and the wife falls down. The women return to the hut and repeat the hunting songs and mime again the killing of the wild pig. Further parts of the rites involve painting the novice with red clay and white flour, miming sexual intercourse and instructing the girl how to perform various sexual acts. These sequences in the ritual are repeated over four successive days. During this period, the girl receives detailed instructions not only through songs, riddles and stories, but also using various clay figurines and plant materials representing the sexual organs and other aspects of women's daily activities (Beidelman, 1964: 366–9). These performances establish homologies between parts of the body, day-to-day objects (hoes, pots) associated with production, key cultural values and symbols, and aspects of femininity and masculinity.

The Ngulu themselves say that the symbolic hunt represents sexual intercourse. The hunting of the wild pig explicitly draws on images of the slaying of a dangerous quarry and the securing of delicious food. The setting of the arrow on the bow is said to represent sexual union. In Ngulu thought, the use of two instruments to perform a productive task is always linked to sex. Grinding flour, making fire with fire sticks, pounding flour – in each case the passive tool is spoken of as feminine and the active as masculine, and the terms for these tools are sometimes used as euphemisms for male and female genitalia. The slaying of the wild pig is explicitly linked to the shedding of blood: the creative blood of the womb, the bloodline of descent, the blood of childbirth and warfare, and the blood of menstruation. In other words, to associations of life and death (ibid.: 370–1). The links that are made between hunting and sex deliberately invoke the relationship between fertility, social continuity and death. The symbolic meanings given to the objects in the ritual shift with context and are multivalent. The long calabash filled with beer, which the hunter's wife carries on her head, is said to represent the penis filled with semen, but since it is placed within a basket it is also said to represent the womb which receives the penis. However, when considered in relation to the meat-plug that stops the calabash, the latter is said to represent the female organs and the beer the reproductive blood of the woman stopped up by the meat-plug which is the penis (ibid.: 373). Concrete objects thus represent aspects of femininity and masculinity, but do so in recursive and folded-over fashion, so that what is once female is revealed in other contexts and forms of practical engagement as male, and vice versa.

The ceremonial acts and symbolic sequences of the full rites are very complex, but they centre on the relationship between the combination of female and male elements to ensure fertility and ordered social life. For Ngulu, the number four represents the repetition resulting from orderly social relations: hence in the ceremony, four attempts to kill the pig, four seeds, four consecutive days of rites. The Ngulu also say that intercourse should take place four times on the night a marriage is consummated, that the newly weds should remain secluded in their hut for four days, that four months of regular sexual intercourse are needed to feed a pregnancy properly, and that there are four parts of the human body formed in the mother's womb (ibid.: 379). The interpenetration of symbols, images and narratives, and their complex interweaving in the form of a long rumination on and practical enactment with the origins of life, Ngulu society and death, are learned over time. Individuals learn more through their successive involvement in the rites over a number of years (Moore, 1997a; 1999a). Through engagement in these ritual sequences, aspects of femininity and masculinity are linked concretely and metaphorically to productive roles, the division of labour and gender roles more generally: that is, to the categorical differences between women and men in Ngulu society.

At the same time, aspects of the body and its experiences become intertwined with theological/philosophical and cosmological principles, and basic daily activities are imbued with wider sets of meanings. These meanings draw on conscious and unconscious fantasies of the body and its relations to parents, clans and matrilineages. During conception a man's semen combines with a woman's blood to produce a child. This child's body is said to be related to the mother and the mother's matrilineage through blood and soft parts of the body, and to the father and the father's matrilineage through the hard parts of the body, such as bone, teeth and cartilage. Semen's whiteness, and its viscosity and coolness associate it with bone, in contrast to the fluidity and heat of blood. Through a series of associations whiteness is also associated with physical rigidity and moral stability. White beads are given to a youth to help him through the operation of circumcision, and are placed on a child's neck to ensure normal development and growth. Whiteness thus encodes ideas about social, moral and developmental features. In this context, the painting of the novice in the Guluwe ceremony with red clay and white maize flour literally inscribes on the exterior of her body the fact of sexual difference, its reproductive combinations, the divisions of Ngulu society in the form of her mother's and her father's matrilineage, and her own multiply gendered nature. Thus, ideas about and images of bodies also invoke themes of the interconnection and multivalent nature of sexuality, its creative, imaginary, productive capacities. They make of sexuality something powerful, both practical and cosmological. Here, there can be no case of a radical separation between the self and the world of objects, between self-reflection and embodied activity, between body and society, or between psyche and culture. There is no sense of a gendered self outside the symbols, images and metaphors that make concrete the relationship of bodies to sexuality and the origins of society. Sexual difference is thus thoroughly cultural.

Ngulu ritual makes explicit use of sexual symbolism. The ritual provides an intellectual and practical exegesis of the way in which masculinity and femininity are constructed within a world of objects. They also show how masculinity and femininity are constituted and experienced through a set of imaginary relations to bodies, fertility, sexuality and production. Material like this can be found in societies all over the world, but what is of interest here is the relation it implies between the imaginary and the symbolic. Representations, images, fantasized connections and motivations from the imaginary are brought into relation with cultural symbols and discourses, and subjected to processes of elaboration and reflection which are both linguistic and performative.[18]

There are two key points here. The first is that we cannot interpret these rites as if they were simply imposing the dominant gender model of Ngulu society. Ngulu girls' initiation ceremonies take place long after the resolution of any oedipal phase could or should have taken place, and the girls involved are already well aware of gender ideologies and their relationships to production, sexuality, marriage and social structure. In any event, the ritual explicitly works over both the categorical, binary distinctions between masculinity and femininity and the fact that they are versions of each other, mutually conjoined and relationally produced. The second point is that both psychoanalysts and anthropologists have a tendency when discussing initiation rituals to miss much of what is important by focusing almost exclusively on the initiates and on what they experience and learn (Moore, 1997a; 1999a). We should recall that adults engage in these rituals over their lifetime, starting as initiates and then going on to be the parents and grandparents of future initiates, and also working over the themes, images, sounds and narratives of the ritual with a cohort of other women and men who were present at their original initiation. Thus, rituals and the cultural formulations of masculinity and femininity they develop, reflect and elaborate on need to be seen in cross-generational and historical perspective. What one has known, seen, understood, danced and felt as an old woman are not the things one knows as a young girl. Here we see the conscious attempt to reflect on and experience the question of what masculinity and femininity do, and mean, and embody, and entail: the puzzling question of what it means to be marked by sexual difference, to accede to its limits, and yet still be alive and productive and part of a society that continues. At this point, we should remind ourselves of a point Obeyesekere made regarding the relationship between the imaginary relations and motivations of childhood, and cultural rituals and symbols: namely, that the latter are not just the reflection or product of the former (Obeyesekere, 1990: 54–62). Unconscious motivations and experiences cannot be seen, but must be inferred from their representations. The imaginary is the context and the content of these representations, and it is in this form that the imaginary enters into and is worked over in cultural symbols, ritual and myth. However, all these cultural productions are not simply the return of the repressed or archaic fantasies in their 'pure form', or evidence of more 'primitive' ways of thinking or any other of the simplistic suggestions that have been made. Cultural forms – symbols, myths and rituals, etc. – are precisely the conscious and unconscious, intentional and motivational, rationalized and reflective, intellectual and practical elaboration of the representations, experiences and sensations which form the gendered self in its cultural and personal context. These cultural forms emerge out of the post-oedipal understandings of gender difference which work by drawing on both the oedipal and the pre-oedipal work to maintain the tensions and ambiguities of the relation of masculinity to femininity, its folded-over and productive nature.

Metaphor and metonym

Ethnographic material and exegesis frequently emphasize the material, somatic, sensate character of metaphor – the way it ties bodies to categories, power relations, images and experiences. One of the criticisms that is sometimes made of psychoanalytic interpretations in anthropology is that they are too abstract, concerned with mapping structural binaries onto the messy configurations of life as lived. Much symbolic work in anthropology – some psychoanalytically inspired and some not – has often been limited by its restrictive dualism, where paired opposites are combined and recombined to form metonymic and metaphoric chains. This way of interpreting cultural material has proved particularly constraining in relation to the analysis of gender, where the binary nature of gender categorization consistently stands in for or refigures the experience of multiplicity and performativity that is also part of the experience of femininity and masculinity. The value of a theory of metaphor developed through the prism of the relation of the imaginary to the symbolic is that we can see that the material dealt with in structuralist analyses is only one aspect of what we need to focus on. A more thoroughgoing analysis of metaphor – both linguistic and non-linguistic – would focus on the way it ties together fantasy, embodiment, power and agency, as well as rationalized, intellectual thought. In such an analysis, the end product is not, as I discuss in chapter 8, a single coherent model, but a set of incomplete and over-determined traces which are the product of specific and situated engagements.

The Aluund of Southwest Zaire (now the Democratic Republic of Congo) tell a story by means of sand drawings during the male initiation rites known as *mwiingoony*. What follows is a condensed version of the tale:

> There was a man Mukaanz, who had a wife Nansoomb. They had two children. Mukaanz provided for them by trapping birds for food. Then one day great hunger came to their village. Nansoomb went begging for food in the villages of her husband and her mother. She crossed the rivers and washed herself in water of Choowal a Mbwaal (lit: 'the washing of the vagina'). She passed the traps in which her husband caught birds. She took the birds' feathers and put them in her hair to make an *nsal* (chiefly hat). With this *nsal* and a ceremonial dress (*vuund*) made from plant fibres, she left from the villages to beg for food. When she arrived there, Nansoomb opened her legs to show her genitals. The people were very happy and she returned home with a lot of food. Before arriving home, she hid the *nsal* and the *vuund* in the bush. The man wondered why his wife came home with so much food, and one day he followed her. He hid himself on the road and saw his wife go by dressed in the *nsal* and the *vuund*. The man got angry and asked her where she got these things. She replied, I made them with feathers from the birds in your traps, but you weren't smart enough to do so. The man took everything from his wife to wear himself and finally killed his wife with an arrow. He hid her body in the hole where the red ants make their nest. From that day on the *mwiingoony* stayed with the men and no longer belongs to the women. (See De Boeck, 1991: 43–4)

This story links the origins of society to the creation of sexual difference.[19] Hunger in the land leads to the killing of Nansoomb and the appropriation of the *mwiingoony* ritual by men. At the same time, the men give women the *chiwiil*, women's initiation ritual, in return. The forced exchange of the rituals establishes both social order and the nature of the relations between the sexes. Men make society through the murder of the mythic mother, and this is symbolized in the fact that the *nsal* is one of the main pieces of royal regalia. The political symbol of male public authority was first produced by the mother. Accounts of Nansoomb's killing are part of both male and female initiation stories, and what they stress is male dependence on female regenerative and life-giving powers as exemplified in the showing of the vagina to collect food. More importantly, they emphasize that women are the origin of the male initiation ritual, that social relations of a particular kind came before the society men created, that being and becoming male depends on something that is female. Thus the ritual ties together chains of metaphor and metonym that link bodily experiences and practices to interpersonal behaviour, social and biological reproduction, economic and social structures, and chiefly power (ibid.: 44–5).

The *mwiingoony* ritual begins with the preparation of the *zeemb*, or initiation ground. This is done by the initiation master, and he is invested in this role by being offered an arrow by one of the novices. By offering this arrow, the novices ask 'to be straightened', literally to become men, and with this arrow they will be initiated or 'killed' as Nansoomb was killed with an arrow by her husband (ibid.: 46). This begins a theme which is common to most male initiation ceremonies in Africa and that is the emphasis on the feminization of the initiates, their death and then subsequent rebirth as male in the course of the ritual. The initiation master marks out the *zeemb* with two sticks representing a hoe and a machete. Luunda proverbs refer to the hoe as female and the machete as male. Once the *zeemb* is prepared, the initiation master plants a long pole made from a white wood in the centre of it. This pole represents the central pole which sustains the roof of the house, and the family male elder who supports the members of the household as the pole supports the roof. For the Aluund, entering a house is linked to the act of penetration, of entering a woman's belly. The initiation ground is thus a house or womb that is literally impregnated by the planting of the pole. The house is the place where the hearth and the fire are situated, and is likened to the womb. Aluund ideas of conception and the origin of life are imaged in the 'water' or 'blood of childhood' – that is, male sperm – leaving the penis and entering the vagina to warm itself by the fire in the womb. The red blood-stuff is cooked in the womb into white life, and the penis provides the fuel that lights the fire (ibid.: 48–51).

The ritual is a rich and complex one, made up of several parts, but its central themes work over the relation between life and death, and between masculinity and femininity. The initiates die in the womb to be reborn, just as a menstruating woman bleeds only to regain a fecund body. These links are made explicit in many of the activities, bodily attacks on the initiates, dances, metaphors and songs that make up the ritual. The rite itself is a long practical and conceptual disquisition on the transformation of female into male principles. Principles that then underpin, and indeed constitute, bodily experiences, personal fantasies, interpersonal interactions, social behaviour, economic activities and social structures. This process of transformation, however, is never final or complete. As Aluund philosophy and cosmology articulate, it is a cyclical process, an unfolding and refolding, a matter of engagement through perspective. What was once female becomes male, and vice versa. This process unfolds at the level of the embodied self. The *zeemb*, as a womb, is a space in which the male initiates have enacted on their bodies the transgression and incorporation of female bodily boundaries and orifices (ibid.: 59). This, paradoxically, is what makes them male. But, the *zeemb*, and the experiences it enfolds, is a space where fantasy is internalized and externalized, where bodily experiences find forms of representation.

In this sense, it is a literal, living encounter with the pre-oedipal, with a space and a time where the imaginary is given form within the symbolic order. Aspects of the maternal body and of the pre-symbolic imaginary – links and connections to, rhythms and fantasies of the female body – are brought into a relation with the symbolic, sexual difference and the paternal law. In consequence, adult sexuality, reproduction, and social and economic relations are not only shot through with aspects of both the female and the male, but are also intimately tied both to the difference that makes sexual difference and to its composite and unstable nature. This is true not just for the initiates, but for all the adults involved. There are very many esoteric meanings associated with the *mwiingoony* ritual and they are learnt only slowly over a lifetime of participation. The meaning and form of an elder's engagement with this ritual is clearly very different from that of a young initiate, but both are engaged through participation with personal and cultural fantasies that develop out of and feed back into cosmological and philosophical principles in ways that are both culturally patterned and highly individualistic. These principles continually produce the key metaphors that constitute bodily experience, individuals' sense of self, interpersonal relations and socio-economic relations. The ritual that dramatizes these principles makes them open to study by the anthropologist, as well as to critical reflection and engagement by people themselves, but the ritual is only part of a lived relation to them. The fantasies that draw on these principles and the metaphors that carry them are there in everyday activities such as cooking, eating and having sex. They are there in the way people think about and relate to persons of specific genders, to their bodies, needs, appetites and capacities. They are the maternal and paternal metaphors that structure Aluund society and Aluund selves. They are sexual difference itself.

Metaphor in these contexts is what links the imaginary to the symbolic, and provides the means for a continuing somatic and representational link between the feminine and the masculine. Metaphor is what ties the body and the experience of the body to language and conceptualization. However, it is not a simple matter of a chain of associations or significations or, as has sometimes been argued, of 'one thing standing for another'. Metaphor here is simultaneously concrete and imaginative, in that it folds and unfolds across space and time, especially within rituals, setting off new sets of meanings and associations. It is more akin to Castoriadis's notion of the radical imaginary in its ability to continuously create images and meanings (see chapter 3). It is through this mechanism that social fantasies engage with the fantasies of the subject. This not only allows for the cultural structuring of desire and enjoyment, but also means that social significations are embedded within unconscious desire in a manner that underpins individuals' understanding of self and other. The explicit aim of the ritual is not just to make men into men, but to provide an opportunity for the psyche to invest representations with unconscious desire, a kind of rumination on the nature of being human and of being gendered, and one that takes place simultaneously on the level of conscious cultural thought and unconscious representation. This demonstrates quite conclusively that the human capacity for representation and symbolism is bound up with fantasies of the feminine and the masculine and their interrelations.

Conclusion

The images in which the subject finds itself come to it from outside. The self forms as a result of an engagement with a lived world of objects and recognizes itself and its desires within certain representations, images, sounds and narratives which attach themselves to bodily sensations and perceptions. It is the fact of the self's location within a physical body that breaks down the validity of the subject–object distinction as an absolute. The materiality of representation means that the gendered body – for a parent to recognize and affirm the physical sex of a child is already for them to engage in an imaginary relation with a gendered body – is at the origin of the self and psychic processes. One cannot engage with the world of objects as a social being without being gendered in this way through the recognition of one's sex. The handling of the child's body from the earliest days engages with the lived reality of gender, with the way a culture or a society engages with the limiting effects of sexual difference and the fantasies of masculinity and femininity that this entails.

The relation of the subject to the symbolic order is itself an imaginary relation, that is set up in representation and informed by the imaginary relations of others. As Freud so persuasively argued, the psychic reality of the ego is one created in the world of objects, and it takes as real its representations of that world. As anthropology demonstrates, the world that forms the cultural self is already a mediated one (Obeyesekere, 1990: 66). The external world is never unmarked by the particular way that representations, images and sounds are part of the evolving self-consciousness of the ego in the context of the developing physiology and neurological coherence of the body. Thus, representations have a reality that is made material and consequently the relations a child has to its parents are both sensate and imaginary. Psychoanalysis frequently portrays the mother and father as self-evident entities or categories, as if all mothers and fathers were the same kind of object in the child's world. This cannot be so. Fantasies are the imaginative representations of instincts and feelings, and as such form the basis for the development of the self in a world of objects in which parents and significant others play a constitutive role. Relations with parents and significant others are thus set up in and through representations. But, the fantasies that sustain the emerging self of the child are not monadic: they are relational, they are themselves engaged by the fantasies of parents and others (Laplanche and Pontalis, 1968). This is in consequence of the fact – if nothing else – that the latter are themselves gendered individuals marked by the limits of sexual difference within the configurations of personal and cultural histories.

The development of a gendered self is a complex process of identification and differentiation, introjection and projection. This process is often characterized as an interaction between objects – child, mother, father – whereas recent developments in psychoanalysis have emphasized that it is not just the relationship between self and other that is internalized, but also the relations between and among others. The child not only internalizes the mother and the father as individuals, but also the relation between them. Psychic processes and the assumption of a gendered identity are thus shaped not just by subject–object relations, but also by relations between objects. This links to earlier work in anthropology (see chapter 2) which emphasizes the inappropriateness of imposing western views of subject–object relations when discussing the notion of the self cross-culturally. The western conception of the subject–object relation implies both the autonomy of the subject and its visual mastery of the object which it sees, interprets and knows. Much of the work on symbolism in anthropology also emphasizes this form of the subject–object relation to explain how individuals know, construct and interpret their world. However, other views of this relation figure the subject as located within a field of relations, where the emphasis is on the subject as constituted through relations rather than being a single, fixed point of knowledge.[20] From this perspective, the world of objects is not just present, awaiting determination (representation, interpretation) by the subject, but is, rather, an active, material, semiotic environment that engages with the subject.

An emphasis on the emergence of the gendered self in a world of 'objects in relations' is important when we consider that ethnographically many of the images of masculinity and femininity we encounter are not images of 'things' or 'essences' or 'whole objects', but of relations, of masculinity and femininity as mutually and multiply constitutive. One of the fantasies that the child has to relinquish is the desire to be all, to be both sexes. Thus, the imposition of sexual difference, the recognition of its limits, works to unbind the composite sex, to unravel the fantasy that powerful others must lack nothing. Whether we equate this with Fast's 'over-inclusiveness' or Klein's 'combined parent', we see ethnographically that this model of masculinity and femininity as being 'in relation' to, 'connected to', 'mutually constituted' plays a powerful role in myth, ritual and symbolism. In the very earliest stages of a child's life, psychic processes are developed through representations involving creativity, imagination and fantasy. This is the space of the imaginary in which the gendered self is formed through engagement with a world of objects. During the oedipal phase, oppositional, binary gender categories are frequently emphasized, and these often shape the dominant gender ideologies of a given society. However, post-oedipal models of gender connect explicitly to the imaginary and draw on more fluid representations of masculinity and femininity, bringing such images and narratives into relation with oedipal categorizations. Post-oedipal representations of gender are concerned with preserving tensions, ambiguity and fluidity, rather than trying to assimilate them. It is this adult use of the imaginary for the purposes of cultural production and intellectual reflection that is the concern of this book.

The reduction of sexual difference to sexual dimorphism is something that all societies have to struggle with.[21] This does not mean that different societies and cultures do not make more or less of categorical gender differences, more or less of the multiplicity of gendered meanings and metaphors, more or less of the body-as-fact. But every culture has to struggle with the fact that conscious and unconscious fantasies about gender and bodies exceed the facticity of socially permitted constructions. There is always more to gender and the body than socially dominant discourses frame. Each individual has to make their individual, lived appropriation of cultural images, stories, metaphors, etc., but such material as is provided by culture, and in particular through language, is not a coherent, easily readable account of sexual difference, but a complex terrain of multiple readings that have to be understood and lived both socially and individually. Unconscious fantasies bearing the marks of others' (parents and significant others) accommodations to cultural images and symbols, and of their social and individual lived and unconscious relation to a specific world of objects, erupt into the cultural material that becomes available to any individual in any specific generation. The result, as discussed in chapter 5, is that images and metaphors from the imaginary erupt into the symbolic, and the oedipal and the post-oedipal are permanently marked by the pre-oedipal. Thus, whatever the dominant ideologies of gender relations and the power differentials that underpin them in any context, these ideologies are disrupted by, folded around a set of images and metaphors, the embodied understandings of gender relations and the meanings given to sexual difference. Sexual difference is not and cannot be culturally invariant.

5

The Problem of the Phallus

[A]ll human individuals, as a result of their bisexual disposition and of cross-inheritance, combine in themselves both masculine and feminine characteristics, so that pure masculinity and femininity remain theoretical constructions of uncertain content.

Freud, 1977c[1925]: 342

If multiple models of gender exist in all societies, then how should we theorize the relationship between bodies and representation? Psychoanalytic theory maintains that biological sex difference does not provide a self-evident basis for gender and sexual identity. This makes psychoanalysis of interest to feminists and at the same time sets up an internal contradiction in their relation. If psychoanalysis provides a non-biological account of the formation of gender identity with all the liberatory potential such a theory offers, what are we to make of the fact that both Freud and Lacan claimed that it is the relation to the phallus that determines sexual difference? Freud argued that the feminine is always configured in relation to the masculine, establishing this as the basis for his theory of the Oedipus complex and object choice. Women are defined as lacking the phallus. Lacan developed this theory further, arguing that the phallus is the signifier of desire and the primary signifier of the symbolic order. As the privileged signifier of the symbolic order, it represents the asymmetrical relations between the sexes, where women and men are differently positioned with relation to power because of their differential relation to the phallus. This links the question of representation back to power.

But what is the status of the phallus? Is it the male penis? This question, which is discussed further below, has been revisited many times. It raises the question, of course, of what bodies mean. Is biological sexual difference not just obvious? Is it not just there for all to see? In this chapter, I provide two ethnographic readings of the status of the phallus and its relationship to the male penis. The first traces the effects of its representation through psychoanalytic and feminist writing. The second explores some material from Tanzania, demonstrating that sexual difference is not obvious, that the phallus is not always the privileged signifier of the symbolic order, and that when it is, it is not necessarily a male organ. I use this material to argue – contra the feminist critique – that femininity does not acquire meaning solely as the other of the masculine, that the relationship between masculinity and femininity is more mutual than this, and that, if anything, the ethnographic material suggests that it is the masculine which is defined as the other of the feminine (see also chapter 8).

What does a penis signify?

Freud's account of sexuality starts with the assumption that there is nothing natural or pre-given about the relationship between anatomical differences and sexuality itself. What he attempts is an account of sexuality at the level of the psyche and through the workings of desire. Freud frees sexuality from biology, but does so in a way that seeks to retain a link between sensation, the materiality of the body, and erotics or the social construction of desire.[1] Controlling the body in response to social demands, as part of an exchange with the external social world, is how the body becomes constructed as an interface between the psychic and the social. It is Freud's persistent linking of the psyche to the materiality of the body that has provided the grounds for so much discussion within feminist scholarship. The body erupts into theoretical debates in an unstable way, always threatening to return the theory of the social construction of sexuality to biology. This is particularly evident in the Freudian treatment of female sexuality, where femininity is consistently figured as a conundrum, a riddle, a problem without an adequate resolution (Moi, 2004).[2] Freud complained throughout his career that he could not understand the sexual life of women, although he did change his views quite considerably over time (Cf. Mitchell, 1985: 9–25). In his early work, he assumed a parallelism between the sexual development of boys and girls, but as his work on the dissolution of the Oedipus complex and the importance of castration progressed, he realized that this could not be the case, that there were certain problems and peculiarities in the sexual development of girls that required explanation (1977c[1925]: 332–3).[3]

The first love-object for both children is the mother, and the renunciation of that desire is not undertaken willingly, but only through the threat of castration. Castration is, according to Freud, the threatened punishment for masturbation, but the boy does not recognize this threat as a reality until he sees the genitals of the girl. As a result, the boy's ego turns away from the Oedipus complex and paternal authority is accepted and introjected as the superego, which thereafter perpetuates the prohibition against incest and the law (1977d[1924]: 316–19). The little girl behaves differently. Her clitoris 'behaves just like a penis to begin with', until she sees the boy's penis and 'She makes her judgement and her decision in a flash. She has seen it and knows that she is without it and wants to have it' (1977c[1925]: 336). The girl assumes castration as a wrong done to her; she sustains a narcissistic wound, and suffers a sense of inferiority. When she realizes that this condition affects all women, she also feels a contempt for her own lesser, female sex (ibid.: 337). This is what Freud controversially refers to as penis envy, and is a key feature in his explanation as to why girls should relinquish their first object of love, the mother, in favour of the father.

Freud's argument here is attenuated and rather weak, but he suggests that what happens is that the girl gives up her desire for a penis and in compensation replaces it with a desire for a child. As a result, she takes her father as her love-object and the mother becomes her object of jealousy. Freud thus argues that in boys castration destroys the Oedipus complex, whereas in girls it leads up to and makes the Oedipus complex possible. The girl is consequently left without a motive for the dissolution of the Oedipus complex: 'The fear of castration being thus excluded in the little girl, a powerful motive also drops out for the setting-up of a superego and for the breaking-off of the infantile genital organization' (Freud 1977d[1924]: 321). Freud suggests that although the girl's Oedipus complex culminates in her making a symbolic equation between penis and child, the fact that she is never able to bear her father's child, that her wish does not come true, means that the Oedipus complex slowly dissolves. Her transference of heterosexual love-object to other men is again a consequence of the symbolic equation between penis and child: 'The two wishes – to possess a penis and a child – remain strongly cathected in the unconscious and help to prepare the female creature for her later sexual role' (ibid.: 321). However, even Freud acknowledges that 'in general our insight into these developmental processes in girls is unsatisfactory, incomplete and vague' (ibid.: 321).

Freud's account of the differential progress and impact of the Oedipus and castration complexes for boys and girls remains problematic for a number of reasons, but at root is the difficulty of biology and the body: 'The difference between the sexual development of males and females . . . is an intelligible consequence of the anatomical distinction between their genitals and of the psychical situation involved in it' (1977c[1925]: 341). There was considerable opposition to and debate concerning Freud's account of female sexuality in the 1920s and 1930s (cf. Mitchell, 1974), and his critics at the time, Jones, Horney, Klein and Deutsch, argued that his account of woman as a castrated man was andocentric and phallocentric: 'there is a healthy suspicion growing that men analysts have been led to adopt an unduly phallo-centric view . . . the importance of the female organs being correspondingly underestimated' (Jones, 1927: 460).[4] Contemporary commentators emphasize, as did Freud at the time, that Jones and other critics attacked phallocentrism, but at the cost of slipping back into a notion of pre-existing biological sex differences where desire and psychical processes simply work on an existing categorical distinction between the male and the female (Chodorow, 1978; Mitchell, 1974; Mitchell and Rose, 1985: 103–21).[5] This is undoubtedly true, but it is equally evident that Freud's theory of female sexuality sees women as essentially castrated men, and thus penis envy is a self-evident explanation (Chodorow, 1994: ch. 1; Benjamin, 1995: ch. 4). Paradoxically, Freud's own radicalism, his insistence on 'bisexual dispositions', on sexual difference as an achievement rather than a given, was always founded on a problem about biology, one which continued to erupt into his theorizing.

Lacan, like Freud, sees the Oedipus complex as the point of the child's entry into culture, but he refuses to see women as castrated in any real, anatomical sense. This is because women and men are defined differently in relation to the symbolic order, and in relation to the third term, the primary signifier of that order, the phallus that splits the mother–child dyad. Contrary to Freud, a woman is not castrated because the child perceives her anatomical lack, but because the child perceives her as powerless in terms of her relation to the father: she desires the father, she is subordinate to the father. The phallus is thus a set of meanings conferred upon the penis, and castration is not a real lack, but a set of meanings conferred upon the genitals of a woman (Rubin, 1975: 190–1).[6]

> It is insofar as the function of man and woman is symbolized, it is insofar as it's literally uprooted from the domain of the imaginary and situated in the domain of the symbolic, that any normal, completed sexual position is realized. Genital realization is submitted to symbolization as an essential requirement – that the man be virilized, that the woman truly accept her feminine function. (Lacan, 1993: 177)

Femininity for Lacan is the consequence of a specific relation to the phallus, since the phallus is the privileged signifier of the symbolic order, and it is the symbolic relation to this signifier that makes women qua women and men qua men. Lacan argues that the phallus serves as the signifier of desire, but why should the phallus play this role and why should it be the privileged signifier of the symbolic order? Since a signifier acquires its value from the signifying system, there is logically no reason why some other signifier could not play the privileged signifier of difference.

> The phallus is the privileged signifier of that mark in which the role of the logos is joined with the advent of desire. It can be said that this signifier is chosen because it is the most tangible element in the real of sexual copulation, and also the most symbolic in the literal (typographical) sense of the term, since it is equivalent there to the (logical) copula. It might also be said that, by virtue of its turgidity, it is the image of the vital flow as it is transmitted in generation. (Lacan, 1977: 287)

In this passage, with its explicit references to erection, sexual intercourse and semen, the phallus is clearly the penis. But the phallus as a mediating term between desire and signification, between the body and language, is necessarily a material symbol. Toril Moi argues that rather than denying this, Lacan makes it evident, but that he wants his readers to grasp the difference between 'the phallus as symbol, as a signifier, and the penis as an ordinary part of the male anatomy' (Moi, 2004: 104).[7] In discussing an analyst's interpretation of a patient, Lacan makes this point:

> There is no better illustration of the function of *penisneid* – it is in so far as she identifies with the imaginary man that the penis takes on a symbolic value, and that there's a problem. It would be entirely

incorrect, the author tells us, to think that *penisneid* is entirely natural in women. Who told him it was natural? Of course, it's symbolic. It is in so far as the woman is in a symbolic order with an androcentric perspective that the penis takes on this value. Besides, it isn't the penis, but the phallus, that is to say something whose symbolic usage is possible because it can be seen, because it can be erected. There can be no possible symbolic use for what is not seen, for what is hidden. (Lacan, 1988b: 272)

Lacan argues that both the masculine and the feminine are defined by their relationship to the phallus. In theory, both sexes can take up either masculine or feminine positions or both, although one or other of these positions will probably emerge as predominant for any specific individual. But the relationship between sexed body and gendered subject is not arbitrary because those with penises usually take up the masculine position and those without usually take up the female position. As Moi argues, for Lacan the relationship between body and sexed subjectivity is 'neither necessary (that would be biological determinism) or arbitrary (that would be a form of idealism, a denial of the material structure of the body), but *contingent*' (2004: 107; emphasis in original). Lacan maintains that the masculine and feminine positions are different because the masculine position involves a wish or imaginary demand to 'have' the phallus, to be complete, not to be split by language, not to be outside the plenitude of the mother–child dyad. The feminine position embodies an imaginary desire to 'be' the phallus, to be recognized as the object of the desire of the other. The penis only comes to be elided with the phallus because female sexuality is considered a lack in a patriarchal order, and the differences between male and female genitals become expressed in terms of the presence or absence of the male term. Furthermore, no one has the phallus, and the penis only ever approximates the function of the phallus.

Why is the phallus the privileged signifier? Lacan answers this query with reference to the subject's relationship to the mother and to the (m)other's desire. The mother is considered initially by both sexes to possess a phallus, and it is the recognition that she does not, according to Lacan, coupled with the recognition that she desires something other than the child, that precipitates the oedipal crisis. This moment of crisis in identity is fused with the entry into the symbolic and into language. In imaginary terms, the penis becomes a form of detachable object because the mother once possessed it, but now no longer does so. The penis thus becomes an object of signification: it becomes the phallus and stands as the symbol of the other's desire. The phallus as a signifier functions as a residue of the child's repressed maternal desire, the desire for mother–child unity. But, as a signifier within a system of signification it cannot be owned or possessed by anyone, but functions through a chain of associations.

The relationship of the phallus to the penis, and its significance as the privileged marker of sexual difference, has been one of the longest running debates in feminist theory.[8] In theory, the penis is not the only object that could serve as the metonym for the phallus, and in other times and other places the phallic signifier, as the symbol of the other's desire, could take a quite different form (Fink, 1995: 102; Grosz, 1990: 121). Theorists regularly assert this possibility, but never provide any evidence to support it. I take up this challenge below, and again in chapter 8, and argue, on the basis of ethnographic data, that the phallus is frequently not the male organ, and that other objects can stand in as the privileged signifiers of the symbolic order, although the manner in which they can be said to mark sexual difference is rather different from that suggested by Lacan.

Representation and power

However, in Lacanian theory the phallus stands in for much more than the symbol of the other's desire, because as the privileged signifier of the symbolic order it also represents the asymmetrical relations between the sexes, and this links the question of representation back to the problem of power.[9]

> The question of whether one can separate 'phallus' from 'penis' rejoins the question of whether one can separate psychoanalysis from politics. The penis is what men have and women do not; the phallus is the attribute of power which neither men nor women have. But as long as the attribute of power is a phallus which refers to and can be confused with . . . a penis, this confusion will support a structure in which it seems reasonable that men have power and women do not. (Gallop, 1982: 97)

The primacy of the masculine term defines its other as the dependent, passive or adjunct term, as other to it. Within the symbolic order, femininity is not defined in positive terms, but only in relation to what the masculine is not. The root of this is the problem of the Oedipus complex itself, and the girl's relation to desire, because since the girl has no ideal exit from the Oedipus complex the relation of feminine sexuality to the symbolic order is uncertain (Adams, 1989). Consequently, women and men are defined differently with respect to the symbolic order and to language: masculine and feminine positions are different ways of being split by language. Thus, the asymmetrical relation between masculinity and femininity is not one that can be addressed simply by arguing that both women and men can take up masculine and feminine positions, because this does not alter the fact that femininity only acquires meaning by virtue of its relation to masculinity. To 'be' the phallus, to be the signifier of the other's desire, is to be the object of a heterosexual masculine desire, and also to represent that desire. Consequently, this being is actually a 'being for', a relation to, if not a function of, a masculine subject.

If 'woman' and femininity are positioned in this way within the symbolic order then what chance is there of changing that order, of developing sexual identities that are not over-determined by the law of the father, of decoupling representation from the phallus? Is a non-patriarchal symbolic order possible? There are several issues here. The first concerns the supposedly universal structure of language which, in Lacanian theory, is invariant and always acts to split or castrate all subjects. This assumption allows for no variation in the formation of sexual identity as a consequence of the child's relations with actual others, in other words no possible variation in relation to specific social and cultural values and practices. This is related to the criticism voiced by object relations theorists, and is of particular relevance from an anthropological perspective because it appears to leave no room for cross-cultural variation (Butler, 1990: 56; Moore, 1994; 1997a).

In addition, the assumption of an invariant symbolic world based on a universal logic of language makes it impossible to specify the historically variable and potentially alterable aspects of relations of domination and power, particularly between women and men, that exist within a given context.[10] As discussed in chapter 3, this occludes the relationship between ideology, power and the psyche, because while the Lacanian critique of the humanist subject assumes that the subject is caught up in a circuit of signification and desire and cannot be fixed or given, there is nevertheless no account of how sexed subjects are produced through concrete sets of cultural meanings, social relations and structures of power. This produces very particular problems for feminists in trying to determine what would bring about changes in gender relations. If it is a matter of changing forms of representation or economies of signification in order to change gender relations, how will this come about? More importantly, gender relations have undergone very significant changes over the last hundred years, but have these changes had no bearing on psychic processes, have they proceeded independently, and, if so, what does this tell us about the relationship between the social and the symbolic? I take up this enquiry again in chapter 9, but here I begin with some ethnographic material that explicitly works over the question of the significance of the phallus, and demonstrates that sexual difference is not necessarily what it seems.

Signifiers and sexual difference

The secret phallus

There is a tension in human life between recognizing the limits of sexual difference and the desire to 'have it all', the wish not to be marked by sexual difference. This is evident in many cultural contexts where people struggle with the problem of what exactly the difference is between women and men. This ought to be self-evident, as I have said, literally written on the body, but it never is. Male and female (physically sexed bodies) are not a problem, but the question of what it is to be masculine and/or feminine is another matter, and this often requires a consideration of what goes on inside bodies, rather than what is evidently there on the outside.

In the past, there were chiefdoms among the Chagga people of Tanzania who first circumcised their young men, and then initiated them through a period of seclusion and instruction in the forest.[11] Children and young women were told that during their time in the forest, the newly circumcised youths would undergo a second operation to plug and stitch their anuses. However, once the young men were in the forest, they were immediately taught that the story of anus stitching was a falsehood, but they were obliged to take a number of oaths never to tell children and young women that they defecated nor ever to allow them to see them defecate or to find their faeces (Raum, 1939: 554–5; 1940: 314–36). No doubt, 'the closed anus was an open secret as far as the women were concerned, but the question which concerns us is how to make sense of this story' (Falk Moore, 1976: 357). Raum notes that the teacher of female initiates in the female initiation rites of the Chagga 'must have discovered the male secret. Then on one occasion observing a man defecate, she waits till he has gone, removes a small quantity of the faeces, and mixes it with ochre and water. On the day of the *shiga*, as the female initiation is called, this mixture is painted on the novice's head' (Raum, 1939: 555).

The form of Chagga initiation involving seclusion in the forest has not been practised for a long time, but it has been interpreted by anthropologists as connecting to broader ideas about the control of fertility, of reproductive power, and of relations between women and men.[12] The organizing idea behind the story of the stitched anus is reportedly that men should be closed, whilst women should be open. A woman is open; as open as the vagina into which the penis is inserted and out of which the child comes. A man has no vagina, he is closed and his closure connects to his fertility and to his control over procreative powers. An initiated man is a socially procreative one, one who can marry and have children. A woman is only closed when she is pregnant, at the time when she retains the blood inside her. During pregnancy, she is at the height of her procreative power and her fertility. Chagga women say that the original *ngoso*, the original plug, the secret of the masculine control over procreative power, once belonged to them, before it was stolen from them by men. This fact is explicitly referred to in the female initiation rite, which takes place after circumcision, the *shiga*. 'In ancient days that which now appertains to men was ours, but those possessed of horns came, and by force robbed us of our manhood!' (Raum, 1939: 557; 1940: 353). Pregnancy, women say, is the female *ngoso*, because a pregnant woman no longer menstruates, and so her body is closed or plugged (Falk Moore, 1976: 358; Raum, 1939: 557). The theft left women not only without a penis, but with an open body which can only be closed during pregnancy.

In Chagga thought, openness and closedness are reportedly associated with human sexuality, with the inauguration of sexual difference, and with life and death. A man's faeces and a woman's menstrual blood make them vulnerable to sterility if these body substances are appropriated by or pass into the control of others. Sterility is connected straightforwardly to death and to the inability to have children and to perpetuate human society (Falk Moore, 1976: 358). Chagga theology/philosophy and cosmology, like that of the Aluund and Ngulu discussed in the previous chapter, makes an explicit link between properly ordered sexuality, fertility and the continuity of human society (Moore et al., 1999). In the case of the Chagga, this traditional link has been reinforced by the experience

of very high levels of HIV infection since 1984, with local epidemi-
ologies emphasizing the connection between disordered sexuality,
social change and death through illness (Setel, 1999). At one time,
around the end of the nineteenth century, the fundamental link
between sex and work was encapsulated for the Chagga in family
and clan-based units of production based on inherited garden plots
on the slopes of Mount Kilimanjaro. These plots growing bananas
and coffee, known as *kihamba* (pl. *vihamba*), were the centre of a
properly ordered set of reproductive activities that included sexual
relations between initiated women and men, bridewealth, marriage,
cattle-raising and the growing of crops essential for the maintenance of life. Male and female initiation drew on a set of cultural
models of productive and reproductive sexuality based on symbols
drawn from things located in, produced by and carried out in
the *kihamba*. Key amongst these were the production of milk, beer,
bananas and cattle (Falk Moore, 1976; 1986; Gutmann, 1932). Boys
were even circumcised sitting astride a banana stem (Raum, 1940:
308). The fundamental precepts of Chagga cosmo-philosophical
thought were based on symbols which themselves had a concrete
relation to daily activities, and thus ideas about properly ordered
sexuality and the importance of sexual difference for reproduction
were part of a set of embodied experiences and practical activities.
Life itself was held to depend on the correct combination of vital
forces, including the female and the male in sexual intercourse and
in marriage more generally. Correct combinations brought life and
fertility and social order, while incorrect ones produced sterility and
death (Falk Moore, 1977: 46).

In Chagga thought and practice, we see a concrete realization of
the relationship between sexuality and the law, with culture and
social relations explicitly dependent on sexual difference and its
management (sexuality). A *mreho* or *mregho* stick was traditionally
used to convey key values to young men and women in teachings
that took place after the initiation ceremony.[13] These sticks were
carved in patterns that simultaneously represented the history of
the chiefdom, its location on the mountain, the scars of circumcision on the penis, the sutured anus and the growth of the foetus in
embryo (Raum, 1940: 327–30). Each band of pattern served as a
mnemonic to a song cycle that contained parables about clan
history, adult sexuality and marriage, work ethics and the importance of honouring the ancestors. Thus, images, symbolism,
metaphors and narratives established homologies between social
bodies and sexed bodies, and between the reproduction of both

through the predominant mode of production, the *kihamba* (Setel, 1996: 1171). Raum describes three types of tally stick: one representing the growing of the embryo in the womb, the rings and notches standing for organs; another the multiple symbolism linking reproductive processes and civic affairs; and a third that embodies the stages of an embryo that disintegrates in the womb (Raum, 1940: 328). The example illustrated in Raum's discussion of Chagga initiation shows 26 abstract patterned bands representing, amongst other things, 'the anus of a man, coved over with skin: he does not defecate'; 'your father's circumcision scar; from this downwards it represents his glans'; 'your mother's vagina, do not look at it'; 'a woman's ribs. They are more bent than a man's because she has to support the embryo'; 'the railings separating the animal's quarters from the central passage of the hut'; 'the chief's eleusine store'; 'royal ornament worn on arm'; 'hoes with which pits were dug'; 'the circumcision knife'; 'top of hut' (Raum, 1940: 327). Following the same logic, the traditional instrument for cursing an unknown adversary would be decorated with female and male genitalia representing the power both of life and death (Falk Moore, 1977: 46).

The tally stick was clearly a phallic symbol, but a phallus that was multiply constituted, made up of both female and male parts. Its relationship to sexual difference and successful reproduction was made clear through the fact that the tally stick of each male initiate would be eventually thrown into the first fire to be lit after the birth of his first child (Falk Moore, 1977: 60–1). The purpose of the tally stick was to facilitate the first conception and birth, to mark the achievement of successful adult sexual relations through the production of a child (Raum, 1940: 36). The exact decoration and meanings of the tally sticks differed, depending on the knowledge of initiates and teachers, and on what lessons the tally was being used for. So the tally stick for girls' initiation might be cut at an angle at one end to represent female genitalia. However, Raum gives the example of one where a hole was made at each end, one representing 'the scrotum by having two beans placed in it, and the other the anus, the seat of the sign of manhood, the *ngoso*' (Raum, 1940: 336). In this case, the tally stick represents more than one phallus; not just a composite one, but a doubled one.

The fiction of the suturing of the anus during initiation ceremonies was linked to the particular role faeces played in the male initiation ceremony in the past. At the beginning of their seclusion, the young men dug two adjacent pits, one for faeces and one for urine. The initiates had to use these two pits during their training, and each morning they rubbed themselves with urine-wet mud from the urine pit, and this coating was the only covering they were allowed during their period of seclusion (Falk Moore, 1976: 359). The faecal pit was consecrated before use, was very deep, and tales were told of previous initiates who had fallen in and been left to die (Gutmann, 1926: 323). A youth could be pushed into the pit by order of the 'king of the camp'. A weakling, a cripple or the son of poor people was often chosen for this sacrifice (Raum, 1940: 316). The ordeals that the boys went through in the initiation camp were real ones, and the dangerous relationship between male and female, and life and death, was made manifest in the fact that some boys did not return from the camp (Dundas, 1924: 221; Raum, 1940: 322).

The central teaching of the initiation camp was the plugging of the anus. The plug or *ngoso* was said to represent manhood and male superiority, and the guarding of its secret was the foremost duty of all those initiated:

> Don't emit wind in the presence of women and uninitiated youths. ... Beware lest you be surprised by women when you defecate.... Particular care is necessary after your marriage.... If tapeworm is troubling you, send your mother or an old woman for the ... medicine ...; they know how to keep a secret. For if your bride gets to know about it, it means misery to you! If you dare to tell anybody of the secret of men, your age-group, the tribal elders and the chief will without mercy deprive you of all you own. For you would have disgraced your contemporaries ... And it will be said that the secret of the men is a lie! (Raum, 1940: 318–19)

If a man were to fall ill, he should be cared for by other men so that the secret should not be revealed (Falk Moore, 1977: 59).

The whole of the initiation rite and the activities in the camp were to be kept secret from women, and the vow of silence was taken using several different kinds of animal caught by the novices in a series of hunting expeditions (Raum, 1940: 319). Ritual or 'mock' hunts were part of the young men's training during seclusion, and the ritual of hunting was connected with the faecal pit, known as the bull. A piece of every animal killed was used to swear the binding oath of silence. The meat was dipped into the pit, and the young men then had to lick the meat and swear that they would keep the secrets of initiation from children and young women (ibid.: 320). On the last day of seclusion, the young men dipped locusts into the pit, licked the covered insects and swore never again to eat locusts. Locusts were a favourite food of women and children (Falk Moore, 1976: 361–2). The initiation instructor was reported as saying:

> 'This is the blood pact of the men! This is your secret. The strokes which you received in this camp prohibit you from eating locusts henceforth. For if you eat the blood pact of man, that is the locust which you licked, the curse of initiation will cut through your connection with the ancestors, and you will bear no offspring! . . . Liberate these creatures for they are our brothers with whom we have made a blood pact. We may not harm them.' (Raum, 1940: 320)

When a youth passes through initiation, he acquires the right to beget children. Falk Moore asks what the association is between the begetting of children and the fiction of the closed anus. Her response is that the explicit link for the Chagga is the prohibition on homosexual intercourse. If a man violates this prohibition, he may die. Once a man has passed through initiation, he is as fertile as any woman, he has assumed his socially reproductive powers. Falk Moore bases her analysis on Chagga statements and on the warnings given to initiates not to let their anuses be used like vaginas when drunk (Falk Moore, 1977: 60):

> Once he can beget children, he runs the risk of becoming pregnant or of impregnating another man through anal intercourse. For a man to become pregnant in this way would mean death because, being closed, he has no birth canal out of which the child can pass. The anus of the initiate is not literally plugged and stitched, but is figuratively so. He is closed to other men. (Falk Moore, 1976: 359)

The idea is that in order to achieve fatherhood, to ensure social continuity, a man must have sexual relations with women and forswear those with men. Falk Moore extends this analysis to explain the oath relating to locusts, where she suggests that the identification between men and locusts established in the rite means that when the young men swear not to eat the locusts – their brothers – they are, in fact, swearing not to eat themselves. Initiated men also had to avoid eating the rectum of all animals (Raum, 1940: 331). Since the analogy between eating and sex is a persistent theme in Chagga symbolism (Emanatian, 1996; Setel, 1996; 1999), as elsewhere, the prohibition on eating locusts and eating faeces is an analogy for the prohibition on anal intercourse.

Traditionally, once a Chagga man had a circumcised child himself, a moment which was said to symbolise the end of his period of procreation and fertility, he could resume defecating. In the distant past, a man and his lineage mates would perform a ritual which involved slaughtering a goat and they would then tie pieces of goat meat to the man's thighs so that the blood ran down over his legs. The meat was removed and the man's wife called. She was told that he was bleeding because he had removed his *ngoso* for the sake of his sons, and that from then on her husband would defecate. Falk Moore notes: 'whether this ritual was actually performed or not matters less than that the report of it was made, that Chagga talked about such an "ancient" custom' (1976: 361). From Gutmann's account it seems very likely that the ritual did take place because of the link between political control, generational succession, fertility and sexual difference: ' "Today I am handing the *ngoso* to you, for I have grown old. You preserve it. . . . The country is a succession. We leave it to you to seize the *ngoso* as we have kept it. Today I step aside and unite with the women. I withdraw the *ngoso* and hand it over to you. . . . I am now on a par with the parturient woman" ' (Gutmann, 1926: 303).

The idea that women and men have to be different in order to be procreative, to produce children successfully, is a common theme in much ethnographic material. What the bleeding man resembles, once he removes his *ngoso* for the sake of his sons, is a menstruating woman, one who has let the blood go and is no longer pregnant. There is puzzlement and envy involved in the constructions of gender difference which initiation inaugurates. The puzzlement has to do with the secret of fertility, both human and natural; with how the power of procreation and fertility is to be controlled and captured. This is not an esoteric question in the context of a rural African society, where human control over the fertility, and therefore the reproduction, of humans, land and animals is frequently precarious. Both women and men are aware that they do not have the secret of life (Falk Moore, 1976: 363). Women state that they once had the secret, but that the men stole it, and all they have left is pregnancy (ibid.: 364; Raum, 1939: 557). The men may have penises, but they do not have the capacity to get pregnant. These two capacities have to be combined for successful procreation.

It might be thought that this should be no problem, that women and men already have the naturally differentiated capacities whose combination is necessary for successful reproduction, but that is not necessarily how the Chagga see it.[14] Chagga statements, rituals and symbolism would seem to suggest that they are preoccupied with sameness and difference between women and men, with the problem of the relationship between masculinity and femininity, and with how it can be managed to ensure social continuity. This preoccupation has endured, and taken on new meaning in the context of the HIV epidemic (Setel, 1999: ch. 5). The contrasting images of women as open, as defecators of faeces and menstruators of blood, and men as closed, as retainers and containers of blood and faeces was traditionally created in the course of the initiation rites, and emphasized through the procreative years of married life to produce and maintain the categories of gender difference. The question is why did/does this difference need to be made? The answer lies in the blurred line between being male and female, or, more accurately, the duality and mutuality of gender identifications as revealed in the ritual of the removal of the *ngoso*. At that moment, the man resembles a menstruating woman and thus reveals that he has been pregnant all along, that his male procreative power has depended on what he has contained in his body, and that that is the purpose of the anal plug.

The point we should note is that the focus of male initiation is as much on the period of seclusion in the forest and the story of a bodily transformation which does not take place, as it is on that bodily change which has been the focus of so much anthropological and psychoanalytic writing on initiation, the circumcision of the penis (see chapter 7). The Chagga view is clearly that there is a link between sex and eating, between digestion, faeces and reproduction, a link that traditionally was made concrete and practical in the use of human and animal manure in the banana groves; a kind of virtuous circle of fertility and reproduction. But, in the case of the *ngoso*, what makes a man fertile is the closing of his body, not the simple possession of a penis: having the external organ is not enough. But, why is it the sutured anus and not the penis that is the phallic representation of sexual difference, the very thing that distinguishes men from women?

Freud made a well-known equation between faeces, babies and penises. He appeared to have derived this equation from children's fantasies about faecal pregnancies, and linked it also to his discussion of developmental sequences and the relationship of the anal-erotic impulses to the later emergence of genital organization (1977f[1917]: 296–302). The interchangeability of faeces, baby and penis was seen by Freud as something occurring in the unconscious. The link between the penis and the baby connected to a woman's desire for a penis, which was then replaced by her desire for a baby. Freud writes: 'It looks as if such women had understood (although this could not possibly have acted as a motive) that nature has given babies to women as a substitute for the penis that has been denied them' (ibid.: 297). On the surface of it, this sounds rather like what Chagga women have to say. The only problem is that the process of analogy, of establishing equivalence, which Freud describes as part of unconscious process, is part of ritual, myth and explicit statement for Chagga women.

In his discussion of this set of equivalences or analogies, Freud goes on to suggest that since a part of the eroticism of the pre-genital phase becomes available for use in the phase of genital primacy, and since babies are often regarded, presumably only by children, as something which comes out of the body by way of the anus, then an identity between babies and faeces can be established. The idea that both babies and faeces are gifts in some way, and that the baby is gifted through the mediation of the penis, somehow binds all three elements in a chain of associations (ibid.: 298–9). Freud goes on to propose, on the basis of case material, that some individuals make a direct analogy between the faecal mass and the penis, and that the mass inside the rectum represents the first penis, and the rectum thus becomes associated with the vagina. The result is that in fantasy the penis and the vagina come to be represented by the faecal stick and the rectum. One cause of this fantasy may be related to the moment when the boy discovers that women do not have a penis, and this leads him to conclude that the penis must be a detachable part of the body, like faeces (ibid.: 301–2).

When we ask ourselves the question, 'What does the body of the closed Chagga man contain?', we might want to respond that not only was he pregnant with a foetus, as the Chagga themselves suggest, but that he also contained a penis inside himself. In short, Chagga men are multiply sexed, but the secret is that they remain so even after the initiation rite which is supposed to render them categorical males. This multiply sexed male is one who, on one level, is pregnant with a phallus, but a phallus that is also a foetus, and like a foetus it is apparently detachable. His body is both female and male, and the fact that he retains this duality inside him accounts, in part, for his procreative powers, since he literally contains the elements necessary both for physical and social reproduction to take place. The Chagga link faeces, phallus and foetus in a series of metaphors and metonyms. Their post-oedipal account, however, of these connections is not explained by Freud's theory per se, but does work over the same material, using aspects of the physical body to symbolize and concretize pre-oedipal and oedipal relations. The problem with Freud's account of equivalences between faeces, babies and penises as seen from the perspective of Chagga theosophy is that the phallus is assumed to be male; whereas what Chagga theories reveal is that this is very likely not the case.

In Freud's account of castration, it is ultimately women who suffer from penis envy and who substitute the desire for a penis with the desire for a child. Chagga ritual explicitly makes that substitution, but sees it as the result of men's agency, since it is they who steal the *ngoso* from women and leave them with pregnancy in compensation. Male initiation and the social fantasy of the sutured anus suggest that it is Chagga men who suffer from penis envy or, rather, they acknowledge the fact that having a penis is not the same as having a phallus: having the organ is never enough.

The ostensible purpose of the initiation rites is to make boys into men, to render them categorically masculine in relation to what is feminine. But, the product of initiation, the sutured anus, is a much more complex material and symbolic figure, and cannot be readily interpreted, as many psychoanalysts and anthropologists writing about initiation might prefer, either as a form of castration or as a straightforward example of submission to the law of the father (see chapter 7). It is, rather, a powerful denial of castration, and a statement about the importance of femininity. We can see this if we ask the question, 'Whose phallus does the Chagga man contain?' In traditional Freudian and Lacanian accounts, the answer would always be the phallus of the father, because this is the phallus that signifies desire and, more importantly, the desire of the other. However, the multiply sexed nature of the Chagga man – the analogy between pregnancy, faeces and phallus – suggests that what the man contains is the maternal phallus: the original object of desire for both girls and boys, the thing which men dispossess women of, and that which confers completeness on the man at the very moment when he becomes categorically male. The sutured anus is thus a story of the denial of the limits of sexual difference or, rather, it is an account of a male fantasy about how they hope the limits of sexual difference apply to the female subject, but not the male one. Men want to retain inside them all that is necessary for reproduction both female and male.[15]

However, a moment's reflection on the question 'Whose phallus is it anyway?' reveals that the phallus inside the body is never unambiguously female or male. It is both maternal and paternal, multiply sexed, the very symbol of sexual difference itself and of its impossibility. Chagga reflections on these matters are very different from those of Lacan, but they work over a similar set of experiential, representational and conceptual difficulties or conundrums. The removal of the *ngoso* and its original association with a ban on homosexual intercourse both reveal the phallus in the body as the phallus of the father and of the law of the father, handed from one generation to another: 'Today I am handing the *ngoso* to you, for I have grown old.' And yet, this phallus is also a part object representing the mother and the capacity to produce a child, to be all-powerful, to reproduce oneself and society simultaneously, to be without lack or loss. An instance of the pre-oedipal and the oedipal conjoined (cf. Jones, 1933; Klein 1998a[1928]; 1998b[1930]).

The relationship of the phallus to the mother has been an intense subject of debate in psychoanalysis beginning with the lively exchanges in the 1930s on the subject of the female Oedipus complex and its connections to castration and penis envy (Chasseguet-Smirgel, 1970; Mitchell, 1974; Mitchell and Rose, 1985). Both Freud and Klein argue that children initially believe their mothers to possess a penis. But the question is, whose phallus does the mother possess? The phallic mother is omnipotent; for the child, she possesses every valuable attribute and is capable of everything, and the child is dependent upon her. Many theorists, since Klein, have thus taken the view that the child maintains both an imago of the good, all–providing mother, as well as one of the terrifying, omnipotent mother who intervenes in the psycho-physiological condition of the child's body. This is true for children of both sexes and accounts for the child's view that the mother possesses a phallus. While the mother may be thought to possess a phallus of her own, there may also arise at a later stage the idea that although the mother is castrated she nonetheless possesses the paternal phallus inside her (Chasseguet-Smirgel, 1970: 117). Jones (1933) argued that the child's theory is that sexual intercourse results in castration, and hence the mother's vagina contains the father's penis. This incorporated phallus is an object of desire for the child. In Jones's view, this results in a fantasy for the boy of castrating and incorporating the father's penis through homosexual relations. In the case of the girl, she wishes to steal the father's penis from the mother, incorporate it and make a child of it.

Fantasies such as these arise out of the earliest stages of a child's life and make use of intense relations to body parts which are themselves idealized and become fantasized objects. The relationship to the mother's and the father's body and to parts of parental bodies is thus a relation to fantasized objects. In the earliest stages of development, children express a desire to have the attributes of both parents – for example, boys may want to be able to have children – but this desire 'to have it all' does not preclude the awareness of physical differences between the sexes. The result is that sexual difference emerges out of and remains based on a prior awareness of interconnectedness. Chagga ritual fuses the fantasies of bodies and body parts to understandings of physical and social reproduction. It provides the indispensable link between personal and cultural fantasies. What Chagga ritual shows is that castration is not bound up with the male penis and its loss, but with an idealized and fantasized phallus that is initially a female organ belonging to the mother, and yet also belongs in aspects and in parts to both parental bodies. Castration is certainly about the experience and the possibility of a limit to or loss of *jouissance*, and in this case is connected to the emergence of and recognition of sexual difference. As Freud said, something always has to be relinquished or given up. However, what the Chagga material also shows is that the content of what might be broadly termed 'castration anxiety' is culturally variable, as is the nature of the privileged signifier that represents the desire of the other. The sutured anus is an orifice filled with a plug, a male vagina filled with a female penis. The plug, the *ngoso*, is both a child and a penis, both a female and a male part, but in ways that are congruent with Chagga symbolic thought. To talk of maternal and paternal bodies, or even mothers and fathers, is misleading unless we recognize that the child's (and thus the adult's) relation to the mother's body and to parts of parental bodies is one set up in fantasy, and is therefore always a relation to a specific culturally and socially valorized mother, father, parent. From an anthropological perspective, we can say that gender is already there in the pre-oedipal fantasies on which sexual difference is based.

6

Being and Having

What differentiates men and women...is not the maleness or femaleness of their sexual organs but *what they do with them.*
Strathern, 1988: 128; emphasis in original

Sexual difference is an uneasy and shifting compromise, but one which has very profound importance for the management of human societies. It is for this reason that the feminist insight that gender identities are never singular, but multiple, never fixed or finished, but reiterative and performative, helps to make sense of the contradictory and shifting nature of gender identities, relations and metaphors. Masculinity and femininity are multiply constituted, and are processually related and over-determined, rather than categorically separated. This does not, however, mean that societies do not make categorical separations in many contexts and instances, but it also means that every time that separation is effected, what is evoked is the fact that the female and the male were once connected and remain so.

Relationships are always socially patterned, and relationships between women and men are structured in terms of cultural assumptions about gender capacities, attributes, roles and resources. Thus, the mother and the father as objects, part-objects and/or individuals can only ever be present to the child as culturally constituted. Unconscious fantasies about love, loss and betrayal are developed out of culturally shared sets of symbols, images, metaphors and ideas. What constitutes the 'maternal' and the 'paternal' are not givens, but must be investigated. There is no masculinity or femininity outside the relations established between them. This applies also to any broader range of kin within which an individual acquires a gender identity (see chapter 7).

Sexual difference calls for attention to the effects of language and signification on the construction of femininity and masculinity. This is necessarily so since human sexuality is profoundly imaginary, in the sense that it is bound up with representation: language and the body cannot be separated. Psychoanalysis argues that sexuality and subjectivity are intertwined in the unconscious, that one cannot become a social being without becoming a sexed being. Feminists and anthropologists want to know whether this means that sexual difference is primary: are all other forms of difference derivative in some sense? This issue has been taken up in different ways in feminist writings and wide-ranging positions have emerged along a spectrum arguing for and against social constructivism as opposed to the primacy of invariant (symbolic) psychosexual structures. Most feminists explicitly argue that gender is not given either in biology or in the body, but is socially constructed. Others want to know whether there are limits to this social construction and, if so, what they are. The perennial question that all feminists have to answer is 'Does gender originate in the body?'. Anthropology has played a major role in this debate, and in early formulations gender was taken to be the cultural inscription and redescription of naturally sexed bodies (Moore, 1994; 1999b). In later formulations, it was not just gender that was culturally constructed; so too were bodies and sexes themselves (Butler, 1994; Moore, 1999b). The cultural construction of sex, which owed much to the work of Foucault in the humanities and social sciences, had a particular emphasis in anthropology, where it was never just a matter of representation and cultural meaning, but always of praxis and lived relations also: in other words, of discourse, in the fullest Foucauldian sense of that term. However, in anthropology the cultural construction of sex did not solve anything very much. After all, what is the difference between a socially constructed sex and a social construction of sex (i.e. gender) (Moore, 1999b: 154)? In these discussions, sex appears and disappears; it is separate from gender, it is not separate from gender. What, then, does the distinction between sex and gender mean? In feminist debates in general, this methodological confusion was handled in two ways, one of which involved asserting that sex was 'always already gender' and the other of which entailed arguing that sex, being performative, was really sexuality and/or sexual practice. The result, unsurprisingly, has been much heat and little light, a new libidinal economy where genitals, practices, identities and desires collide and conflict. In other words, it turns out that the theories of sex, gender and sexuality provided in such writings are just as much about performing gender as the systems of signification, praxis and domination they seek to analyse (Moore, 1999b: 159).

Recent work on the performative nature of gender identity has insistently figured it as an effect of language and symbolic action, as the product of a set of regulatory practices that construct the categories of woman and man and open them to resignification:

> If there is something right in De Beauvoir's claim that one is not born but rather becomes a woman, it follows that woman itself is a term in process, a becoming, a constructing that cannot rightfully be said to originate or to end. As an ongoing discursive practice, it is open to intervention and resignification. (Butler, 1990: 33; see also 1993: 1–23)

Performativity is about the reiterative citation of the regulatory norms of sexual difference; it is not, as Butler has frequently stressed, about voluntarism, choice or manipulation (Butler, 1993: Intro). To say that gender is socially constructed does not mean that it is an act, an event, something that simply takes place; it is, rather, a process – the formation of a subject in process – but never one that is finished or complete (Moore, 1994). The notion that one becomes a gender though an ongoing and ceaseless process of reiteration rather than being born one is not hard to grasp: the difficulties all come later.

One of the problems is how to theorize the relationship between gender difference and other forms of difference, such as race, ethnicity, sexuality, class and so on. Psychoanalysis implies that sexual difference is somehow primary because of the way it is tied to the formation of the subject (cf. Braidotti, 1997; Braidotti and Butler, 1994; Butler, 1995a; Cornell, 1997; Felski, 1997; Frye, 1996). The theory of performativity could in principle cope with the notion of multiple and intersecting sites of difference and treat them all as mutually determining systems of regulatory norms, but would it be enough to claim that all are mutually performative? Would that give us sufficient purchase on the question of the relationship between subjectivity and representation? Clearly, multiple identities are mutually imbricating and not in any sense serial or additional. What is at issue in their relations are questions of power, agency and ideology. As discussed in chapter 3, unconscious desire is deeply sedimented in social practices and systems of domination, but exactly how feminists theorize the intersections of multiple identities has never been easy or uncontentious (e.g. Butler, 1993: ch. 4; Flax, 1990: ch. 5; Hooks, 1984; Mohanty, 2003; Moore, 1994; Zinn and Dill, 1996). What we need is a more cogent way of figuring how the subject gets caught up in representation, one that understands how the subject is founded across the imaginary and the symbolic.

A first step might be to think about the analytical level at which we are proceeding. Multiple and fluid gender identities are maintained at the level of discourse, at the level of ideology, of spoken and enacted practices over time and at a day-to-day level. This is true also of other forms of difference, of the discourses on race, ethnicity, nationalism, class and sexuality, for example, and of their relations with each other. These forms of discourse are open to considerable contestation and renegotiation; they provide multiple subject positions with which social agents can identify, and through which they can construct a sense of self over time (see chapter 2). These subject positions may be contradictory and conflicting (Moore, 1994: chs. 3 and 4), but they provide frameworks for action and for self-realization that are both enabling and constraining. The relationship of social agents to such discourses is not always or necessarily one of self-reflection and self-knowledge. To be effective, such discursive practices and forms of knowledge do not have to be conscious; they do not need to be in language directly, but may form part of the agent's habitus or way of being, as both Bourdieu and Foucault suggest in their different ways (Moore, 1994: chs. 3 and 4; McNay, 2000). But, how do discourses that operate at these levels and in these ways relate to the unconscious, to the symbolic order, to a posited set of invariant psychosexual structures?[1] A potential way forward here is provided by the return to the question of libido and the way it drives the ego forward into the world:

> [T]he libido is not an instinct, that is, an activity naturally directed towards definite ends, it is the general power, which the psychosomatic subject enjoys, of taking root in different settings . . . of gaining structures of conduct. It is what causes man to have a history. Insofar as a man's sexual history provides a key to his life, it is because in

his sexuality is projected his manner of being towards the world, that is, toward time and other men. (Merleau-Ponty, 1962: 158)

What is interesting about this quote is its insistence on history and its materiality, on the fact that the desire for engagement with the world provides an orientation for an embodied psyche both towards that world and towards other people.

If sexual difference is not to be culturally and historically invariant, the product of an invariant symbolic order, then there must be some account of how culture and society could enter into an understanding of a sexed body which is produced through multiple forms of difference. This would involve thinking about sexual difference in terms of the way it is insistently figured through other forms of difference, through the specifics of concrete social, cultural and historical circumstances. It would also entail recognizing that the issue of primacy is misleading because psychosexual structures cannot be treated as contentless and consequently we need to re-evaluate the relationship between culture and the process of how we become sexed beings. In the following sections, I resituate Freud's and Lacan's work on the body ego and trace out its potential for understanding a new way of conceptualizing the relationship of culture to the production of historically situated, sexed bodies. From the anthropological perspective, the terms of debate about sex and gender within the discipline might have shifted, but the methodological question is still intact: what can be learnt from laying anthropological and feminist theories of sex and gender alongside theories pertaining to bodies, sexualities, sexual difference, and gender that originate elsewhere and have their own philosophical and metaphysical distinctions?[2] The issue of the origins of sexual difference is not one that is confined to the musings of feminists and anthropologists. The question of how sexual difference links the psyche to the social and the unconscious to systems of power clearly has to do with how the body is embroiled in representation. In discussing material from Melanesia below, I show how specific ideas about imagined anatomies are located in wider understandings of sexed bodies, social relationships, reproduction and power.

The body ego

In *The Ego and the Id*, Freud sets out how the formation of the ego is tied to a psychic map of the body, and how this arises through bodily sensations on the surface of the body: 'The ego is first and foremost a bodily ego; it is not merely a surface entity, but is itself the projection of a surface' (Freud 1984b[1923]: 364).[3] In this account, there is no body that precedes representations, no body that precedes ideas in the mind. This is so for two reasons: first, because the ego is itself only formed out of identifications and object relations – including taking itself as a libidinal object; and second, because there is no lived phenomenological body prior to a psychic investment in certain parts and surfaces of the body. The map the ego forms of the body allows for no distinction between material and representation, between the physical and the psychical body. For any body part to come into psychic experience, the ego must form a fantasy relation to it – that is, one set up in representation. This is analogous to Freud's idea that what is present in the unconscious is not the drive or the instinct, but its representation. Thus, a phenomenologically accessible body requires and is formed through psychic representations of stimuli. These stimuli can be external, arising on the surface of the body, through both pain and pleasure, but they can also, as the ego develops, be internal, in the sense of being the product or the workings of previously introjected sensations and objects operating within the ego. Where Freud is innovative here is in his insistence that the ego is produced and only grows in relation to its interactions with the external world, and these take place via the perceptual surface of the body. The sexual instincts in the form of pleasure and pain are primary here, and this is so, as discussed earlier, because they are linked to the child's basic needs:

> [I]t is all the more necessary for us to lay stress upon the libidinal character of the self-preservative instincts now that we are venturing upon the further step of recognizing the sexual instinct as Eros, the preserver of all things, and of deriving the narcissistic libido of the ego from the stores of libido by means of which the cells of the soma are attached to one another. (Freud, 1984c[1920]: 325)

Freud argues that it is the erotogenic zones of the body that provide the prototype for the development of a psychic map of the body, and key to this process is the question of narcissism. Narcissism is an intermediate stage between auto-eroticism and object-love. It thus forms a crucial link in the development of the ego. Freud argues that auto-erotic instincts are 'there from the very first', being linked to basic needs, but that the ego takes itself as a love-object as a consequence of pain and pleasure experienced from the erotogenic zones of the body: 'Let us now, taking any part of the body, describe its activity of sending sexually exciting stimuli to the mind as its "erotogenicity", and let us further reflect . . . that certain other parts of the body – the "erotogenic" zones – may act as substitutes for the genitals and behave analogously to them' (Freud, 1984d[1914]: 77). As a result, the ego forms a narcissistic attachment to certain parts of its body, and the body becomes libidinally and psychically invested, takes on a certain form and becomes a materially lived body-ego. The formation of the embodied ego thus follows the contours of libidinal investment first in itself and later in other love-objects. Thus the ego is formed through relations to itself and to others.

However, this is not to say that the ego is the product or the representation of a physical, anatomical body; the ego is not determined by biology. The ego develops out of perception, but this perception includes the stimuli on the surface of the body and the inner effects of psychic processes. Perception thus provides the content of the ego, as well as its earliest sexual objects, including itself (Grosz, 1994: 37). Since the ego is formed out of the representation of the varying intensity of libidinal investment in various body parts and the body as a whole, it is a product of the body's meaning and significance both for the subject and for the other, since the management of the infant's body is literally in the hands of others (ibid.: 38). This implies two things: first, that the body ego is the product of an eroticized fantasy relation to sensation and perception; and second, that bodies being indissolubly tied to egos are the product of self–other relations, that their very physicality only becomes phenomenologically accessible through the social and cultural understandings of sexed bodies. This is particularly true given that the ego is made up of the earliest identifications in a child's life, including its lost love-objects, and its relations to its parents (Freud 1984b[1923]: 368–70). Thus, the ego is formed out of the body's relation to the world, and this is a world that is already informed by representations of sexual difference. It is an intersubjective world, with a history informed by relations of power and difference.

Lacan takes up this idea with his notion of the mirror stage, which he sees as the grounds for the development of the ego. For Lacan, as for Freud, the ego is not a projection of a real anatomical body, but of an imagined lived body, as imagined and represented both by the subject and by others. The mirror stage marks the

earliest recognition by the child of its bodily unity, and she/he identifies with that image. In this sense, it is the first moment of the
recognition of an essential libidinal relation with the body: 'The
imaginary anatomy is an internalized image or map of the meaning
that the body has for the subject, for others in its social world, and
for the symbolic order conceived in its generality (that is, for culture
as a whole)' (Grosz, 1994: 39–40). Lacan emphasizes that the ego is
formed out of imaginary identifications with the infant's own
mirror image, but also out of images of parents and primary
caregivers, and images deriving from them. Thus the body ego is
again formed intersubjectively and historically. Lacan also emphasizes that the unconscious is made up of significations that form the
discourse of the Other and break in and interrupt the ego. This
Other discourse is quite literally the language of others, constituted
out of their desire, and it is this system of signification through
which the child is forced to express its own desire as it acquires
language. Thus, the world, the law of the father, culture, and
wider social and family networks are involved in the formation and
development of the ego.

Lacan suggests that what the child sees in the mirror stage is an
imaginary body, a totalized image of itself, and although this image
will change throughout the individual's life in response to new
experiences, it will derive its stability from the earliest stages of the
child's representations, from the earliest stages of ego formation.
What this implies is that the body ego is not a finished and complete product, but must be continually renewed. This process of
renewal is not one of conscious willing, but of continual engagement with an intersubjective world, in which the relations
established between self and others, between subject and objects,
provide the grounds for agency. An imaginary anatomy, and the
body ego through which it is formed, requires a set of practical
engagements with the bodies and subjectivities of others, with
notions of inside/outside, boundaries, definitions, intimate and
sexual actions. These forms of engagement may be visual and may
be orientational or physical, may or may not be brought into language, may be conscious or unconscious, may be self-reflexively
oriented towards agency and may be unthought. Two consequences
follow from this. First, sexual difference has a history, is a process
of renewal or reiteration and not a matter of an initial definition or
cultural construction of a pre-given sexed anatomy: in other words,
it is part of an engagement with a world in which gender differences are already at work. In the ethnographic material presented

below and in later chapters, this process of reiteration and renewal, the work of sexual difference, is very much in evidence in ritual, mythic and symbolic material. Second, the nature of the embodied ego, the history of its formation and the consequences of its orientation to an intersubjective world mean that the unconscious and the conscious, the unthought and the discursive are formed in relation to each other, and are mutually interdependent. This last point needs further elaboration.

Freud makes it clear that although consciousness and agency are attached to the ego, there is also a part of the ego that is unconscious (Freud, 1984b[1923]: 355–6). The conscious ego is 'first and foremost a body-ego', but he also stresses that the boundaries between the ego, id and superego should not be taken as hard-and-fast: not only is the ego a specifically differentiated part of the id, but the superego is the residue of the earliest object choices of the id (see chapter 3) (ibid.: 366, 373, 378). Thus, this topography of mind is best understood as an analytical device for describing and explaining a set of dynamic interrelations. The result is, of course, that psychoanalysis has always maintained, that representation and symbolism are the interface that allows for the emergence of an embodied, thinking agent that is also tied psychically and culturally to values and forms of difference through sensations, emotions, drives and desires. This being so, subjectivities (gender identities) must always be tied to sexual difference, to what is made historically and individually of an anatomy that is engaged with a world already subject to the workings of gender difference. However, I propose that we recognize that this understanding of sexual difference is not something immutable, something that is everywhere and always the same, something that is subject to an unchanging symbolic law, but is, rather, something that is open to cross-cultural variation and social change over time, and is always constituted in and through its relations to other forms of difference.

It is the process of the formation of the body ego via the medium of representation that makes this possible, because it ties that process to social and cultural valuations and understandings, most specifically as they are inflected by power and difference. This being so, we now have a comprehensible link between the unconscious and the discursive, between the imaginary and the symbolic. The capacity for making representations is essential for the formation of the body ego. Culture and history do not come to the individual from outside, but are part of its evolving constitution and continuing relation to the world. Fantasies of the embodied self are linked to fantasies of relations and identifications with others. The earliest representations of significant others are caught up with forms of gender difference that have no realizable expression outside their relations with other forms of difference, such as race, class and ethnicity. I argue that gender is the ground for the emergence of sexual difference, but it can never be a neutral, uninflected set of categories and relations. Feminist scholars writing on the relationship between race and psychoanalysis make this evident when they point out that 'whiteness' is a racial category (Abel et al., 1997; Seshadri-Crooks, 2000), and that no theory of the acquisition of gendered subjectivity can proceed on an unexamined assumption of neutrality (Leary, 1997; Walton, 1995).

One of the puzzling features of Freud's and Lacan's account of the body ego is why they simultaneously insist on a psychical and cultural understanding of anatomy, while providing an account of the child's confrontation with the sexed body that configures the feminine in terms of the masculine: having or not having the penis. There is no logical reason, as Grosz points out, to regard the phallus as having an a priori privilege in the constitution of the girl's imaginary body/body ego (Grosz, 1994: 59). From the discussion of the formation of the body ego above, it is evident that the body one has must play a role in the formation of the ego, first because of the way each individual/ego makes a libidinal investment in the body, and second because of the way the body ego is formed out of and acts as an interface between others and the world, both of which are already subject to sexual difference. This provides a conundrum in the account of the Oedipus complex provided by Freud and Lacan, where both insist that sexuality and anatomy get marked in relation to the phallus. In this situation, the girl child would need to see herself as, experience her body as, already lacking in the initial stages of the formation of the body ego – that is, before castration can be construed as having occurred. If one takes the arguments made by Cixous and Irigaray about the multiple nature and sites of female desire, a view that is in accord with Freud's own view on the question of multiple erotogenic zones and the plasticity of sexualization, then why, as Elizabeth Grosz asks, would the presence or absence of the phallus play a major role in shaping the girl's body ego (ibid.: 59)? In essence, there is a discordance or disjuncture between the theories of Freud and Lacan with regard to the formation of the body ego and their account of the Oedipus complex (cf. Cixous, 1980a; Flax, 1990; 1980b; Irigaray, 1985). In short, the first suggests a viable general theory for the formation and delineation of a psychically and culturally invested body ego, and the second provides a particular historical account of how that ego is situated within a particular symbolic order. This is not to suggest that we can or should negate the importance of the symbolic order. This is not a viable position, as discussed in the previous chapter, but it does imply, as many feminists have suggested, that we treat their specific account of the Oedipus complex and its resolution as pertaining to a particular patriarchal culture (Silverman, 1992). There is no reason, as the ethnographic data presented below demonstrates, to argue that, because the insertion of the subject into the symbolic order is a necessary process for all subjects, it is an invariant one pertaining to an invariant symbolic order that always constitutes sexual difference in a fixed way.

I suggest that we can develop a theory that allows for cultural variation both in the formation of the body ego and in the nature of the symbolic order, whilst maintaining a commitment to an understanding of the necessity of the processes of representation, separation, identification, differentiation and signification for the emergence and development of the ego/subject. In other words, we do need to recognize and build on the psychoanalytic insight that the construction of sexuality is the condition of subjecthood, but we can do so in a way that takes culture, history and power as being integral to that process of iterative construction.

The woman with the man inside

The Gimi of Papua New Guinea exchange sisters in marriage, and these dual ceremonies ideally take place at the same time as the initiation of their adolescent brothers. Before their marriage, the pairs of future sisters-in-law are secluded inside the house of the mother of one of them, and, while being deprived of food and sleep, they are taught the songs and incantations necessary for successful gardening and the raising of pigs. The women pile wood onto the fire in the centre of the hut and tell the girls that the heat will make them sweat and remove their menstrual blood. Women's gardening and pig-rearing songs are related to their myths, and to their 'blood' and 'Moon' songs that they sing to bring their periods to a close. During the initial phases of initiation and the rites of marriage, a girl receives spells and songs from older women. These food spells are secret and shared only between classificatory mothers and

daughters, and between mothers-in-law and daughters-in-law
(Gillison, 1993: 155–9). Production and reproduction are linked in
Gimi philosohy because a woman is thought to be able to transform
her life-force (*auna*) into food over time. She sends her *auna* into
plants and animals through a repetitive process of singing, talking,
cajoling and caressing. In a sense, she makes things grow by mag-
ically extending motherhood into other objects. Through songs and
chants, a woman joins her *auna* with that of the plant or animal, and
internalizes them as a woman does a child. But her power to make
things grow, to conceive a child, originates in the source of her *auna*,
that is, in her menstrual blood (ibid.: 199–201). Thus a woman's
body and its reproductive potential are imagined in relation to specific sets of social and productive relationships.

According to Gimi myth, women's menstrual blood is something
they stole from men. The Gimi term for menstruation means to
be 'killed/implanted by the Moon'. Women's myths tell the story
of the first man, whose enormous penis awoke in the night and
went out by itself to search for woman. The penis found her asleep,
but could not penetrate her because the vagina was closed.
The penis ate an opening to gain entry and the woman awoke
and cut off the enormous thing that had invaded her: the blood
of the Moon or first man was the blood of menstruation, which
was also the blood of a severed penis (ibid.: 217). According to
the women's myth:

> The woman awoke and took the penis in her hand. She went out of
> her house and cut a piece of sugar cane. Holding the penis in her
> hand, she went to the Men's house and found the man sleeping. She
> placed the sugar cane next to his penis and cut it to the length of the
> cane, throwing the huge severed part into the river. Other men saw
> his penis and cut theirs the same. This is why men's penes have the
> same markings as sugar cane. (Ibid.: 113–14)

Gillison recorded one of her informants as saying: 'When the
woman cut off the man's penis the Moon killed her for the first time.
. . . Moon's blood is blood of the penis. A woman's blood is really
the blood of a man' (ibid.: 114). What the narrative describes is the
first mythic marriage or copulation, and because women continue
to menstruate it implies that they are still filled with the blood or
penis of the Moon, that there is something male inside them.
However, both Gimi women and men also figure menstrual blood
as the Moon's remains, part of his body, and also as the residue of

a dead or failed child. Many Gimi represent sex, marriage and reproduction as a conquest between the husband and the primordial father who already fills the woman, between the man she marries and her own male kin, fathers and brothers. 'When the Moon kills you and your husband demands sex . . . Tell him the Moon has closed you up completely . . . while the Moon is with you the opening is small, and a man who tries to enter you will hurt his penis' (ibid.: 187).

Both women and men state that a child is made entirely from the man's semen. To produce a child, a man must copulate with his wife many times and fill her womb. Once she is pregnant, he refrains from sexual relations until the end of the pregnancy when he returns to 'finish' the child. A man's semen is the product of his body substance and in giving up this substance a man sacrifices part of himself to make a child (ibid.: 201–2). In order to make a woman pregnant, a man has to 'defeat the Moon'. The Gimi account runs parallel to Freud's theory of the primal father, since the Moon, the original father/husband, eats his way into the woman and opens the way for sexual relations, but also fills and closes her, making her inaccessible to others. According to the Gimi, however, this battle between the son and the primal father results not in death but in a negotiated truce:

> When a woman gets pregnant, it isn't only a man who's had sex with her, the Moon has had sex with her, too. The first time a man goes into a woman, the Moon gets rid of his semen. And the second time, too. . . . By the eleventh or twelfth time, maybe, a child lies sleeping in her. . . . When a real child lies inside a woman, the Moon doesn't kill her anymore . . . [but] his semen stays in her and heats (lit: cooks) the child to make it grow. The Moon is not enough to *make* the child! But he holds it. His semen stays on the side, keeping it hot. (Ibid.: 206)

Rather than kill the primordial father, the husband enters into a truce with him. When the husband returns at the end of the pregnancy to 'wake the child' by having sex with the mother, he becomes the true father by dislodging the child from the Moon's embrace. The finishing of the child is the model for brideprice because the husband offers the Moon his semen, offers the Moon meat in exchange for the child, just as the husband and his kin offer the woman's father and her brothers meat in exchange for the bride (ibid.: 215–16).

Thus, for the Gimi the child that is born from successful reproduction depends on a number of transactions and transformations: dislodging the child from the embrace of the primordial father, forcing the mother to give up her phallus in exchange for a child, and turning the father's phallus (the blood of the Moon) into a live child. However, the starting point for the Gimi theory of reproduction is a particular account of an imaginary anatomy, a fantasized relation to bodies and body parts, and specific sets of asymmetrical social relations in which women are multiply sexed, in the sense that they contain male parts inside them. In this account, the mother is complete; containing the father's phallus; she has no need of social reproduction based on sexual difference. This presupposition is captured in the following women's myth.

Once there was a widow whose husband had just died. She left her son and daughter at home to go and collect ferns.[4] She told her children to watch and listen to the banana tree, and that if it cried out they would know she had died. The woman climbed up towards the source of the river collecting frogs as she went. Near the source of the river she found an old man hacking grubs out of a tree. He demanded all the frogs that the woman had hidden in her mourning clothes, and after he had eaten them he killed her by thrusting his long stick up her anus. He pulled the stick out and licked it clean and then cut the widow into pieces. He tried on one hand and it fitted well. He cut off one leg and tried it on. It fitted him well. He cut off one breast and tried it on and it fitted him well. He cut off her head and tried it on. The he put on her mourning clothes. He went back to the widow's house to trick her children. The children were worried because they had heard the banana cry out. The old man in disguise sent the daughter off to fetch water and while she was gone he murdered her infant brother and hid his corpse in the rafters. While the old man was sleeping, the daughter discovered her brother's body because the water/death juice from his nose dripped onto her thigh and caught her attention. She stoked up the fire and saw the old man's penis beneath his mourning clothes. She realized that she had been tricked and taking her brother's corpse, she placed him in her net bag and left, setting fire to the house. The old man was killed. The girl set off to find her true husband who would marry her with bride-price. She found him and told him the story of what had happened to her. He told her to make decorations and he hollowed out a tree in which he put the boy's corpse and the decorations. He told his

wife 'I am going away and when I am gone wonderful sounds will come out of the tree, but don't go near it or hit it with a stick.' He left and the woman heard the sounds and hit the tree. At once all the birds of the forest flew out of the tree and dispersed. (Abridged from Gillison 1993: 159–64)[5]

This is a story of a woman with a man inside her. It is also an account of how violent and cannibalistic relations between women and men are turned through exchange into marital relations based on sexual difference. In Gimi interpretations of this myth, the old man is the Moon. The child he kills and whose nose leaks onto the girl's leg is a symbol of her first menstruation. The girl carries the dead child to her true husband – the one who pays brideprice – and transforms the dead child of the Moon, an incestuous product, into new life (ibid.: 165). The myth, however, contains no simple resolution regarding femininity and masculinity, no categorical account of sexual difference. The girl sees the primordial father inside her mother and recognizes his murderous intent. Yet, when she takes the dead boy/child to her true husband, it is she – despite his prohibition – who actually takes the penis or stick and creates new life (ibid.: 152, 166). What the myth reveals is that, even with exchange and the establishment of social relations between the genders based on the inauguration of sexual difference, the woman retains her male part. As the Gimi emphasize elsewhere, the result is that the husband always has to enter into a negotiated relation with the Moon/primordial father who resides inside the woman. The fact of sexual difference does not banish or extinguish women's multiply sexed nature, the enfolded relation of femininity and masculinity. This is made most evident in male initiation and in the rites surrounding marriage.

During male initiation, which ideally takes place for boys at the same time as their sisters are being married, the adult men play secret bamboo flutes in the men's house where the initiates are secluded and sing of how men are born of women. At a key moment in the rite, the flautists reveal themselves to the initiates, and at that moment the mother's brothers of the boys hold stone axes to the boys' throats and tell them that if they reveal the secret that it is men who play the flutes then their throats will be cut. A flute is placed across the thighs of each initiate and a piece of salted pork is put in his mouth. This, the big men tell the boys, is the faeces of the flute: 'we give you this food to make you grow quickly' (Gillison, 1991: 177–8). During the initiation ritual, men repeat

various versions of the secret flute myth and recount for the boys
how it was women who first owned the flutes and had the powers
and prerogatives men now own.

The First Woman had no husband and she made and played the
flutes. In the male myth recounted during initiation, the flute was
stolen by a boy from his sister, the First Woman, and this theft
caused her to menstruate or, as the Gimi say, 'to be killed by the
Moon for the first time' (ibid.: 180–2). However, the myth not only
recounts how women acquired menstruation, but also how men
acquired masculinity. The original flute or *kamiba* had a mouth
which was plugged with the woman's pubic hair. When the boy
stole his sister's flute, he did not realize that the hole (vagina) was
closed. He put his mouth to the hole to make sounds and that is
how men came to have beards. Gimi men's account of the original
flute is that the First Woman created it in her own image and thus
it represents not only her body, but also the penis of the Moon. What
men stole from women was thus the phallus, or rather a composite
vagina/phallus, and what women gained in its place – as in the
Chagga case discussed in the previous chapter – was the ability to
have children.

Woman's first husband is both the boy who stole the flute
and caused the woman to bleed by severing her from her penis
as recounted in the male myth, and the father of the Moon whose
penis ate its way into the woman, making her complete as
portrayed in the women's myth. In both accounts, the first husband
is a male part of the woman, simultaneously father and brother.
Women make this explicit in the 'blood songs' they sing while
secluding girls before marriage, a process that takes place as
boys are being initiated and listening to the flute myth. These
'blood songs' reveal that the origin of women's blood/menstrua-
tion is connected to her brother's body, as well as deriving from
the severed penis of the Moon, as told in the women's myth
discussed above. In secret rites at the end of initiation, Gimi men
let blood from their noses to get rid of accumulations of female
blood that are said to sap their strength and vitality. Menstrual
blood enters a man's body through intercourse and through ordinary contact, including the ingestion of food. When a man lets
blood from his nose, he is said both to be expelling Moon blood,
and to be sending the blood of his sister back to his sister. Women,
on the other hand, talk of ridding their bodies of their brother's
blood in order to produce a child. This connection is made explicit
in the women's myth of the 'man inside the woman', discussed

above, where the 'nose-water' of the brother's corpse drips onto the girl's leg, symbolizing both her menstruation and the deathly product of the activities of the Moon/primordial father. One of the major messages in the myth is that, in taking this dead child to her true husband, the girl is able to produce new life (Gillison, 1993: 183–4). To put it more succinctly, the female and the male are indissolubly linked, and the role of initiation and marriage is to unbind that link, create socialized sexual difference in order to allow reproduction to take place. What happens during marriage rites makes this evident.

Before the rites begin, a man has a design tattooed around his daughter's mouth. He then cuts a pair of flutes for his new son-in-law that have the same design incised around the blowing hole or mouth. A man identifies his daughter with the flute not only by matching their 'mouths', but also by referring to the flute he sends to his son-in-law as the 'child' of the 'mother' he still possesses. The flute a man gives to his son-in-law consists not only of the decorated instrument, but also of the right to play his own named 'cry', a distinctive combinations of sounds and rhythms. Blowing into a flute, the men reveal, is like going into a woman, and the sounds the player blows out are the cries of his child. The father sends these flutes to his son-in-law without the knowledge of the bride/his daughter by hiding them in her netbag. But, before he does so, he stuffs each flute with salted pieces of cooked marsupial or piglet. The Gimi describe these pieces of meat as 'killed', 'covered with hair' and 'like the unborn'. Like the flute the boy steals from his sister the First Woman, the flutes are unplayable because they are stuffed with hair, with something dead, with the head of an unborn child (ibid.: 268–73; 1991: 180–4). The father instructs the son-in-law to take out the meat and feed it to the bride when she arrives, indicating that before the groom can play his father-in-law's flutes, he has to unplug them, to dislodge what fills the woman so that a new, live child can be born.

However, it is usually the father of the groom (acting for the groom/son-in-law) who takes out the meat and feeds it back to the bride, taking the contents of one 'hairy vagina' (the decorated blowing hole) and putting them into another (the bride's newly bearded mouth) (Gillison, 1991: 185–6); taking the penis of the Moon/father out of the body of the bride/First Woman and feeding it back into a newly created vagina that is appropriate for social reproduction. This is the reversed and paired operation of brothers letting blood from their noses to send it back to their sisters. As a symbolic operation, it inaugurates sexual difference, separates the male from the female, creates the possibility of society through the disavowal of incest. Yet, the results of this operation are not clear-cut, they do not result in an unambiguous femininity or masculinity. Ideally, marriage involves sister exchange, and thus the father who sends his son-in-law the plugged flutes also receives in his turn a pair of plugged flutes carried by his new daughter-in-law. He receives them on the part of his son, and removes from them the meat symbolizing her father's penis and his child. But, by feeding the meat into the bride's mouth, symbolizing a new vagina receiving a male part, he reveals three things. First, that the daughter is still filled with her father's penis/ child, which he demonstrates by (re)filling the bride in the very act of emptying her father's flute and with the very same substance (Gillison, 1993: 275). This thus underscores the more general Gimi view that the husband always has to establish a relation/negotiated truce with the father who resides within the woman. Secondly, he reveals that, sexually and symbolically, he and his son (the groom) are conjoined. The act of removing the meat from the flute, detaching the woman from the phallus, recalls the action of the boy in the flute myth who steals the flute/phallus from his sister. Thirdly, the emptying of the flute discloses that sister, father and brother are one, that what the flute symbolizes is a female body both shaped and plugged by a phallus (Gillison, 1991: 188). Ideal sister exchange marriage involves reciprocal naming, so that parents give the name of the intended spouse of their child to the cross-sex sibling next in birth order. The result is that when a bride marries, her husband has the same name as her brother, just as her brother's wife will have her name. Thus, every marriage, whether it conforms to ideals or involves classificatory kin, always symbolically unites a 'brother' and a 'sister'. Consequently, marriage rites, while appearing to resolve mythic incest and inaugurate sexual difference, simultaneously reaffirm the conjoined nature of femininity and masculinity, the folded-over relation of father–son/sister–mother. They paradoxically reveal the fact that every woman has at least one man hidden inside her.

The Gimi material emphasizes that reproduction is only possible after masculinity and femininity have been differentiated, and the practical discursive nature of this process during initiation and marriage is intended to unbind the composite sex, to accede to the limits of sexual difference so that the male and the female can be combined to make new life. Gimi exegesis of such matters does not just focus on parents and children, but on a wider set of kin relations essential for an understanding of what masculinity and femininity mean and entail, including brother/sister, and father-in-law/son-in-law. From this perspective, it is evident that the ways in which we become sexed beings are culturally variant because sexed subjects can only be produced through concrete sets of cultural meanings, social relations and structures of power. To put it in other terms, the symbolic order is not invariant, and thus the detailed ways in which the body ego as self develops in a specific world of objects cannot be invariant either. The specific fantasies about female and male bodies, their capacities and attributes, are actively constitutive of any under-standing of the maternal and the paternal, and of mothers and fathers, as well as of wider kin and significant others. They are also actively and simultaneously constitutive of the asymmetrical relations of women and men, and of older and younger men in Gimi society, and of the distributed relations of power within kinship systems.

Processes of differentiation are only ever temporary because masculinity and femininity can never really be separated, and thus differentiation has to be iteratively performed. The images of masculinity and femininity that the Gimi work over-emphasize relations rather than categories. It is, as Marilyn Strathern has said, almost as if the masculine and the feminine are variants of each other (Strathern, 1988: 126). If this is so, then how do we know whether something is definitively female or male? Strathern sees this as part of a larger set of western assumptions about persons and property, the assumption that 'breasts belong to women or that phalluses are the property of men' (ibid.: 127). This leads to a further set of assumptions that we should be able to identify things by their attributes, to decide whether a flute, for example, is female or male. But the Gimi flute stolen by the brother in the myth is evidently a vagina stuffed with a penis or a penis-shaped vagina (Weiner, 1995: 104), and the flute carried by the bride at marriage is, similarly, a female body shaped as a penis, stuffed with a phallus/child. Strathern argues that our under-standing of Gimi ideas about masculinity and femininity are con-siderably enhanced if we move away from 'ownership' models towards transactional ones. What differentiates men and women is not the maleness or femaleness of their sex organs, but what they do with them. Melanesian knowledge of masculinity and femininity is never simply written on the body, never a matter of inspection, but always a question of the outcome of relational inter-action (Strathern, 1988: 127–8).

The Gimi material encourages us to reflect on two matters. The first is that 'ownership' models encourage us to over-naturalize body parts, to see them as self-evidently sexed by the bodies to which we think they belong. Hence the long-running anxiety in feminist theorizing that the phallus might be/is a penis in mas-querade. The second problem is the assumption that attributes must add up to identity, that identities and body parts must go together. The Gimi, it would seem, do not share either of these assumptions. What acts as the marker of sexual difference, the privileged signi-fier of the other's desire, is a phallus, but a phallus that is defini-tively not the male organ, a phallus shaped like a vagina. The analyses we produce of such complex cultural representations are always shot through with our ideas about gender, ideas which precede any theorization of sexual difference. Such theories, whilst appearing to describe invariant structures, are caught up in a self-referencing circulation of images and attributes where what is masculine and what is feminine are assumed to be givens, and where we consistently configure other people's fantasized relations to their bodies and to those of significant others in terms of our own.

Conclusion

What the Gimi material invites consideration of – as does the African data presented in the previous chapter – is that when dealing with ethnographic material, it is essential to make a dis-tinction between different levels of analysis. On the one hand, there are multiple and fluid post-oedipal discourses on gender that exist at the level of discourse, in myth, and narratives, and ritual, and also at the level of performance, in spoken and enacted practices over time and in day-to-day activities and encounters. However, these multiple, performative discourses are situated in contexts – as in the examples discussed above – where power differentials between women and men are very marked, and where the cate-gorical differences between women and men are a salient and per-vasive feature of social life. Yet, having made this point, what is equally evident is that it does not make much sense as a generality to claim that in these contexts femininity is defined in terms of what masculinity is not. The examples I have discussed are most certainly patriarchal societies in the given sense of the term, but they are not in any simple way governed by the abstract and invariant paternal law presumed in much psychoanalytic theorizing, if by invariant, we mean either that cultural variability and history are contingent and subordinate to structure, or that the law is itself monolithic and has only a particular kind of phallus as its privileged signifier.

One of the most striking features of the ethnographic material is the way that the imaginary erupts into the symbolic, the manner in which the paternal remains permanently linked to the maternal, the way that masculinity is always part of femininity. This provides the grounds for multiple and shifting post-oedipal interpretations of masculinity and femininity, and their relations based on pre-oedipal and oedipal materials. Such interpretations are both conscious and unconscious, embodied and linguistic, practical and symbolic. What is evident is that sexual difference is itself produced through concrete sets of cultural meanings, social relations and structures of power. The symbolic is always culturally variable. Such variability exists on two levels. First, in the character of the link between the imaginary and the symbolic, the concrete sets of metaphor that fold and unfold across space and time within specific cultural idioms. Secondly, in the very definition and comprehension of the maternal and the paternal, and their role, and the role of significant others, power differences and social institutions in the inauguration and delineation of sexual difference.

The image of femininity that comes over from the ethnographic data is not one that is simply subservient to male oedipal needs. While it is true that femininity is indissolubly linked to questions of reproduction and fertility, the very nature of the maternal in these contexts seems quite different from the repressed maternal of much feminist and psychoanalytic writing. The form of femininity that is evident in the ethnographic material, while different in each context, is one that is shot through with a notion of the maternal as constitutive of the social, law and exchange. It is true that in each case, categorical gender discourses represent the maternal/imaginary as being overthrown by the paternal/law: a kind of 'world historical defeat of the female sex'. And yet, in each instance the dependence of the paternal on the maternal, of masculinity on femininity, of the symbolic on the imaginary, is constantly revealed in myth and ritual. In theoretical terms, this may fall far short of an account of feminine subjectivity, but it is quite categorically not an account of femininity defined in terms of what masculinity is not. The ethnographic examples discussed here and in the previous chapters are societies where, in many contexts, culture and value are portrayed and valorized as male, but they are also societies in which the originators of culture and society were once women, and where what is now most highly valued and associated with men is consistently revealed as being dependent on its female or feminine part.

7

Kinship and Sexuality

The sexual behaviour of a human being often *lays down the pattern* for all of his other modes of reacting to life.

Sigmund Freud, 1985c[1908]: 50

> Malinowski, Rivers
> Benedict and others
> Show how common culture
>   Shapes the separate lives:
> Matrilineal races
> Kill their mothers' brothers
> In their dreams and turn their
>   Sisters into wives.
> W. H. Auden[1]

The debate between anthropology and psychoanalysis has traditionally turned on whether the Oedipus complex is universal or not. The Oedipus complex involves relations with parents, and this being so it raises the question of how kinship relations connect to individual psychosexual structures and processes. Since anthropology is committed to cross-cultural variation, this raises the inevitable question of how variability in kinship structures impacts on sexual difference, and consequently on femininity and masculinity. What this chapter demonstrates is that there is a series of linked questions, one of which is how kinship relates to the socialization of desire and how parents (and others) determine the formation of the gendered self in the broader context of masculine and feminine identities. Anthropology, of course, is concerned with two issues within this broad domain. The first is the question of what we might mean by kinship: who makes up the set of significant others? how are those affective relationships lived and experienced? The second related point, as discussed in previous chapters, is exactly what is entailed by terms such as 'maternal' and 'paternal', mother and father. If kinship variability is to have any significance at all, then it must operate at two levels: variation in the definition and range of kin, and their affective relations; and differences in cultural understandings of parenting, and of what it is to be a mother and a father. These levels are clearly related. In this chapter, I begin with a brief discussion of the debate on the Oedipus complex in anthropology, as a way of situating my larger claim that we need to shift our focus away from the Oedipus complex to the more general question of how we become sexed beings.

Kinship and variations in the conceptual and lived understandings of what it is to be related to others are crucial because 'family' relationships (however defined) are the intimate and passionate context for the development of sexual identity. Sexual identities are the product of a complex set of interactions between processes of identification and separation. In orthodox psychoanalytic terms, object choice arises out of identification, and sexuality is the inevitable precipitate of object choice. This raises the question of whether parents and kin are responsible in some way for sexuality. Do failures in identification lead to problems with masculinity or femininity and thus to failures in object choice? The anthropological data on absent fathers, initiation and ritual homosexuality in Melanesia are reviewed below in this light. However, once we begin a discussion of the relationship of identification to object choice, we are drawn into the debate on bisexuality, homosexuality and heterosexuality. Freud's theory of bisexuality contained a paradox because it had to be fashioned into an account of how heterosexual femininity and masculinity emerge. The acquisition of sexual difference is a process, as discussed in previous chapters, which is not only shaped by understandings of masculinity and femininity, but transforms the ego. Gender identity thus becomes the fulcrum that links self to culture. However, empirical data from anthropology, and recent work in psychoanalysis, suggest that it is exceedingly problematic to treat masculinity and femininity as necessarily singular or categorical, and/or to see them as fully differentiated from each other. The result is not just that we require a much more nuanced account of how identification with the same-sexed parent leads to erotic object choice, but we need to go further and ask: Is this the right way to be approaching the question of how gender identity is related to sexuality? One of the key issues here is that we need to recognize that fantasy is part of relationality, and thus the question of how we become sexed beings is not about kinship structures and their variability per se, but about how we imagine our relation to our bodies, to others and to the wider social and cultural world we inhabit.

Oedipus once more

The debate in anthropology about whether the Oedipus complex is universal has hinged on whether it is family relations or psychosexual structures that should be given precedence: 'Do the conflicts, passions and attachments within the family vary with its constitution, or do they remain the same throughout humanity? . . . If they vary, as in fact they do, then the nuclear complex of the family cannot remain constant in all human races and people; it must vary with the constitution of the family' (Malinowski, 1955[1927]: 19–20). Malinowski famously argued that the Oedipus complex did not exist in its classic form in the Trobriands, because in this matrilineal society, the boy feels hostility toward the mother's brother rather than the father. His incestuous feelings towards the mother get eliminated naturally over time and it is the sister rather than the mother who becomes the object of incestuous desire. The debate which followed this assertion has retained its irritable edge, if not its theoretical saliency. Many anthropologists have taken the view that Malinowski made a major contribution to anthropology and psychoanalysis by showing the existence of an alternative Oedipus complex, and this is a view forcibly expressed in many textbooks and introductory courses (cf. Ingham, 1963: 8; Spiro, 1982a: 1). However, others have suggested that Malinowski understood little of psychoanalytic theory and that the evidence from the Trobriands suggests that there is well-developed hostility towards the father, incestuous desire for the mother and evidence for a strong classic Oedipus complex (cf. Ingham, 1963; Kluckhohn, 1943; La Barre, 1958; McDougall, 1975; Parsons, 1957; Roheim, 1950b; Spiro, 1982a). In this, they follow in large part the position set out by Ernst Jones in reply to Malinowski, where he argued that the avunculate complex arises as a defence against oedipal conflicts, and thus the Trobriand case is one where the classic oedipal complex is particularly strong (Jones, 1925). In consequence, far from revising psychoanalytic theory, Malinowski merely confirmed its basic principles.[2]

This debate has moved on considerably over recent decades, and it is probably fair to say that the general position on the Oedipus complex in anthropology now is a loose consensus that a 'family romance' in some sense must be universal, but that its content is cross-culturally variable and open to empirical investigation (Levine 1981; Parsons, 1969). For example, Melford Spiro, who has been one of Malinowski's fiercest critics within anthropology, argues that there must logically be variation within the Oedipus complex cross-culturally:

> [T]here is no theoretical reason why the adult members of the oedipal triangle must consist of the boy's biological mother and father; it might well be the case that in some society this triangle consists of the boy, his sister, and his mother's brother. Malinowski's claim that this is the case in the Trobriands was rejected . . . not on theoretical, but on empirical grounds. (Spiro, 1982a: 164a)

Spiro discusses the Oedipus complex in terms of its structure, its intensity and its outcome. While he postulates that the structure could logically be variant, he argues that there are in fact no examples where this is the case for the totality of a society, as opposed to individuals or sub-sections of society. On the question of intensity and outcome, he boldly asserts that the ethnographic record provides empirical evidence of such variation. His theoretical model suggests that since the boy's hostility to the father is directly related to his oedipal love for the mother, the entire Oedipus complex may be either extinguished, repressed or incompletely repressed, depending on what occurs in relation to incestuous desire for the mother. All three of these outcomes may exist in a single society, but one of them will usually be dominant. What is important for Spiro is that these different outcomes go on to have different social and cultural consequences in specific societies (Spiro, 1982a: 164–7a). These different consequences relate to such things as intergenerational behaviour, kinship and household composition, and the performance of certain rituals, specifically initiation rites (cf. Lidz and Lidz, 1989; Stephens, 1962).

Spiro's view is that the Oedipus complex is a normal and inevitable stage in human psychological development, and that while its structure could vary logically, there is no evidence that it does so at the level of the totality of a culture. Gananath Obeysekere takes a different position and argues that there is no nuclear Oedipus complex of which other forms are variations, but rather 'several possible forms of the complex showing family resemblances to one another' (Obeyesekere, 1990: 75). Obeyesekere's argument is that sexuality and authority are bound together in indistinguishable ways in oedipal conflicts, and that interpersonal relationships within the family, relationships with significant others and kinship structures must therefore have a determining influence on the nature, structure and resolution of oedipal conflict.

Obeyesekere argues that one cannot speak of a universal (Greek) oedipal complex in relation to Hindu familial relationships, which are constructed around the boy's erotic attachment to the mother and submission to the father. He argues that the unity of the joint family depends on those ties that bind the boy to the family unit and continue into adulthood. In contrast to the Greek myth, where the boy marries the mother and overthrows the father, in the Hindu myth the son is erotically dominated by the mother and obtains the father's love by submitting to him: the Hindu son thus duplicates the father rather than displacing him (Obeyesekere, 1990: 82–4; Ramanujan, 1999). The result is a complex psychic identification with both parents, but most crucially with the mother.

Obeyesekere points out that Freud himself had suggested that identification with the mother might be one outcome of the resolution of the Oedipus complex:

Along with the demolition of the Oedipus complex, the boy's object-cathexis of his mother must be given up. Its place may be filled by one of two things: either an identification with his mother or an intensification of his identification with his father. We are accustomed to regard the latter outcome as the more normal. (Freud, 1984b[1923]: 371)

Obeyesekere thus shows that, even for Freud, the Oedipus complex is much more complex than a process of a simple triangular relationship where the boy hates the father and loves the mother, and deals with this problem by relinquishing love for the mother in order to identify with the father. The following passage from *The Ego and the Id* makes this point explicitly:

It would appear, therefore, that in both sexes the relative strength of the masculine and feminine sexual dispositions is what determines whether the outcome of the Oedipus situation shall be an identification with the father or with the mother. This is one of the ways in which bisexuality takes a hand in the subsequent vicissitudes of the Oedipus complex. The other way is even more important. For one gets an impression that the simple Oedipus complex is by no means its commonest form, but rather represents a simplification or schematization which, to be sure, is often enough justified for practical purposes. Closer study usually discloses the *more complete* Oedipus complex, which is twofold, positive and negative, and is due to the bisexuality originally present in children: that is to say, a boy has not merely an ambivalent attitude towards his father and an affectionate object choice towards his mother, but at the same time he also behaves like a girl and displays an affectionate feminine attitude towards his father and a corresponding jealousy and hostility towards his mother. (Ibid.: 372)

What Freud suggests here is that the resolution of the Oedipus complex is not a singular process resulting in a unidimensional outcome, and such resolution as there is results in a series of emotions towards and identifications with both parents. The complicating factor here is 'bisexuality', that is the coexistence and intermingling of both feminine and masculine dispositions: 'It may even be that the ambivalence displayed in the relations to the parents should be attributed entirely to bisexuality and that it is not ... developed out of identification in consequence of rivalry' (ibid.: 372–3). As discussed in the previous chapter, Freud's views on sexual difference are based on the fact that both women and men may take up masculine and feminine positions. Freud thus correctly realizes that 'bisexuality' may be a more powerful explanation for the complexity of oedipal resolution than a simple model of love for the parent of the opposite sex and rivalry or hostility with the parent of the same sex.

As Obeyesekere remarks, Freud never relinquished his triangular view of the Oedipus complex or its theoretical saliency, and, given his view of its importance in the development of religion, 'moral restraint' and social law, this is not surprising (ibid.: 377; see also chapter 3 above). However, Freud did mention in a number of essays the importance of erotic attraction and rivalry with siblings as well as parents, and was clearly aware of the importance of wider familial relations. In his discussion of the female Oedipus complex, Freud was forced, as we saw in chapter 5, to relinquish the idea that the experience of the girl was parallel to that of the boy, and, in particular, he came to the realization that the threat of castration inaugurated the complex for the girl rather than resolving it.

Freud recognized that the problem that the theory of the Oedipus complex never resolved is why the girl should shift from her first love-object, the mother, to her second, the father. This brings into focus the importance of the pre-oedipal phase in coming to an understanding of the Oedipus complex: 'a number of women remain arrested in their original attachment to their mother and never achieve a true change-over towards men. This being so, the pre-Oedipus phase in women gains an importance which we have not attributed to it hitherto' (Freud, 1977f[1931]: 372). As Freud makes clear in the passage that follows, this insight suggests that the classic Oedipus complex is not the universal fulcrum for the development of female sexuality. He suggests that this problem can be dealt with by extending 'the content of the Oedipus complex to include all the child's relations to both parents; or . . . we can take due account of our new findings by saying that the female only reaches the normal positive Oedipus situation after she has sur-mounted a period before it that is governed by the negative complex' (ibid.: 372). The negative complex referred to is one where the girl establishes an object choice towards the mother and hostil-ity towards the father. Freud remained somewhat confused on the question of the female Oedipus complex, as noted in chapter 5, but he also argued that the girl might, having relinquished the father as the love-object, 'bring her masculinity into prominence' and identify with the father (Freud, 1984b[1923]: 372). Chasseguet-Smirgel goes as far as to suggest that in his essay on female sexuality Freud implies that the girl's positive Oedipus complex may not actually exist at all (Chasseguet-Smirgel, 1970: 94).[3]

What Obeyesekere seeks to point out is that Freud was well aware that female sexuality rendered the notion of the classic Oedipus complex problematic. Beyond this, Freud's theoretical speculation on the oedipal resolution for both boys and girls acknowledged the complexity of understanding object-relations and the processes of identification and separation that are at the core of oedipal conflicts (Obeyesekere, 1990: 86–7). This acknowl-edgement led him to the realization that even for the male child, a much more expanded circle of kin than the traditional triangle of relationships is significant for an understanding of how oedipal conflicts are resolved, and, as the passage quoted earlier makes clear, that the classic Oedipus complex is not necessarily 'its commonest form', but, rather, a simplification or schematization. Obeyesekere builds on this insight: 'The idea of the negative complex discovered so late in his career effectively demolished any simplistic notion of the Oedipus complex. . . . Add homosexuality and the sibling complex and what we have is, in my phrase, an "erotically desirable circle of familial kin" ' (ibid.: 88).

Obeyesekere's position is that within this circle each culture isolates certain relationships that are central to the oedipal conflict; these become the oedipal kin and it is the conflicts engendered within these charged relationships that become the Oedipus complex relevant to the psychic development of the child. Thus, Obeyesekere's larger point is that the classic Oedipus complex is not universal in the sense of exhibiting an invariant structure, but that oedipal conflicts of some sort must be since they arise from the erotically charged nature of familial and kin relations (ibid.: 88, 95–6). He concludes that 'the Oedipus complex is not only culturally variable but . . . even within a single culture there might be several oedipal models with one form dominant insofar as it is the most frequent form or reflective of the ideal cultural value configuration' (ibid.: 105). On this last point, he concurs with Spiro (Spiro, 1982a; and see above).

Obeyesekere has been criticized by Stanley Kurtz, who takes issue with his characterization of the Hindu complex as equivalent to the Freudian negative Oedipus complex. Kurtz asserts that Obeyesekere unintentionally reinforces Freudian orthodoxy as opposed to using his ethnography to make a more radical critique of psychoanalytic theory (Kurtz, 1992: 226). In fact, the argument that the Hindu complex is classically 'negative' is one made by a number of psychoanalytic theorists writing on India (cf. Carstairs, 1967; Kakar, 1978; Ramanujan, 1999).[4] However, Obeyesekere's analysis is much more subtle than Kurtz implies, and he explicitly states that the Oedipus complex within the Indian family cannot be structured in terms of the western model (Obeyesekere, 1990: 82).[5] Kurtz makes his criticisms because he is interested in emphasizing the importance of group relations, as opposed to simply the idea of the significance of wider kin relations. His argument is that anthropologists and psychoanalysts have misunderstood the nature of the boy's tie to the mother in the Indian context. The psychical closeness between mother and son is not to be understood in a western sense as simply erotic or seductive or indulgent, but as part of a broader pattern where children are kept physically close, but emotionally are encouraged to move out from the tie to the mother towards larger social groups.

In the case of boy children, this is achieved through the intervention of the mother's sisters-in-law and mother-in-law – what

Kurtz terms the in-law mothers. Kurtz's contention is that Hindu mothering is multiple mothering, and it is the care of the child by these several 'mothers' that consolidates the child's ego and moves him away from a narcissistic merger with his biological mother. This group of mothers may be augmented by other kin, including siblings and cousins. Kurtz's larger point is that psychoanalysis incorporates into its theoretical frameworks western notions of individualism that are inappropriate for understanding the role of the group in ego formation. In the Hindu context, pleasure is not defined by exclusive love relations with individual parents, since personal satisfaction rests on identification with, and activity taken on behalf of and within, the group. Multiple mothering is thus what underpins group identification and also personal pleasure, and, by extension, guarantees the continuity of the extended family: the child learns to understand that 'all mothers are one' or, rather, that the mother is multiply constituted (Kurtz, 1992: 102–8).[6]

Kurtz's argument is interesting because it draws attention once again to the necessity of a critical understanding of what is meant by the 'mother', and it explicitly recalls the pre-theoretical assumptions of much psychoanalytic theorizing as regards discussions about the roles of mothers and fathers (see chapter 5 and below). Kurtz explicitly argues that the child relinquishes incestuous desire for the mother through a process of sublimation, where he gains satisfaction from being 'the shared plaything of the group'. Ultimately, he incorporates his mothers as a group – as they incorporate him – and thus he can turn outwards from the group to seek a mature sexuality (ibid.: 147–8). For Kurtz, the male child's incestuous desires are played out not in a triangle of father, mother and son, but in an expanded triangle of in-law mothers, mother and son. Thus the incestuous desires for the mother have been broken before the boy transfers into the world of men, and the sense of being an ego within a group can be transferred from the group of women to the group of men (ibid.: 169). The son, by submitting to the father, thus loses an individual self, but gains the power and the satisfaction of a group ego. Kurtz is clear that the sense of individual immersion in the group in the Hindu context is not a mere extension and displacement of an unresolved narcissistic union with the mother, but rather the opposite, a mature resolution of early, primary narcissism (ibid.: 160–4). The Hindu path to maturity is based on a loosening of individual bonds for the sake of a fusion with the group (ibid.: 172).[7]

Kurtz's argument is that where infantile pleasures in the West are denied and then repressed, in the Indian context they are willingly renounced in return for inclusion within the group (ibid.: 173). He has made a similar argument for the Trobriand Islands based on a notion of 'polysexualization'. Kurtz's contention is that we cannot understand the oedipal drama in the Trobriands without taking into account the group: 'Wherever multiple companions or caretakers have an integral role in the early life of children, these groups transform the "universal" Oedipal triangle into a more complex structure ... the role of the group, like that of the parents, is *primary*' (Kurtz, 1991: 69). Trobriand children enter the sexually active children's play group between the ages of 4 and 6, and Kurtz argues that it is this set of experiences that seduces the child away from infantile pleasures and objects, and from the exclusive relation with the mother (ibid.: 70–71).[8] His contention, based on both the Indian and Trobriand material, is that collective social attachments are involved in breaking the boy's exclusive relation to the mother prior to the oedipal phase, and not just subsequent upon it.[9] He also argues that the psychoanalytic view of the seductive pre-oedipal mother is inappropriate for understanding mothers and mothering in non-western contexts (see below).

Both Obeyesekere and Kurtz emphasize that a range of significant others, in addition to mothers and fathers, are involved in shaping gender identity and love-object choice. They also stress that the classic model of the triangular structure of the Oedipus complex is over-dependent on western notions of individualism, underpinned by specific assumptions about the desirability of autonomy and separation, that are inappropriate for understanding gender identities in non-western contexts. The wider implication, however, in line with the general 'waning of the Oedipus complex' in psychoanalytic theorizing, is that oedipal conflict may not be the primary or the once-and-for-all determinant of sexual identity (Loewald, 1980). This change in the centrality of the Oedipus complex to psychoanalytic thinking raises further questions about the relationship between identification and object as the primary determinant of gender identity. We can explore these difficulties further by examining the question of initiation rituals which have long been seen as the paradigmatic arena for the acquisition of gender identity both by anthropologists and psychoanalysts, largely because of their assumed role in the resolution of oedipal conflict and in achieving separation from the mother.

Masculinity and initiation

[T]he beginnings of religion, morals, society and art converge in the Oedipus complex. (Freud 1985d[1913]: 219)

Anthropology has always seen sexuality as tied to social organization, reproduction, cosmology, symbolism and culture: all the patterns of life. This is nowhere more evident than in the work on male initiation. The extravagance and violence of many of these rituals led early anthropologists to pose the obvious question, 'What do these rituals do for society?' The answer seemed straightforward enough: they make boys into men. In other words, initiation seems self-evidently about sexed identities and their acquisition or imposition. Initiation may be about many things, but anthropologists and psychoanalysts have generally agreed in seeing such rituals as being about the channelling of sexual interest in culturally appropriate ways.[10] From this perspective, it is an easy step to see initiation as resolving oedipal conflicts in some way or another.

Early discussions of initiation rites focused on circumcision as a form of symbolic castration intended to prevent incest, and a specific link was established between initiation and socialization. Most often, this socialization was portrayed as submission to the authority of society via the authority of the father.[11] The symbolism of castration was not, however, limited to actual circumcision of the penis, but was extended to include other forms of traumatic marking, such as nose-bleeding, cane swallowing, forced feeding and forced abstention, scarification, tooth removal and head hunting. Interpretations focused not only on the hostility of the boy to his father as the agent of his frustrated incestuous desires, but on the father's hostility to the son arising from the memory of his own childhood desires and hostility towards his father. It was consequently said that it was on the basis of his own experience of incestuous desire that the father feared retaliation from the son, as well as rivalry for the love of the mother (Reik 1962[1946]: 105–6, 125–6; Roheim, 1942: 372–4).[12] Indeed, the traumas of initiation in general were seen simultaneously as punishments for hostile wishes against the father, as explaining the identification of the adult men with the monsters, spirits and other forces who inflict the painful ordeals on the boys, and as accounting for the enthusiasm and energy with which the adult men carry out these traumatic activities. The theme of death and rebirth so common in initiation rituals was interpreted as punishment for the primal parricide discussed by Freud in *Totem*

and Taboo and *Moses and Monotheism* (cf. Paul, 1976; Reik 1962[1946]:
116). The aim of circumcision was thus seen as the suppression and
control of sexual and aggressive impulses. What the boy receives in
return for this loss is identification with the father, introduction into
the community of men, and socially approved sexual access to non-
incestuous love-objects. Or, to put it in simpler anthropological
terms, he becomes a man and is allowed to marry! The masculinity
thus acquired might be hard won, but it was essentially unprob-
lematic and enduring. It was also by definition something quite
separate from femininity.[13]

The assumption that masculinity had to be defined against femininity became the major theme of later analyses of male initiation
which focused less on relations with the father and more on the
necessity for, and difficulty of, separation from the mother. John
Whiting was one of the anthropologists most influential in this area,
and he and his colleagues posited a connection between initiation
rites and absent fathers. They argued initially that in polygynous
households fathers must necessarily be absent much of the time,
and children thus form a close relationship with their mothers. This
close relationship is compounded by exclusive mother–child sleeping arrangements and long post-partum sex taboos (cf. Kitahara,
1974; 1976). Whiting and his colleagues took the view that oedipal
conflicts were of varying strengths depending on the specific relationships between fathers, mothers and boys, and that initiation ceremonies must needs be most severe and brutal in situations where
mother–son relations are very close in early life and where bonding
between adult males is important for the functioning of society.[14] In
such contexts the boy identifies with the mother, and the result is a
situation in which his primary female identity will necessarily come
into conflict with his later secondary male identity.[15] This will particularly be the case in societies where masculinity is dominant and
patriarchal (cf. Burton, 1972; Rogers and Long, 1968; Stephens,
1962). Primary identification with the mother has to be replaced at
some point by a 'normal' identification with the father, and hence
the necessity of initiation rites to break the bond with the mother
and to repress the boys' hostility to this father and other adult males
(Whiting et al., 1958: 360–2; cf. Brain, 1977).[16] In the absence of these
rituals, the boy may try to resolve the conflict through compen-
satory hypermasculine behaviour. If, by contrast, the male role is
not dominant over the female one, the boy will continue with
aspects of his feminine identity and feminine behaviour (Munroe
et al., 1973).

The work of Whiting and his colleagues has been extensively criticized (cf. Barry and Schlegel, 1980; Levine, 1973; Norbeck, Walker and Cohen, 1962; Parker et al., 1975; Young, 1965; see also below), not least because of the way correlations between social and psychosexual structures are asserted, but cannot be shown to be causal. However, many of the key assumptions underpinning their work remain intact in contemporary writing in anthropology on initiation rituals. The central thesis continues to be that father absence, or low-level attention from fathers, gives rise to over-identification with the mother. In consequence, initiation and circumcision are connected to child-rearing practices, and thus we can expect oedipal conflicts to be systematically linked to kinship structures and gender roles (see above; cf. Ottenberg, 1989; Parin et al., 1980). However, as Langness has pointed out, the necessary details on marriage and child-rearing necessary to document the systematic nature of such links is frequently absent (Langness, 1990: 389).[17] Even where data on such practices exist, their causal links to processes of identification are difficult to establish empirically. In addition, relative father absence and primary responsibility for childcare by mothers does not mean that it is the biological mother alone who cares for the child. Langness argues for the Bena Bena that children are multiply cared for and nurtured by women of the clan, including grandmothers (ibid.: 389–90), something that he notes that Watson described for a nearby group as 'the community-as-parent' (Watson, 1983: 273). He also points out that children play in sex-linked groups from an early age and are taken care of by both men and women. Here, his argument clearly parallels that of Kurtz discussed earlier. He notes that the use of terms like 'exclusive' to describe the mother–child relationship based on sleeping arrangements is misleading, and the further use of words such as 'feminized' to describe the consequences of certain parenting behaviours has little analytic meaning (Langness, 1990: 392).

Psychoanalysts reflecting on the necessity for separation from the mother have focused less on a shift of identification from mother to father and more on the complex and multiple nature of identifications with both parents. Lidz and Lidz argued that, as the boy becomes an individual, he internalizes something of his mother and thus acquires a basic feminine component that remains at the core of his self. The motivations for such identification have a dual basis: men's envy of women's inherent capacity for fertility and nurturance, and a desire for a symbiotic reunion with the mother, a return to the pre-oedipal. According to Lidz and Lidz, boys and men both fear and wish for re-engulfment by the mother, and this is what initiation rituals work over. The paternal prohibition on the libidinal relationship with the mother provides support to the boy against the threat of the engulfing mother/womb, and, rather than being a threat, it is actually a support of a very powerful nature (Lidz and Lidz, 1989: 74). Lidz and Lidz argued that differentiation for children of both sexes is what is at issue, and that the oedipal transition impelled by castration anxiety is only one means of reinforcing 'a fundamental series of transitions that are essential to the development of children everywhere' (Lidz and Lidz, 1977: 27). The conflict in question is not between a primary and secondary sex identity, or between masculine and feminine positions or identifications, but between the desire for symbiotic reunion with the mother and a desire for an autonomous self.[18]

Bettelheim also argued that it was impossible to understand initiation rites without giving attention to constitutional bisexuality, and said of his own study that he hoped it would show 'how much more that is feminine exists in men than is generally believed . . . and how greatly female influence and female strivings have affected social institutions that have been explained on a purely masculine basis' (Bettelheim, 1954: 22). Bettelheim's basic suggestion was that initiation rites could not be explained in terms of castration anxiety and the prohibition on incest alone, but had to be seen in terms of men's envy of women's reproductive powers, and the desire to control fertility in general (ibid.: 124–7). He pointed to the ethnographic evidence of the analogies drawn between subincision and other forms of blood-letting and menstruation (cf. Hogbin, 1970), and to the themes of rebirth in initiation ceremonies (Bettelheim, 1954: 144–53, 165–206).[19] Bettelheim argued that if internalization/identification with the mother as love-object leading to separation anxiety was the key to understanding initiation rites, then such rites could plausibly be interpreted as an effort to deny separation from the mother by internalizing her. Hence, the focus on female powers and bodies (ibid.: 126). The issue then is not penis envy, but vagina envy (ibid.: 20), and the implication of Bettelheim's analysis is that male initiation rites are not self-evidently about trying to alter the boy's feminine identity into a masculine one, nor necessarily concerned with permanently expunging or removing aspects of a feminine identity, self or substance, but with retaining and internalizing aspects of the mother/femininity.

Most anthropologists and psychoanalysts who have analysed initiation rituals have been hampered by their adherence to a classic form of the oedipal model, where identification and object choice are the inverse of each other, and act as the primary determinants of gender identity. Although Freud himself linked the process of identifying with both parents to the fact that individuals take up both masculine and feminine positions, in other words to constitutional bisexuality, the fact that his own model was so strongly tied to the emergence of heterosexuality has effectively straitjacketed the evolution of alternative frameworks until very recently. The presence of fathers and other significant males in the process of identification and separation is, like the presence of mothers and other significant carers, essential and does have a profound impact on the formation of the gendered subject. However, it is equally apparent that parents alone do not determine gender identity and love-object choice. As Benjamin and others have argued, multiple identifications are formative of gender identities, and it is only possible to see this when we recognize that identification and object love do not break down along the clear lines suggested by the oedipal model (Benjamin, 1995; 1998; see also chapter 4 above).

Identification and object choice

In the past, among the Sambia of Papua New Guinea, male initiation was dramatic, involving bamboo flutes of great and mysterious power, exacting physical ordeals and repeated acts of semen ingestion.[20] In the accounts provided by their ethnographer Gilbert Herdt, there are six initiations in all, beginning between the ages of 7 and 10. Following the first initiation, a boy lives in the male clubhouse for as long as fifteen years, before he marries and builds a house with his wife.[21] The first three stages of initiation are collective and involve, sequentially, semen ingestion and semen insertion; the fourth stage is linked to a man's marriage, the fifth to the menarche of his wife and the sixth to the birth of his first child (Herdt, 1981; 1987; 1999). Flutes are blown during all collective initiations and once during the fourth stage. Women and children, who must never see them on pain of death, are told that their sounds are those of old female hamlet spirits (*aatmwogwambu*) who are already familiar to them from folklore. The flutes are always blown in pairs, referred to as *phalli*: the longer one is the male penis and the shorter one the female glans penis. They are said to be married, and their size and tunes are associated with phratry membership and political alliance (Herdt, 1999: 97).

Sambia cultural values emphasize extreme forms of gender polarity. Men believe themselves superior to women in terms of status, physique and character. They actively fear female pollution in the form of vaginal fluids and menstrual blood, but also through the semen depletion which results from heterosexual intercourse. This ideology of male superiority and disdain strongly pervades all social institutions and relationships, including intimate relations between women and men, and their domestic life (ibid.: 93).[22] At the core of this is a view of sexual and biological growth that necessitates the ritualized creation of masculinity as part of the initiation rites. Sambia men believe that a girl is born with all that she needs to achieve sexual and reproductive maturity because she possesses a menstrual-blood organ (*tingu*) which ensures these processes. The *tingu* of boys, however, is inactive, and although they possess a semen organ (*kereku-kereku*), this organ cannot naturally produce semen, it can only store it. Only oral insemination by other men can activate the boy's organ, stimulating sexual and physical maturity, and providing the manliness necessary to become a warrior. Masculinity is thus a cultural achievement (ibid.: 94). The physical maturity of boys and their masculinity is further imperilled by the closeness between boys and their mothers; hence boys not only need to be separated completely from their mothers when the time comes, but purified of female pollutants which will inhibit growth (ibid.: 95).

During first-stage initiation, the boys are beaten with switches to ensure growth, have their noses forcibly bled in a painful and traumatic ritual and are rubbed all over with stinging-nettles. These experiences set the stage for the flute ceremony, and as the men dress the boys in ceremonial and warrior garb, they begin to joke about sexual relations between men, and the boys' coming role as fellators of the older (third stage) initiates. The flutes are shown to the boys and used to teach the mechanics of fellatio. The boys are told that in order to grow they have to 'eat' the penises of men, but that if they reveal the secrets of the flutes to women and children they will be killed. Semen is repeatedly and explicitly likened to mother's milk. Later, in the cult house, bachelors arrive in disguise playing the flutes; they are impersonating the female hamlet spirits, and the boys are told that they must relieve her desire, suck on her penis (the flutes, like children, are crying out for milk/semen), an implicit command to serve as fellators to the bachelors. The erotic horseplay that follows soon leads to private homoerotic encounters outside, and these encounters continue during the rest of the initiation, and for many years to come (ibid.: 98–104). These same-sex encounters are between older and younger boys, and the younger boy is explicitly feminized by being subordinate to the older and referred to as married to the flute, thus becoming in some sense the 'wife' in the interaction (ibid.: 108). One of the reasons for the secrecy of the male cult and the violence with which it is guarded from women and children is presumably to hide the fact that all men have earlier in their lives played this feminized role (ibid.: 80).

In this society marked by strong sex antagonism and separation, boys who are initiated by being separated from their mothers and subjected to overt forms of brutal masculinization effectively learn that the male penis is a version of the female breast (ibid.: 117; Strathern, 1988: 210). Herdt explicitly argues, following Bowlby (1969; 1973), that the flutes are a symbolic substitute for the boy's mother, and that the flute as a detachable phallus is a substitute for the female breast. In this context, the flutes – and the awe and fear they inspire – 'supplant the mother as the preferred attachment figure by offering the culturally valued penis and homoerotic relationships as sensual substitutes for the mother's breast and for the mother as a whole person'. The secret that the flutes defend is the existence and significance of the homoerotic relationships, and thus the flutes become the boys' other 'mothers' and 'wives' (Herdt, 1999: 117). This analysis is a compelling one. As Herdt advises, it certainly does not suggest that we should view male initiation purely in terms of the resolution of the oedipal conflict and the father's punitive threat of castration as a way of securing the incest taboo (ibid.: 119). The situation is a puzzling one, since boys need to be separated from their mothers in order to become men, the very painful and traumatic rite of nose-bleeding is performed to rid them of mother's blood, and they are taught that all contact with women is debilitating and could impede their growth.[23] Yet the rite explicitly maintains a link between the pre-oedipal symbiosis of the mother–child and the oedipal institution of binary gender categorization and separation. Consequently, it is not just that the penis is a substitute for the mother's breast, as Herdt argues, but that, as eroticized objects, they can never be radically separated from each other, as symbolized most directly by the flutes which are simultaneously mother's breast and phallus.

During their years in the clubhouse, the boys move through the first three stages of initiation and shift from being fellators to being the fellated, and during this time all heterosexual contact is strictly prohibited.[24] Once they become stage three initiates, they can no longer ingest semen, but only provide it for younger boys. Once married, all homoerotic behaviour should cease, although in practice many men continue to have sex with boys, whilst also providing their pre-menarche wives with semen through oral fellation. It is said that this provides a young wife's body with the means to prepare for childbirth and to produce breast milk (Herdt, 1999: 66). Once a man is living with his wife after her menarche, he should be strictly heterosexual, and he is definitely so after the birth of the first child. In this sense, Sambia homoerotics prepares men for heterosexuality.[25] What this shows is that all sexual contacts in Sambia are strictly controlled and related to specific life stages, involving sexual and physical maturity, as well as the capacity to reproduce. Thus the relationship between what is male and what is female, between semen and mother's milk, has to be understood in the broader context of social relationships.

Semen can only be transacted between persons of groups who can intermarry.[26] The Sambia practise sister-exchange, and the preferred semen partner for a boy is his sister's husband. This man is thus inseminating his wife to make her ready to procreate, as well as inseminating her brother to make him grow. The senior man is thus a 'spouse' to a brother–sister pair, and through his acts of semen insertion he finishes off their growth, completing a process that their parents had begun through earlier semen and breast milk transactions. Semen as an eroticized detachable object associated with masculinity and femininity circulates through the bodies of significant others, linking homosexual desire to heterosexuality through the literal reproduction of the generations. A woman contributes womb-blood to a foetus and a man contributes semen. A child is only grown in the womb through repeated acts of sexual intercourse (semen insertion). The Sambia have no notion of conception in the western scientific sense, and a father will continue to 'grow' the child in the womb with semen until late in the pregnancy (Herdt, 1999: 67). A man's inseminations (especially oral) also collect in and are transformed by his wife's body into breast milk (ibid.: 69). Semen and breast milk are not just bodily fluids pertaining to already gendered bodies, but detachable and eroticized substances (objects) that circulate through the generations, linking specific individuals in concrete ways.

In this system of reproduction through sister-exchange, a male ego may receive semen from his brother-in-law, as does his sister and his sister's child. Once this child becomes a man, he knows that his father's semen made his mother, his mother's brother and himself. He ingests his father's semen in the form of his mother's milk. The ramifications of this circulatory system do not stop there because in cases where direct sister-exchange is not involved, the younger man who receives semen from his brother-in-law will eventually receive a return wife, the brother-in-law's daughter, created and grown with the latter's semen and the breast milk of his sister (ibid.: 84). This is not an abstract notion of kinship or social relations, one that merely provides a cultural context for historically specific understandings of sexual difference and object choice, but a symbolic system involving an exchange of objects that is constitutive of the psychic and social processes that make up body image, self–other relations and gendered identities. The significant others in this eroticized circulatory physics are not just mother and father, but sister, brother and brother-in-law, as well as potentially other kin.

The sister–brother pair that are at the core of this set of object exchanges between kin are complemented by two other pairs – mother–son and husband–wife – in such a way that an explicit analogy is drawn between breastfeeding and oral fellatio (ibid.: 69, 116). The management of bodily substances as detachable body parts is integral to the processes of identification and separation underlying self–other relations and the formation of the ego. This begins at birth for the Sambia child who is born into a context of explicit tension between her/his parents over the question of contamination through sexual fluids and the consequent management of the circulation of objects between intimate partners. Men reside with their wives and children, but take elaborate precautions not to come into contact with menstrual blood and/or women's sexual fluids. In such circumstances, they need also to be careful with their own children, who could easily contaminate them with female substances as a result of their close proximity to the mother. The management and circulation of bodily substances as detachable parts therefore form the context in which the maternal and the paternal are fantasized and take shape as part of self–other relations. This process continues through the life-course. The combined object semen/breast milk links a man's earliest conceptions of self as identified with and distinct from his mother to his later experiences as gendered masculine self engaged in sexual activities which involve semen ingestion and then the simultaneous insemination of boy and wife. The masculine and the feminine are thus conjoined as internal representations constitutive of the self and self–other relations.

It is not just that penises are also breasts, and that the violent oedipal nature of initiation retains a manifest link to the pre-oedipal, but also that the issues of identification and separation which underlie masculinity and femininity cannot be separated from the relationships within which they make sense as dual attributes. Sexual identities and the ideas of masculinity and femininity which sustain Sambia understandings of sexual difference cannot be easily reduced to the forms of individuality, with their concomitant ideas about autonomy and separation, which are often dominant in the West. This is evident not only through the circulatory physics of semen/breast milk, but also through the practice and symbolism of blood-letting. Blood-letting has been accounted for both as a mechanism for purification and as a way of psychologically conditioning boys who must become warriors. In this sense, it is always seen as related to masculinization. Herdt maintains this perspective, but he does point out that the forced blood-letting of the initiation rites gives way to the voluntary blood-letting of mature men, who ritually purify themselves after marriage on each occasion their wife has a period. Nose-bleeding among the Sambia is associated with separation from the mother and the removal of female pollutants which allows for male growth, but it is also part of the regulatory 'physics' throughout an adult man's life that are associated with his interactions with women (Herdt, 1982: 190–3). For example, the fifth stage of male initiation, which culminates in nose-bleeding, is triggered by the occurrence of the menarche in the youth's young wife. Ritual knowledge of the other purificatory techniques that protect men from the potentially lethal effects of heterosexual intercourse are taught during the same period (ibid.: 206–7). The result is that, while nose-bleeding is associated with purifying the body first of the mother's contamination and then of the wife's, it is also permanently connected to the reproductive act, heterosexuality, fertility and continued well-being. It is thus attached both to the sense of, and the experience of, being a male self, as well as to heterosexual union, to what ties a man to a woman (mother/wife): the blurred, conjoined and dual nature of masculinity and femininity.

Herdt is ambivalent throughout his work on the question of how much importance to give to oedipal conflicts and their resolution. The all-powerful father, representing culture, who wrests the child from the all-powerful, dominating, seductive mother, is an important theme not only in psychoanalytic theory and psychoanalytically inspired anthropology, but in western culture more generally (see chapter 3), so we need to be cautious about it when it appears too easily in ethnographic interpretations. Herdt is absolutely correct when he says that part of the difficulty here is the western assumption that homosexuality is linked to a failure of masculinity and to effeminacy, to a kind of flaw in normal heterosexuality (Herdt, 1993b: xii; 1999: ch. 9).[27]

Herdt has reviewed the arguments on father presence and ritual homosexuality in Melanesia to see whether absent fathers and dominant mothers correlate with ritual homosexuality in male initiation rites, and concludes, after a detailed ethnographic discussion, that societies which practice ritual homosexuality have varying patterns of father presence in childhood, and that many societies that lack ritual homosexuality have absent fathers (see above). As Herdt points out, the idea that parents alone determine gender identity and love-object choice, and that both of these are determined in early childhood by child-rearing practices, is open to question from a cross-cultural perspective (1989: 329; cf. Riesman, 1983). This is, first, because of the role of wider kin and social groups in parenting and thus in the resolution of oedipal conflicts and, second, because in societies that practise initiation and other powerful rituals, there is no evidence that child-rearing practices are more determinant of gender and sexual identity. 'We need a different framework that recognizes a boy's development as occurring in contexts wherein it is not merely an individual problem to create separate male sexual identity but rather it is a *relational* task to take on new and complex roles and symbolic relationships that far transcend the earlier ones' (Herdt, 1989: 331). One of Herdt's points here is that theories that focus on the 'lone child model' of development need to be replaced by ones that take into account the psychosexual structures and experiences of specific historical societies. Herdt's argument has similarities with those of Obeyesekere, Kurtz and Kakar, discussed above.

Gender and the repetition of sexual difference

However, Herdt's argument can be developed more radically in ways that help us reflect not only on the instability of sexual difference and the multiple nature of gendered identities, but also on the question of how identification and object choice are related to both. What the Sambia data show is that when we speak of the importance of objects or part objects – such as the flutes, semen and breast milk – in the formation of individual fantasies of masculine and feminine selves, or fantasies of self as both masculine and feminine and/or self–other relations, we are already speaking of a self in relation to specific cultural others. It is not only the self and the object that are internalized, but also the system of perceived relations among others, as well as their relations to objects. Thus, the child does not just internalize an aspect of the mother, but also the relationship between the mother and the father, and their relations with others (Aron, 1995: 215; Goldner, 1991: 262). When semen is internalized as an object, so too is its relation with other objects. Masculinity and femininity as internalized aspects of self not only retain a relationship with each other, but also with the objects and social relationships that give them form, as in the example of the circulatory physics of masculine and feminine relations in Sambia. Anthropological and psychoanalytic analyses of oedipal conflict, mother separation and initiation rituals have tended to work with a 'thin' notion of the social, one that sees social relations simply as the framework within which psychic processes take place – hence the emphasis on such things as child-rearing practices and forms of behaviour or types of kinship structure. Whatever masculinity and femininity are for a specific experiencing self, they are always modelled on the multiple and fantasized nature of one's own and other people's experience of them in concrete social relationships.[28] Thus, when we refer to the importance of kin in the formation of gendered identities, we must mean to say that these relationships are simultaneously psychic and social, that there are no social relations with significant others outside our fantasized relation with them and no fantasies about masculinity and femininity outside our lived engagement with them in a concrete world of objects (including other gendered individuals).

This argument gives a whole new perspective on an old debate (see chapter 1) about cultural (historical) variability and psychic structures. The terms of this debate have tended to shift across time, but they are all derived in one way or another from a problem put in place by the claim that the Oedipus complex is universal. One version treats gender identity as subordinate to sexual identity because to be a self at all one must identify as either female or male. The cultural elaboration and content of the subsequent categories are fascinating, but basically epiphenomenal. At this point, the battle is between ideology and ontology, and ontology prevails because being is necessarily a sexed being. A more sophisticated variant on this theme sees the divide as falling between phenomenology and ontology. The way we perceive the world as gendered beings and our experiences of our gendered bodies and their relation to history and memory are important, but make no fundamental difference to the invariant nature of psychic structures, and the primary division of sexual difference. In both cases, culture is epiphenomenal, interesting, but not in any sense constitutive of sexual identity (see chapter 5). Culture operates on the level of gender; psychoanalysis works at the level of sex (Mitchell, 1991).

This omnipotent theory is, however, consistently threatened by the return of the repressed. This takes the form in Freudian theory of the problem of bisexuality or multiple identifications, leading to increasingly contorted manoeuvrings throughout the history of psychoanalytic thinking, positing primary and core identities to be superseded or not by later identifications. All of these theories are struggling more or less successfully with the apparent paradox of categorical and binary sexual difference, interwoven with complex, multiple understandings of masculinity and femininity. Lacanian theory works especially hard to clarify Freud's notion of bisexuality and arrive at a view of the subject as constructed in language which allows the masculine and the feminine to be constituted through a relation to the signifier. Individual men and women may, however, take up positions on either side of the equation. The male and the female appear relatively clear-cut in this context, but the masculine and the feminine remain a problem. (Hence, the regular accusations of biologism that arise against psychoanalysis from time to time.) This is precisely the problem that object relations and relational analysts seek to solve: how can we develop a theory that takes account of intersubjective relations with specified others and deals with the multiple and complex understandings and experiences that individuals have of their gender and their sense of being masculine and feminine selves in light of the fact that we are all subject to the dictates of sexual difference?

The Sambia data shed light on these debates in two ways. The first concerns the relationship between gender identities and sexual difference, and thus addresses the antinomy of cultural determinism versus invariant psychic structures. The second focuses on the relationship between gender identity, identification and object choice. In addressing the first question, we should return to Freud's insight that neither biology nor convention accounts for sexual difference. I take up this point in more detail in chapter 9, but for the moment I want to argue that this is amply demonstrated by the Sambia material, because if sexual difference were a matter of one

or the other, then Sambia men would not need to ingest semen or
let blood from their noses. Sambia society is highly patriarchal,
male-dominated and constructed around rigid binary gender divisions, and yet the problem of sexual difference recurs. It repeats constantly throughout a man's life: initiation grows a man, but it is not
enough to keep him one.

Sexual difference is a very human concern. While other species
find the male and the female quite sufficient for reproduction,
humans have other things on their minds. There is no problem
about males and females, but there is a problem about masculinity
and femininity. Sexual difference is not just a cross-sex problem, it
is also a cross-generational one. This is why Freud's Oedipus
complex has exerted such fascination. In order to acquire a sense of
self, the child has to recognize that she/he is separate from the
mother, inhabit a body image, take up a position in the symbolic
order, relate to the world of objects. Each part of this process,
regardless of which type of psychoanalytic theory is being invoked,
involves representation, and all of these representations are already
gendered, they are already bound up with the world of others, with
culture (see chapters 4 and 5). This is true at the level of fantasy and
at the level of social relations, which are in any event mutually constitutive over time. Masculinity and femininity, and their complex
relation to identification, introjection and projection, are already
bound up with gendered representations. As I argued in the previous chapter, even if one were to adhere to the classic oedipal triangle, one cannot talk about mothers and fathers as if they were either
contentless or invariant categories or entities. The real individuals
who inhabit these roles are already peopled with masculine and
feminine others, body parts and self–other relations. If mothers and
fathers were just mothers and fathers, unambiguously male and
female, singular and distinct, then sexual difference would not be
an issue. The irony is that it is gender that creates the problem of
sexual difference: it accounts for the necessity of the latter's repetition; gender is why the male and the female are never enough.

Human societies make much of gender and they struggle with it
in particular ways. One of the major difficulties is that the term
'gender' as used in the social sciences refers to representations,
ideas, models and discursive practices that operate on a number of
different levels. The unstable natures of the masculine and the feminine, and of their relation to each other, are accompanied in most
societies by models of gender difference that are often very clear-
cut and clearly correlated to power, resource and status differen-

tials. Discourses in many societies speak explicitly of the imperative of establishing definitive gender distinctions through the necessity of marking the body, separating the child from the mother, feminizing or masculinizing particular individuals and so on. The resulting cultural elaborations, models, practices, social roles and statuses are equally designated by the term gender. Anthropologists often talk about gender ideologies as opposed to gender roles to try to capture something of the way gender operates at different levels and in different domains of social life, but the distinction is a crude one which occludes more than it reveals. Benjamin (1995; 1998) and others, working from a psychoanalytic view point, have sought to tackle this problem by distinguishing between the pre-oedipal, the oedipal and the post-oedipal, where the creation of dominant binary gender categorization is a feature of oedipal concerns. These stages should not be taken as necessarily linear, although they are in part developmental – oedipal conflicts cannot arise before the recognition of the self–other relation – and their consequences persist and fold over each other creating new dynamic forms of interrelation from adolescence onwards (Aron, 1995; Benjamin, 1998: ch. 2; Goldner, 1991; Coates, 1997).

From the perspective of the argument made here, the relationship between gender and sexual difference is not one that can be established in a strictly causal or linear sense, first because gender operates at several levels simultaneously and second because the relationship between gender and sexual difference evolves within the lifetimes of individuals and cultures which in any event do not operate on the same time scale. Binary gender differences are violently instituted at initiation, by which time the children already know that some of them are boys and some of them are girls. The maintenance of masculinity, and of gender differences more generally, is a life-long process exemplified by various bodily practices, including blood-letting. The truly historical nature of the relation between gender and sexual difference means that while oedipal conflicts might be important, they cannot be the once-and-for-all defining moment. Sexual difference repeats itself as a conundrum and both subjects and cultures are produced in response to that conundrum. What time reveals is not that sexual difference is settled, but that it is never settled. The male and the female are obvious in their clearly evident nature, and yet representation teaches us all that things are never what they seem.

In the case of the Sambia data, this is brought home very clearly with regard to the relationship between gender identity, identification and love-object choice. Sambia men are a problem for oedipal theories because their erotic life consists of an exclusive period of homosexuality followed by an equally exclusive period of heterosexuality, with men reporting both types of sex as exciting in their different ways. This has led quite understandably to an obvious question about whether or not Sambia men are homosexual in the western sense of the term, and whether sexual practices are related to sexual identities cross-culturally (Elliston, 1995; Herdt, 1999: ch. 9; Herdt and Stoller, 1990). Does it make sense, and is it possible to distinguish between homosexual and heterosexual, since in the Sambia case male homosexuality is in the end actually about heterosexual object choice? This being the case, is it really connected to an individual's sexual identity? If not, then what is the relationship between masculinity (that is, an individual's gender) and their sexual identity (Elliston, 1995: 849)? There is plenty of scope here for muddled thinking, most of it on the side of anthropologists and psychoanalysts. The Sambia, of course, make no distinction between sex and gender – the sexed body and the culturally and socially constituted identity (Herdt, 1981: 168).[29] This should not surprise us, since this distinction is itself culturally and historically specific. However, 'sex' – understood as sexual practices – in ordinary English usage implies an erotic object. Herdt has posited this question for the Sambia, and asked if homosexual activity is linked to erotic pleasures and erotic object choice. His answer is that this is indeed the case for certain individuals, but that it is not the case at a societal level (ibid.: 4).[30] As Herdt himself notes, the Sambia have no category term or cultural representation for 'the homosexual' or 'homosexuality' (Herdt, 1991: 612), just as they have no term for heterosexuality.[31] This leaves the anthropologist with the strange worry 'What then does sex imply, what does it "mean"?' If sex is not about object choice, then how can it be linked to identity, and if it is not linked to identity then it cannot really be relevant to sexual difference (Greenberg, 1988; Herdt, 1997). Gender becomes split off from sexuality.

What is evident is that Sambia ideas about how masculinity and femininity are related and how sexuality emerges out of and in the context of gender differences are not necessarily well served by terms like homosexual and heterosexual. The idea that object love and identification are mutually exclusive is the product of a certain kind of oedipal thinking common to much anthropology and orthodox forms of psychoanalysis. This is a theoretical position underpinned by binary conceptualizations both of gender difference and of sexuality (homosexuality versus heterosexuality). Freud saw the Oedipus complex and the socialization of desire as pivotal because he viewed it as providing an account of how normative hetero-sexuality arises out of constitutional bisexuality. Shorn of its normative pretensions, Freud's theory of bisexuality can be seen to undercut any simple notion that masculinity and femininity are entirely separable or separate from each other, or that pre-oedipal identifications with both parents or with fantasized aspects of mas-culinity and femininity do not continue into adult life. Herdt, however, rejects the label bisexual as a way of understanding the Sambia case. His chief disagreement is with the western assumption that terms such as bisexual or homosexual designate ontological cat-egories. Such categories, he argues, are culturally specific and based on particular assumptions about subject–object relations and their connections to identification–object choice, and sex–love relations (Herdt, 1999: 296–8). Herdt's larger point is that western ideas about sexuality, and particularly those influenced by Freudianism, link the nature of being (ontology) to a particular account of the erotic (ibid.: 297). Thus, when we ask whether the Sambia are homosexual or bisexual, we impose a culturally inappropriate frame.

Once again, we can push this argument further. Herdt points out that Sambia society requires a very specific view of sexual devel-opment and gender identity, one that is based on multiple desired objects (of both genders) (ibid.: 295). This brings us back to the ques-tion: is culture epiphenomenal in such a context interesting, but not actually constitutive, of gendered subjectivities? Anthropologists have long argued (see chapter 2) that cultural ontologies do have a determining impact on the shape and form of what it is to be a self. These arguments have sometimes been fatally weakened by the failure to take into account desires, fantasies, drives and emotions as opposed simply to ideas, practices, intentions and rationaliza-tions. In the Sambia case, however, becoming a gendered person requires – for a man – the experience and management of multiple object choices. It seems logical that any account of how the subject is marked by sexual difference – to put it in rather more Lacanian terms – must take this into account. The route to developing such an account is perhaps a little less rocky if we ask not only how, but why.

The normal answer to the 'why' question is that every being must necessarily be a sexed being, and must assume a position in rela-tion to sexual difference. Given their views about masculinity, it seems likely that the Sambia would agree strongly with such a statement, and yet it is equally apparent that identification and object choice do not break down along the clear lines set by the western oedipal model. Despite this, the Sambia maintain strong binary gender distinctions, and each individual is powerfully marked by sexual difference. It is helpful here to recall that sexual difference is a conundrum: it is a difficulty that repeats itself. For the Sambia, masculinity has to be grown, sexual difference has to be made to appear. Why should this be so? What question is sexual difference the answer to? Anthropologists and psychoanalysts often begin their answer from the wrong starting point, because they look at initiation and ask what it does for the initiates, and perhaps what it does for society. The response is that it makes initiates into men, and thereby produces the kind of men that society needs. However, the problems of masculinity and femininity are not so easily solved, and the difficulties they present are not the confusions of young children, but the dilemmas of adult women and men. A Sambia man lets blood from his nose on the occasion of each of his wife's periods, thereby linking the maintenance of his masculinity to a cyclical process that rids him of the contaminating effects of femininity. If the male and the female were sufficient, this would not need to be so. Sexual difference is the retroactive consequence of the effects of masculinity and femininity, and of their careful management within symbolic systems and social relations. The irony here is that sexual difference is maintained through its impossibility, through the failure of representation to capture in any lasting and fixed sense the distinction between masculinity and femininity. Nose-bleeding reveals that masculine subjectivity is founded on that impossibility which becomes both the 'how' and the 'why' of sexual difference itself.

8

Mothers and Men

Society's self-representations make no sense outside their engagement with specific forms of subjectivity.

Castoriadis, 1997: 89

The origins of sexual difference

The First Man was walking along when he heard the sound of laughter. He went to investigate and saw a group of cassowaries bathing in a pool. Having removed their skins, they had become beautiful human women. The man secretly stole the skin of Nambweapa'w, the cassowary-woman he desired, and when she emerged to put on her skin, she could not find it. This led to the man taking her home with him. Once there, he secretly placed a sharpened piece of quartz at the base of a pandanus palm and told the cassowary-woman to clean herself by rubbing against the tree. As she did so, the stone pierced her groin to form a vulva, and blood started to flow which was the first menstruation.

Man and wife advanced to old age, producing a long line of alternately sexed children, who later intermarried and became the ancestors of all the world's peoples. The father would take the older children to the garden, while the mother stayed home to look after the youngest; the next day the parents would reverse the roles.

The youngest boy was about 6 years old and one day, when he was crying for his mother, the father put on the cassowary skin that he had kept in order to frighten the boy. The next day, in exchange for some food, the boy revealed the secret to his mother, who found her cassowary skin, realized her husband had been deceiving her all these years, put it on and went back to her home in the forest. However, she gave her children instructions on how they were to find her later.

After some months they followed her, taking their father with them. The father hid, and the children climbed trees to try and locate their mother. The mother went to them and ordered the children down from the trees and told the boys to take up their spears. She noticed that one spear remained, and identifying this as her husband's, she found him and crushed his head with it. The children were very afraid of her.

The mother took the children to a place in the forest and, as they slept, she caused spirit houses, menstrual houses and a whole village to appear. This made the children aware of the great power of her magic. They stayed in the village and each brother took the sister following him in the birth order as his wife, all except the youngest boy who had no sister and stayed with his mother. One day the mother decided that it was not good for the descendants of her children all to speak the same language. So she sent the boys up a tree in birth order with the eldest at the bottom, and, as each descended, he was bitten by a certain kind of insect, causing him to speak a different language. The eldest spoke Ilahita, the others spoke languages of neighbouring groups, all except the youngest who spoke a language utterly different from all the others, now known to be English.

Everything was provided in the village, gardens cleared themselves, and harvested food appeared in neat piles on the sides of the garden. They were all provided for by their mother, and there was no death or sorcery. But one day, one of the elder children ate some food that the mother had forbidden them to eat; the others followed suit, all except the youngest son. The mother was very angry and, turning herself into a tree kangaroo, she tricked her youngest son into killing her. He tried to pull the spear out, but she commanded him to wait, saying from now on there will be death and sorcery, there will be much pain in childbirth, and both men and women will have to work hard for their food. The magic is finished. The boy pulled the spear out and his mother died.

The youngest son railed at his siblings, and so great was his fury that a huge wave rose up around him and carried him to America, from whence he will one day return.

This is an abridged account of the Nambweapa'w myth, a story told by the Ilahita Arapesh of Papua New Guinea (Tuzin, 1980: 1–8; 1997: 69–71). It begins with the First Man, or primordial father, capturing a figure representing the fusion of the human and natural worlds. Through an act of deception, he traps the cassowary-woman in her human form and splits the human from the natural world. Through a second ruse, he tricks her into piercing herself to form a vulva and reproductive human sexuality is initiated with the first menstruation. The First Man thus inaugurates a social world, but he does so through trickery and deception. But this world is not a fully social one. Nambweapa'w, the cassowary-woman, is a primordial figure, and what she represents, as is evident in her magical powers, is a plenitude, an impossible *jouissance*, a completeness which symbolizes a closed cycle of auto-reproduction. Under her watchful eye, her perfectly paired children marry each other and remain within the paradise-like womb she has created. Nambweapa'w is a very daunting figure: she not only kills her unfortunate husband, the First Man, but she has the power to create a world, and to inaugurate language. Her children have seen what she has done to their father and are frightened of her.

Freud's proposition that something must be relinquished for society to come into being was more explicitly formulated by Lacan, who claimed that what the individual gives up to attain a speaking place within culture is *jouissance*, the imaginary plenitude of the mother–child union. The myth of Nambweapa'w is very clearly about the inauguration of the social, the birth of society and yet this is not a classic oedipal story. The all-important father, while he initiates the possibility for human sexual relations and reproduction in the form of alterations to the cassowary-woman's body, is nonetheless not a world-maker. It is the terrifying Nambweapa'w who has the power to create worlds and to destroy them, and yet we are left in no doubt that the world she fashions is not a living, sustainable, social world; it is too perfect, too closed, too symbiotic. The world she crafts for her children is ultimately a womb-like prison rather than a world of exchange and growth. When that world is sundered through the breaking of her prohibition, which incites her wrath, the result is a curse of death and deprivation which is also somehow life. This story is a useful starting point for a discussion about origins and mothers because it reprises themes which are of major concern to societies all over the world, but most especially in Melanesia.

Origins are a curious phenomena in human culture and in the human mind because they can only ever be approached, narrated or accounted for in retrospect, and consequently they bear the imprint both of the present and the future. Origins are never originary moments *strictu sensu*. In myths, for example, every beginning presupposes a pre-existing world within which the 'origin' takes place, as in the Nambweapa'w story just recounted. The origins of society and social relations are an enduring preoccupation of Melanesian societies and they are almost always linked explicitly to the inauguration of sexual difference, human sexuality and human reproduction. Before the First Man tricks the cassowary-woman into leaving the natural world for the one of proto-social relations and then goes on to deceive her into creating a vulva, there is no possibility of human sexual relations and reproduction. These two things are impossible because sexual difference does not yet exist in the pre-social world. Sexuality of some sort is there, but sexual difference is not. Bernard Juillerat takes up this theme in his recounting of a Yafar myth.

The women or garboango lived by themselves in the village and the men or suwomp lived in the forest. The women celebrated the rite of Yangis. Sometimes the men hid and observed the public parts of this rite, but were unaware that it was the women who performed it hidden under their body paint and masks. One day a young man came upon a village of women. He surprised them as they were preparing for their ceremony Yangis, and hid. He observed them making masks, preparing colours and painting their bodies. He climbed a bread fruit tree and watched a young woman washing off her body paint in the river. When she had finished, she saw a reflection of a man in the water and looked up at him. He climbed down and they had sex. She hid him on the edge of the village and went home. The other young women noticed that she smelt strange and questioned her, but she revealed nothing, except to show her younger sister where the young man was hidden. The younger sister went to the man and had sex with him. Both sisters gave off a strong smell of man and the other women fainted.

The sisters hid the man in their house. Meanwhile, the women carried out their ceremony and sang sacred songs just outside the house. Unable to get out, the young man urinated inside the house. The women outside smelt the odour and fainted. They said to the sisters, that is the smell of man, and forced the door and discovered the young man. They all wanted to have sex with him and he had sex with several of them simultaneously, using his penis, his hands and his feet and he fainted.

Then the women left to go hunting. The young man stayed with the two sisters, and told the younger one to stay at home while he went to collect firewood with the elder. They collected firewood, made a bed and had sex. The young man conducted a rite mixing their sexual fluids with other materials. This opened up the way for other young men to come out of the forest. They came and hid at the edge of the village. The women came back from the hunt and cooked their game in the sacred enclosure, put on all their finery and went into the village blowing their horns. The young man pretended he was going to urinate, but went and sealed off the sacred enclosure. Then he informed all the young men and they had sex with all the women. The eldest man had a very big penis and the eldest woman had a very big vagina and they had sex. At first she was frightened, then began to laugh and then her vagina roared. After that the men resided in the village with the women. But soon they killed all the women, took over their masks and colours, and spared only very young girls who were ignorant. (Translated and abridged from Juillerat, 1991: 192–3; 2001: 137–8)

This myth recounts a moment of transition from a world of sexual segregation to one of male dominance. The men discover the secrets of the women by deception and then wrest them from the women by force and murder. All this is made possible largely through the agency of sexual desire, but this desire is of a natural kind, it is not based on social relations between the sexes or embedded within a cultural form of sexual difference.[1] Rather, it is the outgrowth of a connection to the natural, biological world, and this is made evident in a series of other myths which contextualize this moment of transition, all of which liken human reproduction and sexuality to plant and animal processes of growth and reproduction (Juillerat, 1991: ch. 5). The story as presented is one about the simultaneous foundation of society and sexual difference, where the inauguration of sexual difference follows the sealing off of the maternal womb (the sacred enclosure) by the male hero, and the installation of procreative sexuality symbolized by the orgasmic response of the eldest woman, literally the moment of conception. In line with many mythic and ritual representations in Melanesia and principles of kinship organization, the difference between younger and older siblings of the same sex often translates into the difference between generations. Hence, the use of the terms translated as 'eldest man' and 'eldest woman' at the end of the story makes them represent the father and the mother. Consequently, the story is one about the birth of society, the installation of sexual difference and the imposition of a paternal/phallic law.

After the men steal the secret, there are no women left to remember that it was once theirs. The content of the myth in representing women as the performers of Yangis and the holders of its knowledge marks them as guardians both of sociality and of sexuality. Living in the village, they control the totality of reproduction, both literal and imaginary, and have no need of men. In other words, they possess the phallus and their world is unmarked by sexual difference. As in the story of Nambweapa'w, the 'origin' of society takes place in a pre-existing world and so cannot be a truly originary moment. Bernard Juillerat's accounts of this myth all emphasize its processual nature, its portrayal of transition and transformation. The hero of the myth, one Pépi, has an earlier incarnation which precedes his actions here.

A man kills game (wild pigs and cassowaries) and leaves them on a platform in the forest to rot, taking back to his wife and daughters only lizards, snakes and other small things. The youngest daughter finds him out. The women kill and bury the man, and take the game they have found home to eat. The man emerges little by little from the ground and returns to the house. He discovers the theft of the game and kills his wife by dropping a large stone on her head. He cuts off her breasts and eats them with sago jelly prepared by his daughters pretending that they are mushrooms. The daughters discover he has killed their mother and set fire to the house with him inside.

The daughters find their mother who has given birth to a child. The girls capture the boy, giving him game to persuade him to leave his mother's body. They leave to collect bread fruit, but the youngest sister is taken by spirits in the tree and immobilized (impregnated). The elder sister and the young boy leave and meet a python who asks to go with them. The python transforms himself into a man during the day and helps the young woman (killing game, cutting down sago palms, building). The boy discovers the python is a man and, as a result, the man can no longer transform himself into a python. He announces that he will not be able to provide for them and that they will go hungry. He leaves with the sister and they abandon the boy.

The boy lives on sago. He meets two sisters whom he marries. His brothers-in-law give him a penis sheath, a bow and some arrows. He kills a female possum with two babies in her pouch. The eldest sister hides the male one and keeps it as her child. The man searches for his little possum and finds that his wives have stolen it. With no success at hunting, he asks his brothers-in-law to kill a pig, but to leave the cassowary alone. They kill the pig, but Wefroog (cultural hero/trickster) kills the cassowary. The hero cries and asks for the cassowary to be cut up, but the heart to be kept for him. He returns from the hunt, but the heart is not there. Five nights later he hears a possum cry (it is the heart of the cassowary metamorphosed) in five different trees. The brothers-in-law cut down the trees and find magic plants that they give to the hero. Pépi is painted and adorned by his son the possum, transforms himself into a bird and perches on a branch from where he baits his wives. They are furious and camp at the base of the tree. The younger drinks the water that has accumulated in the roots of the tree and becomes pregnant. (Translated and abridged from Juillerat, 1991: 154–68)

This myth works over in a much more explicit fashion the connection between asocial human sexuality and the natural world. It also establishes a series of connections between social continuity, human fertility and the ability to extract resources from the natural world, including the very capacity for reproduction and subsequent growth. The myth makes it very clear that this is a proto-social world where humans, plants and animals are not entirely separate. The father who is murdered at the beginning of the myth re-emerges out of the ground like a plant, and his name Riyu (rii = 'tree', yug = 'young shoot') makes this link apparent. Juillerat notes that Riyu is, in particular, associated with the coconut palm, and his wife with the mature coconut (mother's milk), while Pépi is the sprout which germinates from the rotting coconut (dead mother) (Juillerat, 1991: 168). The instances of reproduction described in the myth are forms of parthenogenesis rather than procreative human sexuality. This makes sense, as Juillerat demonstrates, of the strange report at the beginning of the myth that the man is letting the game rot rather than bringing it home to his family. This indicates that, rather than a true hunter, he is actually managing reproduction as a form of germination/gestation, just as the sprout emerges out of the rotting coconut. At the centre of this is the image of the coconut palm as androgynous, as something feminine which contains the phallus of the father while continuously producing sons (Juillerat,

1995: 41). This vegetable world is a productive one, but not yet one marked by human sexual difference. This is made evident in the myth through the way that sexual relations do not produce human offspring. Pépi's sisters enter the story as the product of the relations of Riyu and his wife, but their subsequent fates suggest that they were never really fully human and they return to the natural world. The sexual relations between Pépi and his wives produce nothing, their offspring is something captured from the natural world, a form of game (Juillerat, 1991: 184), just as Pépi is himself when he is 'captured' by his elder sisters and lured out of his mother's stomach/vagina with promises of more game (ibid.: 170–1). The story turns on how humans are not separate from the natural world and on how more is required than sexual coupling and proto-social exchanges (the penis sheath, bow, plants, etc. from the brothers-in-law) to create social life. Relations between women and men need to be marked by sexual difference to bring society into being.

All the myths discussed here link the origin of human society to the inauguration of sexual difference. This moment of origin is of continuing concern, but can never be accurately located. A world without sexual difference has to be back projected from one in which it is already installed as the defining principle, and stories of how this transformation comes about thus deal with the question of the emergence of humans qua humans.

Figures of the maternal

Three sons go hunting and return empty handed. Their father opens the door of an underground store at the foot of a tree and takes out a pig, kills it, shuts the door and returns to the house. The sons ask him where he got the pig, and he replies that the game is nearby. This continues for some time. The sons are always unsuccessful and the father always brings game home. The three elder brothers consult and decide to send their younger brother to spy on their father. The next day the youngest son follows the father who goes straight to a door at the foot of a tree near the house. The son hears the sounds of pigs, cassowaries, possums and kangaroos. The father chooses a large pig, kills it, shuts the door and takes the animal back to the house.

The youngest son tells his elder brothers what he has seen. The following day, the parents leave to prepare sago. The older brothers prepare their arrows. The youngest opens the door and the brothers let fly, killing some animals, but the rest escape into the forest. The father returns later and finds the subterranean store empty. That night he digs a deep hole and inside it he pretends to be preparing for a rite by playing a drum and blowing a trumpet. In the morning he asks his sons what they heard. Each night he continues to dig a deeper hole until the sons report that they can hear nothing. He throws his three eldest sons, houses, fire, firewood and all things that were previously abundant into the hole. He seals the entrance with his sperm. (Translated and abridged from Juillerat, 1991: 56–61; 1995: 45)

This is the public version of the myth; esoteric variations include one where, when the youngest son spies on the father, he sees him prepare his bow and arrows, but instead of leaving the house he turns to his wife and pulls the game from her vagina. Another has a dwarf-sized father sitting on his wife's coccyx and by blowing a trumpet he creates a great wind which pulls the three sons, their houses, goods, sago palms and tools into their mother's stomach/vagina. The father then seals the entrance with a mixture of his sperm, the petiole of a coconut, the plumes of the cassowary and the sap of the bread fruit tree (Juillerat, 1991: 63–4). Juillerat makes it very clear throughout the whole corpus of his work that for the Yafar, meaning is never univocal. There are links between ritual, myth and cosmology, but these do not constitute 'an absolutely logical system of meanings'. Even when the public and esoteric forms of ritual and mythic knowledge are taken together they do not 'constitute a cohesive story of creation or one perfectly coherent worldview' (Juillerat, 1992a: 22).[2] This is a system of thought that circulates around and through its own contradictions, resonances and ambiguities.

In this regard, the Yafar make it very plain that representations are not flawless, nor are they complete. The relation of language to the world is not a self-evident one and not everything is given in language. No set of representations could provide a complete account of the world and of people's relation to it. This must logically be true for anthropologists as well as informants. However, to make such a claim is not just to say that knowledge is situated, embedded, partial. The latter view point is undoubtedly accurate, but it does not capture the 'generative principle' that is at the core of Melanesian myths of origins. This principle is not explicitly stated in cosmologies, myths and rituals, but acts as the point around which metaphors, metonyms, partial representations and contradictions slip and slide. It is not itself present as a positive appearance, but rather as a negative whose 'signature appears in language' (Copjec, 1994: 9). Lacan comes out against the post-structuralist proposition that language/texts are worlds in themselves, that 'reality' is structured through language, and that because the relationship of signifier to signified is never fixed and stable, this process of structuration is always incomplete. The Lacanian view starts from a different proposition and suggests that even when language is caught up in a web of self-referencing signifiers, there is a reference point to its movement, its play, its ambiguities. The point around which language slips and slides is what Lacan terms the *objet a* (see chapter 3). This object cannot be present as a positive appearance in the symbolic system because it is a lost object (Žižek, 1989: 158). It nevertheless acts as the point around which the social regime functions and yet simultaneously works as a negation of the principle of the rules that appear to govern society (Copjec, 1994: 10–13).

Žižek illuminates this point by describing a joke about 'Lenin in Warsaw': 'At an art exhibition in Moscow, there is a picture showing Nadezhda Krupskaya, Lenin's wife, in bed with a young member of the Komsomol. The title of the picture is "Lenin in Warsaw". A bewildered visitor asks a guide: "But where is Lenin?" The guide replies quietly and with dignity: "Lenin is in Warsaw" ' (Žižek, 1989: 159). The poor visitor's mistake, as Žižek notes, is to imagine that the title refers to what is depicted, that the sign denotes an object. Whereas the point is that the title does not refer to what is positively depicted, but to the negative principle around which the representation circulates and from which it gains its form, a present absence which is not portrayed in the picture. This lack or void does not itself have a content, it is an object produced by the signifying system, in and through its workings (ibid.: 159–61), but this negative object cannot be absorbed into the symbolic system itself. From an anthropological point of view, we can say that it is the thing that cannot find expression within a given symbolic form, it is the absent signature of culture (Copjec, 1994: 14). The *objet a* represents for Lacan the surplus of the real over every symbolization, the idea that there is always a 'kernel' of the real that resists symbolization, something that, while it cannot be integrated into the symbolic system, nonetheless shapes it. This non-integrated element produces a series of structural effects (displacements, repetitions, substitutions). It has a series of properties, but as an entity it does not exist, in the sense of 'taking place in reality'. Žižek, who is good on apposite stories, illustrates this point with an account of the original anecdote behind the Hitchcock MacGuffin. Two men are sitting in a train and one asks, 'What's that package on the luggage rack?' 'That's a MacGuffin.' 'What's a MacGuffin?' 'An apparatus for trapping lions in the Scottish Highlands.' 'There are no lions in the Scottish Highlands.' 'Well, then, that's not a MacGuffin!' (Žižek, 1989: 162–3). This object which does not exist can only be inferred from a series of effects, including its impact on the symbolic reality of subjects.[3] It is in a logical sense impossible. But, we must be careful here and not mistake the character of the Lacanian real. The real is not a positive entity, existing somewhere before or beyond the symbolic order, stubbornly resisting incorporation. It is itself a nothing, a point of failure in a symbolic structure, something that marks a central impossibility (Žižek, 1989: 173). It is the negative within the symbolic that functions as the object cause of desire and thus structures the symbolic. Starting from this position allows us to read and interpret anthropological material in quite a different way.

The Yafar Yangis

This point can be exemplified by the Yafar Yangis ritual which, in its broadest sense, is a fertility ritual that enacts in sequence the coitus of the divine couple, the loss of virginal blood, conception, gestation, the announcement of the birth of sons, the birth itself, the quest for the mother's breast, the appropriation and the loss of the breast, and accession to the law of the father. In the long period of preparation (eight to nine months) that precedes the rite, a number of taboos are instituted that prevent the men from the opposed male and female moieties of Yafar society from entering each other's territories. Noise, singing and dancing are prohibited, as are the collection and exploitation of certain natural products, the cutting of hair, the building of houses and the use of certain words that recall reproductive processes. Life forces are kept strictly controlled so that when they are re-released at Yangis, they burst forth with huge power and vitality (Juillerat, 1992a: 77–8). The male and female moieties are associated respectively with the sago palm and the coconut, but their sexual differentiation is more usually represented by two clones of the sago: *fenaw* (female) and *afwêêg* (male). The preparation of huge quantities of sago for the Yangis ritual begins with the simultaneous felling of one *fenaw* and one *afwêêg* palm by men of the opposite moiety. These will be processed into sago jelly by the men (normally this is women's work) and eaten at a ritual meal. The sago is referred to as the vegetable incarnation of the divine sperm. A small part of this jelly will be used in the preparation of the sacred jelly from which in the course of the rite two totemic sons or *ifegê* (one for each moiety) will emerge. The preparations for the rite thus involve the sexed moieties in preparing and consuming the divine sperm and then using it to produce a symbolic act of fertilization and reproduction carried out in the course of the Yangis ritual (Juillerat, 2001: 182–3).

Prior to the main ritual, an intensive hunting period is initiated as part of the process of preparing and stocking the food necessary. All the women and children are sent to work in the forest and the men gather at the foot of two coconut palms – one for each moiety. The two men who will perform the role of *ifegê* climb the palms saying: 'Mother give me, give me pig, give me a cassowary.' As they cut open a spathe and shake out the flowers, they make further demands: 'Bring forth the possum children, bring forth the cassowary children.' The flowers are explicitly associated with mother's milk. The men below stand with their palms upturned, those who get a flower in their hands are said to be in mother's net bag (in her womb or being carried like a baby), those who do not, say: 'Mother abandoned me.' The *ifegê* climb down and are verbally associated with the mother's breast and milk. The men eat a ritual meal of animal hearts, blood, magical rhizomes and the flowers received by the lucky participants. In doing this, they speak of eating 'the blood of mother's milk' (Juillerat, 1992a: 79–81; 2001: 183–5).

Next to the river, the men create a ritual enclosure where they can prepare themselves during Yangis and make their ritual masks away from the eyes of women. At the centre of this enclosure, a small shelter is erected, divided into two parts: the 'mouth' for the male moiety and the 'vagina' for the female one. In creating the ritual enclosure, the men rediscover and reconstitute the body of the mother. In their part of the shelter, the men of each moiety plant a petiole of the sago plant of their totem. These petioles are the young shoots of the totems or the totemic sons embodied by the *ifegê* in the Yangis ritual who incarnate the principle of phallic regeneration which liberates itself from the body of the dead mother, as Pépi did in the myth. The esoteric knowledge of the Yafar makes it clear that the mouth and the vagina are two sites for the emergence of the phallus as the active principle of reproduction (*hoofuk*). Each orifice grows a shoot, representing respectively the uvula and the clitoris. The ritual enclosure symbolizes the uterus, and the two moieties manage a process of birth that gives them both access to the fecundity of the mother (Juillerat, 1995: 52–3).

The ritual proper lasts for two nights and two days, and sees a series of figures enter the central space of the village and perform their dances. Although some chants are performed and trumpets played, the main ritual is essentially non-verbal. On the first night, when the first pair of masked dancers (*êri*) enter the scene, two masters of the moieties who have danced as *êri* in a previous Yangis throw to the ground two bundles of leaves containing the totemic hoofuk, that is sago from the palms ritually felled earlier, the flesh of tubers associated with both sexes, magical plants and the sexual fluids of the two masters and their wives. Each master throws down the hoofuk bundle of the other moiety, and this represents the sudden encounter of the sexes represented by the two totems and the mutual exchange of sexual substances that prefigures the main narrative of the rite (Juillerat, 1995: 55–6).

The Yangis rite is a singular cosmological and intellectual achievement; its range, diversity and complexity when linked to the myths, other rituals and secret knowledge of the Yafar are awesome. It would be impossible here to summarize the care and brilliance with which Bernard Juillerat has collected and analysed his material. The rite has also been reinterpreted by a number of anthropologists and psychoanalysts (cf. Juillerat, 1992b; Weiner, 1995: ch. 1), each offering evocative and crafted re-analysis of the materials. The point I wish to draw out is, as Juillerat makes very plain, that it is only possible to understand the shape and content of the public rite when it has been linked to myth and other forms of esoteric knowledge. Such linkages do not form a coherent story or reveal a secret core, but rather set in motion metaphors, resonances and associations that allow particular kinds of movement through the narrative(s) that Yangis creates and the broader symbolic system of the Yafar. For example, the *êri* are replaced on stage by two dancers representing the *yis* (sago jelly) and, with the help of the masters of the moieties, these two performers throw pieces of hot sago jelly made from the two varieties of sago palm ritually felled, shouting incantations for growth. On the public face of it, this part of the rite is to enhance the growth of the sago palms, the main food staple of the Yafar. However, secret knowledge reveals that the Yafar see the sago palms as penises full of sperm, while the cooked jelly represents the coagulation of the sperm in the uterus, and the *yis* becomes a metaphor for the embryo. The full purpose of this part of the rite is thus revealed as bringing into being – through the agency of two communities of men – the two totemic sons whose birth, growth and final emergence as social beings the rite of Yangis traces (Juillerat, 1995: 57). Yet, without the esoteric knowledge, the inter-pretations and representations that the society conceals, the rite is indecipherable, a figure whose proper shape cannot be discerned (ibid.: 65).

It is evident from the myths and the details of the rite, and from the secret knowledge imparted by senior men, that what gives Yangis its shape is a series of interconnected themes, not all of which operate on the same analytic level. Juillerat argues that Yangis deals with the Oedipus complex, the origins of the social order, the emergence of the masculine subject and the instauration of mascu-line domination. Through these means, it brings into play a series of affects, representations and emotions which link the develop-ment of the masculine subject to the origins of society, and both are encompassed by the narrative of conception, birth and social emergence that Yangis narrates (Juillerat, 1995: ch. 3; 2001: ch. 7). This audacious interpretation is a compelling one, is marvellously worked through the material and provides the most comprehensive theorization currently available in the anthropological literature on the relationship between the psyche and the social. In analysing material of this kind, one cannot work at a single analytic level, but must move from questions about gender roles and the sexual divi-sion of labour, to power relations between women and men, to gender as a structuring principle of the symbolic realm, to accounts of the formation of the subject, and the structures of unconscious thought. These different levels have interconnections, but they are not reducible to each other and are not the logical outcome of each other, often embodying contradiction and conflict. Multiple levels of analysis entail multiple interpretations, but should not necessarily be taken to imply a hierarchy of representations and interpretations, such that those that are more 'secret' are also more 'true'.

The shape of Yangis, including the way it is run by and for men, comes at one level from the way ideas, representations and emo-tions slip and slide around the problem of deception. Not just the fact that men have knowledge that they are keeping from their sisters and wives, but that – as the myth of Pépi demonstrates – this knowledge was once owned by women before men stole it. Thus, all men know that in some sense their knowledge is not rightfully theirs, and that the present state of male domination is based on a deception. This gives gender relations themselves a palpable shape because men have a strong sense that women, or rather the feminine principle, are genuinely powerful, as opposed to the fragility of their own powers obtained through murder and trickery. The male arrogation of female powers is given substance in Yangis and in various myths where it is clear that men are constructing an account of male communities producing male children, imaginatively and materially involving themselves in the growth and regeneration of the phallus. This is a kind of 'response' or 'reply' to the fact that women once owned the phallus and the knowledge of the secrets of reproduction, and lived in the village and had no need of the men from the forest. Many Melanesian and Australian cultures work over this theme of male envy of women's reproductive function, their desire to be able to reproduce both sons and societies in the way that women can (Juillerat, 1995: 93–4), but they always strive to hide the fiction of their success at giving birth from women (Silverman, 2001: ch. 4).

Male envy of women's fecundity and reproductive power is a common theme in Melanesian anthropology and is often put forward to explain masculine domination, male solidarity and violence, the nature of gender relations and the character of male rituals. This is a major preoccupation for Yafar men, as Juillerat notes, but it is not simply this that gives Yangis its ultimate shape. It is not just that men want to arrogate women's powers to themselves, hide their deception and institute control over women – no doubt all these things are in play – but that what structures the ritual is a particular relation to the maternal, a profound desire to return to a nurturing mother, to the *jouissance* of plenitude attached to the mother–child bond. This 'maternal schema' has been noted for a range of New Guinea societies (e.g. Lipset, 1997; Silverman, 2001), as has the particularly strong emotional valence that the image of the nurturing mother and the memory of her solicitous care has for adult men. Maternal plenitude is powerfully associated with mother's milk, with food and with hunting (Juillerat, 2001: ch. 7). The primordial mother is the origin of game, as the myth makes apparent, where the mother's stomach/vagina are explicitly linked with the subterranean store under ground. The unsuccessful hunter is one who has been abandoned by the mother, as the ritual linking mother's milk, blood and game makes plain in the preparatory rite for Yangis (ibid.: 186–7). The actual shortage of game in Yafar country, and the threat of hunger, give emotional valence to forms of material production that emphasize dependence on the mother and indeed natural fertility as guaranteed by and enclosed within the primordial mother. In the myth recounted earlier, the sons liberate the game from the control of the jealous father and thereby gain direct access to the mother. The price they pay is that they are engulfed by her, forcibly returned to the womb. The mother is an object of desire, in her idealized state very much a lost object, but she cannot be approached too directly because to do so results in annihilation. Thus, the mother is a split figure, both nurturing and frightening, as in the case of Nambweapa'w. The paradox of everyday life is that the maternal must be approached to secure production (food) and reproduction (children and society). Links with her must be maintained for life to continue, but if one gets too close then there is no social, no exchange, no masculinity and no life.

The Yafar have an image of the universe as created from the body of the mother. According to one myth, the primordial mother dies of a haemorrhage whilst giving birth and her body is dismembered by her divine companion, who uses it to create the universe. Her single (central) breast is hung in the sky by the divine father and becomes the sun (Juillerat, 2001: 185). This is all given dramatic form in the closing stages of the Yangis ritual – one from which women are rigorously excluded – where the two *ifegê*, with drawn bows and arrows, accompanied by their guides ('maternal uncles'), march around the area with eyes and arrows pointing downwards. This is a quest that is secretly described as the search for the mother or the search for the breast. The penises of the *ifegê* are said to point downwards towards the stomach/vagina of the mother from where they emerged and to where they desire to return. The maternal uncles, however, draw the eyes of the *ifegê* to the sun representing the single breast of the primordial mother pulled into the sky by the father, and they let their arrows fly towards it (Juillerat, 1992a: 60–3; 1995: 62–3). Various interpretations have been given of this climactic moment (see Juillerat, 1992b; Weiner, 1995). One clear theme distinguishes the two antagonistic forms of the maternal and reinforces the choice between them that the maternal uncles dictate. The one is the engulfing womb/earth into which masculinity could be reincorporated, and the other is the socialized breast of the nurturing mother held at a distance, at once the lost detachable object and a legitimate object of desire (Juillerat, 1995: 99–100).

Juillerat notes that associated with these split versions of the maternal is an underlying theme of the relation to the maternal which is 'the law of all or nothing'. The mother can give everything or nothing, as in the myth of Nambweapa'w. Thus, the desire to receive is indistinguishable from the anguish of not receiving, and both are marked by lack. The subject's desire is to be loved by the mother, recognized by the mother or, in Lacanian terms, the subject's desire is the desire of the (m)other. The rite of Yangis is thus a *mis-en-scène* of this lack, an attempt not to lose the object of desire totally, but its inevitable result is the re-enactment of that loss, the affirmation of lack (Juillerat, 2001: 186–7).[4] This Lacanian analysis can be developed more radically. The desire for the mother cannot be incorporated into the symbolic system as a positive presence, it is rather the negative within the symbolic that functions as the object cause of desire and thus structures the symbolic. In this guise, it is the generative principle of Yafar society and symbolism and yet it simultaneously works as a negation of the principle of the rules that ostensibly govern society.

Yafar society is patriarchal and male-dominated, women are rigorously excluded from male knowledge, and sexual relations between women and men are subject to considerable constraint. The desire for the *jouissance* of mother–child unity, the desire for the desire of the mother and the return to an imagined world of plenitude are a structural impossibility in such a society. The symbolic system of the Yafar is the product of this desire, just as it works around and covers over the lack in the place of desire. And yet, Yafar society is irreducible to the relations of male power that can never obtain absolutely anyway. This secret is part of the esoteric knowledge of men and yet this same knowledge sets up feelings of panic that threaten the relations of male power, block their resolution and betray their origins (Copjec, 1994: 11). The mother, not the father, is apparently the generative principle of Yafar society and it is the impossibility of relations with her that acts as the object of desire and sets in motion the magnificent achievements of Yafar culture. However, we must be clear here that it is not a matter of claiming that a desire for mother–child unity produces Yafar culture directly, because we must recall that it is, strictly speaking, its negation, the failure on which it is founded. It is the oscillation or movement of the positive in relation to the negative that is the condition of desire.

This point needs pursuing further. We are not speaking simply here of a society built on repressing the mother or on the repression of desire for the mother, because culture does not work by constructing a subject who simply and straightforwardly has desire(s). Our relationship to desire is much more elliptical than this. We are dealing most often with subjects who reject their desires, who do not want to desire them, are willing, as Freud said, to give something up. Therefore, we should not approach the desire for the maternal, for mother–child unity, as if it were the 'hidden secret' of Yafar society, its esoteric exegesis, its true origin. To do so would be to mischaracterize the nature of desire. Desire is something unrealizable, but beyond that we need to acknowledge that it is not necessarily committed to realization. By this, we mean that we cannot understand desire as that which would seek to be realized if the law did not exist. So that, if the world were a different place, men would actually desire to be reunited with their mothers in a pre-social plenitude. What Yafar myth and ritual tell us is that men do not actually desire this or, rather, what they desire is contradictory. A desire for maternal nurturance has to be balanced against the terror of reincorporation. But more than this, the masculine emerges out of the split with the mother. Thus, the subject is split from its desire and this makes the subject dependent upon the negation of its own desire for its existence (Copjec, 1994: 25–6). Desire is an impossibility and remains unrealized as a condition of social existence. The key point here is one of negation. Anthropology works consistently within the realm of the positive, and from this perspective it can be claimed that the desire for the maternal produces distinctive cultural forms, including social relations in Melanesian societies (cf. Lipset, 1997; Silverman, 2001). However, from the position of psychoanalysis, which starts with the problem of splitting and negation, the social is reconfigured as the result of the impossibility of desire for the mother. This is an important shift in analytical perspective because, instead of figuring culture or the social as the realization of its founding principle, it refigures it as the product of its impossibility.

It is important here to recognize the importance of analytic levels. We are not necessarily speaking of individual desires or specific mothers. The longing for a return to the mother in Melanesian societies, in so far as it is part of a putative cultural schema, is clearly not going to be experienced by all men in the same way and to the same degree. Culture has no such determining power, no possibility for complete closure. Individuals will thus engage with the imagos of their parents, their oedipal conflicts and the cultural representations of desire, separation, filiation, mothers, fathers, reproduction and death in particular ways. Anthropological material does not often work ethnographically with exactly how individuals link their personal experience of parenting and sexuality with dominant cultural representations (see chapter 7; Obeyesekere, 1990). Anthropologists have traditionally had little interest in desire, and ignoring its effects explains why we are still so impoverished when it comes to theorizing the relation between the psyche and the social. In practice, we have had until now no way of linking the constitution of subjectivity to the emergence of particular forms of the social.

However, the Yafar material does reinforce a particular point about the relation of oedipal structures to the specificities of cultural history. As Lacan emphasizes, entry into the symbolic, into language and the law of the father, divides the subject, splits and dismembers it. Parts of the body – the breast, voice, gaze, phallus and faeces – become separated off through the process of constituting ourselves. These separated parts become the object cause of our desire because as lost parts of ourselves their absence constantly prevents us from becoming whole. However, constituted in and through language and the symbolic system, our desires are not wholly our own: they belong to others. Building on this, I would argue – and here contra Lacan for whom entry into the symbolic is tied to the 'hard kernel' of the Oedipus complex, which returns as the same through all forms of historicization – that while the act of separation is a constant, the content of and the way in which the symbolic system constructs and invests certain objects, and notions of the maternal and paternal are culturally variable (see below and chapter 5). In other words, the particular way in which each culture slips and slides around what resists symbolization provides a distinctive shape to culture. Desire is always socialized in a specific form.

However, the Yafar alert us to something more. They emphasize that the purpose of cultural representations is not to produce a single, coherent system, a single secret that is its origin and provides a unitary explanandum.[5] The experience of gender and the question of sexual difference and of how societies and subjects come into being strikes at the core of human understanding. Let us take, for example, the mother's breast, which from one perspective is a part object covering over the lack at the core of the subject, the impossible desire for reunion with the mother, the memory of her solicitous care and closeness. Yafar exegesis makes it clear that this breast is also a phallus, not only the phallus originally possessed by the mother who created the world as an enclosed womb and the women who celebrated Yangis, but the phallus of the primal father who monopolizes and inhabits the mother's womb and the game that comes from it, as well as the phallus of the social father represented by the maternal uncles at the end of Yangis as they direct the totemic sons towards a non-incestuous relation with the mother (Juillerat, 1995: 104–7; 2001: 202–3, 211). The breast and the phallus are not wholly distinguishable objects: they do not unambiguously belong to the mother or the father.

A more general version of this point is frequently made with regard to Melanesian ethnography. From a comparative perspective, as discussed in chapter 6, Strathern has pointed out that western ideas of gender as forms of property – 'breasts belong to women' and 'phalluses are the property of men' – are thrown into relief by Melanesian gender models which figure gender as transactional and mutable, processual rather than fixed, where things and body parts are defined more by their relations than their attributes (Strathern, 1988: 126–8). Strathern correctly posits the question: what then is male and what is female? (ibid.: 126). The answer she provides focuses in large measure on questions of agency, but others reading her frequently converge on the notion of androgyny that she inserts into the debate, the idea that women and men are composite. This notion, however, presupposes – as does Freud's notion of polymorphous perversity – that distinct genders exist prior to their combination. It would be possible – and Strathern often seems close to this position – to conceive of androgyny in terms of the female and the male as transformations of each other. In other words, it is not just that the breast and the phallus do not belong unambiguously to the mother and the father, but that they are not wholly distinguishable objects in the full sense, their whole status as gender-attributed objects is in doubt, they do not form the basis for a stable set of representations of sexual difference. So that, in terms of the Yafar exegesis of Yangis, the secret which the Yafar men guard so assiduously is not that men desire their mothers or want to return to them, but that there is no ultimate secret – except perhaps that cultural symbolism reveals uncertainty about the relation of language to the world, and that this provides for a constant process of contradiction, from which derive representations, interpretations and reinterpretations. Secret knowledge does not produce origins, it does not produce authoritative closure; rather, it demonstrates the limits of all representations, their fundamental and radical uncertainty.

Naven and the maternal

We can, however, use Strathern's insights into Melanesian gender to push our understanding further. Strathern discusses gender in two registers: one as a limiting aesthetic – everything must take one of a pair of forms – the other as something that evinces the capacities that people have in their minds and bodies, and the effects of these on others (1988: 142). Persons can only be apprehended in gendered form, but that form will depend on whether what is being expressed is a same-sex form or a cross-sex form. This applies not only to relations between individuals, but also to relations internal to them: 'Gender refers to the internal relations between parts of persons, as well as to their externalization as relations between persons' (ibid.: 185). In particular circumstances, female and male persons may be opposed as discrete reference points from which specific relations flow. In others, they will be conceived as androgynous – that is, cross-sexed. There are two consequences of this position. The first is that we cannot assume that biological attributes place male and female persons in 'a perpetual relation of difference' and, second, that the differentiated single-sex state cannot be taken as a 'natural' reference point (ibid.: 185). Weiner argues in his re-analysis of the Yafar Yangis that the female and the male are never presented in a monolithic or permanent form in the ritual and its accompanying myths, but in relations of encompassment and detachment that 'make male and female capacities appear momentarily, only to allow them to collapse back into their essentially mediatory, relational constitution' (Weiner, 1995: 15). From this perspective, gender is a relational capacity rather then a series of attributes, but nonetheless a relational capacity that has a very problematic form, or what Strathern would designate a limiting aesthetic.

In straightforward terms we can say that many of the difficulties we have in asking the question, 'What is female and what is male?', or in trying to determine how gender relates to sexual difference, arise because of this limitation. The limitation itself has multiple sources: the first is the human body and its physical manifestations and capacities, the second is language and the forms of representation which shape and encompass the body, and the third is the relationship of anthropological language to other forms of representation, both linguistic and non-linguistic. We can explore some of these difficulties by looking at another famous Melanesian ethnographic example, the Naven rite.

First-time cultural achievements among the Iatmul of New Guinea – such as paddling a canoe, buying an outboard motor, spearing fish, wearing spirit masks and, in the past, killing – are honoured by means of a rite where women are adorned with male finery and mothers' brothers dress like old women. The tenor of the rite is a strange mixture of celebration, mockery and pathos, and it culminates in a gesture known as *nggariik* in which a maternal uncle honours his nephew by sliding his buttocks down the young man's leg.[6] As the rite concludes, those honoured present gifts to their matrikin and to other participants. Naven was first analysed by Gregory Bateson (1936), and has been the subject of much subsequent discussion and reinterpretation (e.g. Handelman, 1979; Houseman and Severi, 1998; Juillerat, 2001; Silverman, 2001; Stanek, 1983; Weiss, 1987a; 1987b). A variety of theoretical approaches has been applied, but as a general gloss it is evident that, over time, explanations for Naven have moved from those based on social integration and kinship structures to those more concerned with mother–child ties, psychodynamics and psychoanalytic frameworks.[7]

The transvestism of the rite and the fact that it works over encounters where women and men assume the attributes and body parts of the other sex chime well with the androgynous, processual nature of Melanesian gender, but there is still much about the rite that puzzles. Naven are performed to honour individuals who have accomplished something or attained a social skill, and yet these moments of achievement are often marked by men in tears. What do these tears signify? Weiss describes the moment when at the end of the male initiation rite of scarification, the women dance a Naven for their brothers, sons, nephews and grandsons to welcome them back from the world of men. The women are seductive and aggressive, while 'the young men look fixedly at the ground trying to hide their tears with their hands' (Weiss, 1987b: 183). The combination of seduction and aggression is a potent one. In the Naven rites described by Silverman, women spit red betel-nut juice (representing menstrual blood) into the faces of men who are affines or potential affines, daub men with substances representing faeces, beat them about the head and chest, and shout flirtatious insults, such as 'Are you pregnant with my child?' In response, men flee from these assaults (Silverman; 2001: 141–54).

Certain forms of Naven culminate in *nggariik*, which Eric Silverman describes as 'an unparalleled moment in men's emotional lives'. Men feel pity for the main protagonists, particularly for the mother's brother who is said to be shamed by this gesture, while the nephew and the uncle are regularly reduced to tears, tears of humiliation (ibid.: 160–1). Both the pity and the humiliation are intensified if it occurs in front of women (ibid.: 162). The women, on the other hand, caricature *nggariik* itself during Naven, along with other male behaviours, and laugh about it outside the context of the rite. While men speak of the act in hushed voices, women may shout out loud and tease men, saying: 'Go defecate and *nggariik* on this tree' (ibid.: 167–8). This central act, which is such a source of trepidation for men, is apparently quite peripheral to women's emotional and practical concerns, and even the subject of a certain amount of ridicule.

Various commentators have seen in Naven a series of reflections on the relation between men and their mothers, between masculinity and motherhood. Bateson saw *nggariik* as incorporating both a sexual act and a birth, while Silverman sees it as an enactment of a male anal birth involving the recognition of masculinity's reproductive limits (Juillerat, 2001: 218; Silverman, 2001: 37). This latter interpretation is a variation on the theme of men's arrogation of women's reproductive powers and the symbolic re-enactment of male control of birth which is such a feature of male initiation ceremonies and cults in Melanesia and elsewhere. Since the mother's brother stands in for his sister and for her clan and is yet a man, various interpreters have delineated both incestuous and homoerotic themes in the evidently sexualized submission of the mother's brother to his sister's son. Juillerat further develops the theme of the maternal and sees the rite as a threefold reflection on relations with the mother: separation (birth, initiation, autonomy), return and ongoing emotional and libidinal attachment (2001: 219).

Silverman asserts that eastern Iatmul men retain a life-long wish to return to an ideal nurturing mother (ibid.: 9, 69), and he suggests that men achieve a return to their mothers in two ways. The first is through the building of a magnificent domestic dwelling modelled on the mother's body. Such houses are a huge drain on a man's resources, take many years to build and are in all senses a labour of love. Such houses do provide shelter, warmth and food just like real mothers, and their front doors are mouths and vulvas, while their rear doors are anuses (ibid.: 66–70). Once his sons are married with children, a man is expected to move out to a modest dwelling and cede his house to his son. Thus inheritance is unequivocally an oedipal act where men relinquish the maternal body to their sons (ibid.: 73). This has to be understood in the context of ambivalent relations between fathers and sons. Once a boy reaches the age of 5 or 6, he has limited contact with this father, and emotional connections between them are not encouraged (ibid.: 72). But one thing a father does do for his son is to make resources available to the young man so that he can compensate the mother's brother who performs *nggariik* on him.

The second way a man can be said to return to his mother is through marriage. The eastern Iatmul have a preference for the union of a man with his father's mother's brother's son's daughter (FMBSD), a woman termed *iai*, which is also the word used for a woman's belly or womb, as well as the interior of a house (ibid.: 73; 105–6).[8] *Iai* is what a potential husband calls this woman, but his father actually calls her 'mother' (*nyame*).[9] Thus, a man is said to reacquire his mother as his son's bride (ibid.: 73). The basis of *iai* marriage is the long-term relationship between maternal uncle and sister's son. The maternal uncle feeds his nephew, gives him jewellery and celebrates Naven for him. The nephew reciprocates with wealth and thus it is said that the maternal uncle feels inferior, a situation he redresses by asking his own son to give the nephew a woman he calls mother (*nyame*), although it is the nephew's son who will marry her (ibid.: 106–7). It is *iai* women who are most sexualized and ferocious in their attacks on men, especially their affines or potential affines, during the Naven rite. The paradox of this form of marriage is that no sooner does a man 'get his mother back' than he loses her to his son, just as he cedes his maternal house to him. There are clear oedipal themes here, as the father uses the building of his house (a mother's belly) and his sons' marriage to act on his oedipal desires, while the son uses his inheritance and his marriage to dispossess his father of the mother and effectively annihilate him (ibid.: 110).

The very overtness of Naven, its energetic performance, suggests just how misleading it would be to see the social (culture) as something that exists simply to repress desire; rather, as we saw in the previous section, it is the product of the effects of the impossibility of desire, its circulations and contradictions. Any actual return to the mother, either the real mother or the fantasized phallic mother, is impossible – there can be no return to pre-oedipal *jouissance* – but the circulation of this desire produces a number of effects. However, the elliptical nature of desire, the way it works by attaching individuals as subjects to its negation or denial – hence fathers marry their sons to their mothers and when *nggariik* comes close to incestuous and homosexual desires grown men weep with shame – is not only constitutive of the social, but of the subject also. This raises a particularly salient question for anthropologists about the relationship between ideology and ontology. The human body is a lived relationship of the signifier and the flesh conjoined. Lacan's insight that the organization and experience of the body are not given at birth and have to be constructed, and that this is accomplished through a certain relation to language, ties sexuality to representation. Yet, these representations are themselves bound to Strathern's limiting aesthetic, to the fact that the human body has a particular material configuration, has two forms. But, this is not a matter of natural fact, but an imaginative engagement with an ongoing set of attempts to ascertain in what these two forms might actually consist. Sexual difference is not therefore the origin of this limiting aesthetic, but its outcome, a set of unstable, vanishing representations that are the consequence of an imaginative engagement with it.

Two points follow from this. The first is that since there are no lived biological attributes without representations of biological attributes, the actual consequences and effects of such attributes cannot be known in advance, and certainly do not place male and female persons in perpetual relations of difference. Everyone knows that mothers have penises! The second point is that sexual difference is itself radically unstable. Since the meaning of this difference circulates in language, there can be no fixed set of meanings associated with it. This instability is not, however, to be taken as a simple outcome of the multiplicity of language, the range of its polymorphous metaphorical capacities, but rather as a consequence of the incompleteness of language, the fact that something always escapes representation, that representation is never complete. What cannot be represented moves into the circuits of desire and becomes the grit of fantasy, the present absence of culture. But this thing that cannot be represented, this leftover, *objet a*, is itself contentless. We cannot specify what our representations of sexual difference leave out, we just have to engage with the fact that they are not and cannot be complete. Anthropologists are, in fact, used to thinking of cultural productions and social systems in a somewhat analogous way, but not sexual difference.

Using Strathern's argument that body parts and persons do not always go together and that gender difference is internal as well as external to persons, we can see a link with Lacan's theory that sexual difference is all about a relation to the phallus (being or having) and that both women and men may be on either side of the relation. It is important to stress here that this is a step further on from the usual anthropological acceptance that women and men are composite. It is, rather, that they are caught up in a circulation of body parts and representations where it is not possible finally to know what is male and what is female. The very concreteness of body parts makes it easy to misinterpret the radicalism of this point, but a return to Naven might clarify the issue further.

A cursory reading of the ethnographic material on Naven is enough to know that any single explanation for the rite would certainly be reductionist. Reflections on mothers, fathers, wives, sisters, affines, agnates, sociality and exchange are all in play. It is not enough to say that it is about a desire to return to a pre-oedipal *jouissance* or the envy of female reproductive powers or a man's oedipal desire for his mother. These are all present in cultural performance and in the matrix of meanings that sustain it, but we should be cautious that in formulating an explanation we do not re-import binary gender distinctions in an effort to stabilize the meanings given to sexual difference. One form this trap might take in relation to Naven – and more generally in relation to the notion of 'maternal schemas' in Melanesia – is to focus too exclusively on the separation from the mother as a condition for the emergence of a masculine subject. Both Juillerat and Silverman acknowledge the importance of continuing affective and libidinal ties to the mother, and the fear of re-engulfment by a castrating or phallic mother. This position is sound, but leaves the question of sexual difference resting on the ambiguity of separation/attachment relations and the resolution or not of oedipal desires. This is ultimately unsatisfactory because it presupposes that we can know what the difference between the masculine and the feminine is, that sexual difference is knowable, if not always achievable.

An alternative position might begin from a slightly different vantage point. Why is it that men should become separate from their mothers? The answer in brief is that they need to develop a relation to the world and to subjectivity, but beyond that they need to identify themselves as men, a process achieved by identifying with the father. Hence the extreme anxiety evinced in initiation rituals, discussed in earlier chapters, that boys should be physically separated from women and cleansed of female substances. Ethnographic material often focuses on men becoming men by repudiating their feminine selves, from whence comes the peculiar shame of being discovered by women to be claiming to control birth, a quintessentially female capacity. But, what is it then that men identify with when they identify with mothers or the maternal? The standard oedipal thesis is that the boy has to give up his sexual desire for the mother, but in so far as he continues to identify with her, does that mean he is identifying with her feminine capacity for nurturing and birth? It is certainly possible, but it is equally possible that what he is identifying with is her activity, her masculinity, particularly the masculinity she embodies as the phallic mother. Mother possesses a phallus, and the extraordinary thing about this organ is that it gives birth. Women once owned the phallus before it was stolen from them by men – and what did it allow them to do? It allowed them to create society. In envying women's reproductive power, in simulating birth through *nggariik*, secret cults and forms of initiation, it seems unlikely that what is being sought is the female biological capacity to give birth as a feminine attribute.

Here we can make sense of Benjamin's contention, following Chodorow (1989), that the boy first defines himself as not-mother before he defines her as not-male (Benjamin, 1998: 51–2). The conflict *nggariik* works over is that masculinity does not emerge solely as a consequence of a split from the mother, but is also based on forms of identification. The corollary is an irresolvable tension where the man cannot both be her (be the phallus that gives birth) and simultaneously have her (have the phallus that reunites with her).[10] This tension is partially resolved through splitting the mother into her phallic, nurturing and feminine aspects. Once the boy begins to recognize that the mother is not omnipotent, not self-sufficient and complete, does not have the father's penis inside her and thus she desires someone else to complete her, she becomes 'feminine' (ibid.: 51). The feminine then becomes the antidote to the power of the phallic mother, the space in which the male subject lodges passivity, reception, accommodation, those things from which, from one perspective, he must separate himself if he is to attain masculine subjectivity. This form of the feminine is very evident in heterosexual relationships in many contexts where women are denigrated, and men fear sexual passivity, female body substances and so on. But, the feminine is also desired since it neatly positions the masculine subject as the possessor not just of the penis, but also of a phallus which can complete the mother. Heterosexual desire thus comes about as the consequence of the mother's castration (ibid.: 51).

However, this is only one perspective on the issue. We must recall the arguments in chapter 6, where the phallus the mother contains within her is both hers and the father's. The feminine is a position constructed around the lack of the phallus, and the desire for it, but the phallic mother, with whom the man identifies, has no such lack, she retains her phallus. In consequence, the phallus is never unambiguously male or female, not just because it can be either male or female or even both simultaneously, but because it is never simply one body part or another. An additional problem arises because in defining the phallic mother, possessor of the phallus that gives birth, as having a masculine attribute, we import binary gender categorizations into the analysis. In fairness, it seems impossible to avoid doing this because the language we have at our disposal is necessarily shaped by Strathern's limiting aesthetic. However, this should not blind us to the point that the dual nature of the maternal phallus, its doubly masculine sense, reveals that sexual difference is literally undecidable. It also means that when masculinity emerges as the split from the mother, it splits off also from a part of itself. Surely, this is what *nggariik* works over.

The problem, then, is that the relation of sexual difference to the signifier(s) is a disjointed one, but this is not simply because gender identity is performative and multiple, that sex is unstable because meaning proliferates and is undecidable. Rather, it is because sexual difference is not founded on a binary that maps onto bodies and psyches in predictable ways, and so no position defines a resolute identity. From this point of view, we can say that sexed subjects come into being retroactively as the effects of social discourses, but they are not in a straightforward sense realizations of them, *pace* Foucault. Sexual difference is the product of the failure of signification, the gap in every culture between signification and the flesh. Melanesians make it evident how very difficult it is to know in any resolute sense what is male and what is female. Their reflections on these matters demonstrate how unwise it is for anthropologists and psychoanalysts to label body parts and other objects with binary gender labels that are often wholly inappropriate. More than this, Melanesians show us how sexed subjects are produced as a particular kind of answer to the problem of the origins of the social.

9

Social Transformations

Ideology and ontology

Initiation rituals bring ritual, myth and bodily transformation into close relation with the practicalities of day-to-day living, intimate relations and productive labour. The result, as discussed in previous chapters, is a series of metaphors and imaginary connections that establish a sensate link between body processes and social processes, a set of concordances between the inner rhythms and functions of the body, and social structures and cosmological understandings (Moore, 1997a; 1999a). In such contexts, the body is both the starting point of one's own experience and the origin of a set of culturally constructed imaginative domains (Beidelman, 1997). Bodily experiences are thus tied to the imaginative and practical possibilities of being a gendered individual in a specific context. What initiation rituals do is to present staged narrative sequences of symbols, which provide opportunities for reflection and for an enlargement of understanding of self and others as gendered individuals. In the course of the rites, hitherto separate images, sounds, colours, emotions and aspects of life are brought into relation with each other in ways that reveal new connections and understandings. This is true not only for the new initiates, but for the adult men and women who act as the initiators and whose comprehension of symbols, tropes, bodily sensations and imaginary links changes over time, with each new performance, and as they age.

Local exegesis is thus a matter of making connections: some of these connections will be linguistic – in the sense that they will be made in language – while others will be physical, practical and experiential. Reflections on bodily experiences and their metaphoric transpositions – whether through practice or linguistic exegesis – enlarge one's sense of agency and of self. It is one of the paradoxes of gender that, because it is relational, it is only possible to understand the gender of the other through reflection on one's own gender, and to comprehend one's own gender through engagement with that of the other.

Anthropologists have thus often interpreted initiation rituals as condensed and sensate reflections – a kind of practical philosophy of the body – on the ontological nature of being, and on the origins of gendered difference and human society itself. As we have seen in previous chapters, the predominant and overt themes of initiation rituals are often concerned with gender and fertility, but their larger import is as an imaginary engagement with the origins of society and with the processes of self–other relations. It is in this sense that we can speak of initiation rituals as encompassing the 'social imaginary relations' that hold society together and that provide the foundation for the emergence of self and subjectivity. They are, so to speak, a moment of condensation where the emergence of subjectivity is tied to specific cultural understandings, and to the emergence of a particular form of the social. Society's self-representations make no sense outside their engagement with specific forms of subjectivity (Castoriadis, 1997: 89).[1]

We are talking here of the production of cultural and symbolic systems that are also the conditions for the emergence of the subject. What is remarkable about much Melanesian material is the way that this co-production is itself an explicit part of cultural production and reflection. Not all Melanesian material works over the same set of concerns, and ethnographically we can see that cultures differ with respect to what comes into symbolism, myth and ritual, and with regard to the degree of elaboration and conscious reflection to which it is subjected (Obeyesekere, 1990: ch. 3). However, much of the material reviewed in this book takes as a major preoccupation the emergence of the subject, and how it comes into being alongside the social and the symbolic. One might go further and say that these materials engage with the matter of how the sexed subject is produced as a particular kind of answer to the conundrum of what constitutes the social. This is what I take Juillerat to mean when he says that Yafar myth and ritual trace the trajectory of the emergence of the masculine subject. However, in acceding to this argument concerning a subject indivisible from – but not reduced to – the social, a number of difficulties remain. The first is the question of whether sexual difference, understood as a founding difference, is open to historical change. And, if it is open to change, which part of it changes, what are the conditions for change and how are changes made manifest? Connected to this series of questions is the old quandary of what is the difference between sexual difference and gender? There are a number of ways to approach this issue, but one that reveals the traditional incompatibilities of psychoanalytic and anthropological theories and methods focuses on whether social and historical transformations have an impact on the formation of the sexed subject – that is, on the relation of the subject to the symbolic. As a way of approaching this question, let us begin first with an ethnographic example.

The Tambaran[2]

In Melanesia, what is revealed to men during initiation often goes by the name of the Tambaran. Tambarans are manifestations of a terrifying being that must be appeased and fed by men to secure the continuity of human society. Ritual Tambarans take the form of masks and loud sounds, all of which are produced secretly by men. A key part of the initiation rituals in many parts of Melanesia is the revelation made to the initiates that the thing they hold in terror is actually a set of representations made by men. A larger secret, though, underlies this secret, and that is that the Tambaran were once owned by women until they were stolen from them by men.

Until 1984, male initiation among the Ilahita Arapesh of Papua New Guinea centred on an elaborate and secret male cult with a series of five grades. Cult activities focused on ritual communication with spirits (Tambaran) thought to be the source of all life's necessities, whose terrible powers of destruction were only contained by the elaborate ritual feasts provided for them by men. Although women were rigorously excluded from the cult, it actually depended upon them, not only as providers of the enormous amount of food consumed on ritual occasions, but also as excluded spectators terrified of its power (Tuzin, 1980: 26).

A man is successively initiated into each stage of the cult, where various secrets, mostly in the form of paintings, statues, flutes and other objects, are revealed to him, along with knowledge that many of the acts of the Tambaran are actually the acts of men. Admission to the lowest grade (*falanga*) occurs after about the age of 3. The aim of the rite is to rid the boy of the polluting effects of mother's milk and her physical presence, and to separate him from her through entrusting him with ritual secrets. The boys and their mothers are told that the Tambaran will force the boys to slide down the spiked trunk of a sago palm that will rip open their soft parts. The reality is that three or four men attired as pigs lacerate the boys' penises with bamboo razors, while younger boys have their penises and scrota rubbed with stinging nettles. All the boys are then thrown into a stream full of stinging-nettles, but they are usually helped in this ordeal by their mother's brothers who jump into the water to lift the boys clear. Food taboos and periods of seclusion are also part of the rite, as is the revelation that the *hangahiwa* figures are not spirits incarnate, but men wearing masks. This is no small thing given that the *hangahiwa* were responsible in the past for the murder of those who had offended against the Tambaran in some way (ibid.: 39–54).

Entry into the next grade, *lefin*, comes in late childhood and is seen as the final stage in purging female influences. This stage consists of mock battles with enemies and the revelation that the terrifying voice of the Tambaran is actually made by men swinging bull-roarers. The main ordeal comes when the boys are led down to a roofless shelter over a stream, where two men attired as pigs come up through the floor; while the initiators hold the boys and peel back their foreskins, the men-pigs slash at each penis with bamboo razors. The boys are then ordered to lie down so that the blood may flow freely into the water below (ibid.: 58–72). This spilling of blood is a forerunner to the regular blood-letting from the penis that all sexually active males perform during their lives to cleanse themselves of feminine influences and the polluting effects of intercourse with women.

The third stage of the cult (*maolimu*) takes place in young adulthood and involves a long seclusion in the forest in a secret village built for the purpose, during which the initiates are given instruction in various male skills, including the art of formal speechmaking. The main themes of this grade are sexuality and fertility, and novices are likened in its early stages to girls who are experiencing their first menstruation. Just before the period of seclusion starts, the boys are suddenly told that they will be turned into flying foxes, an animal associated with sorcery and male lust. The period of seclusion represents the boys' enclosure within a totally male world, where all domestic and ritual tasks are performed by men, and where symbolism and experience strongly reinforce the notion that men can do perfectly well without women. If a ritual enactment of marriage or a high part in a song is required, then the part will be taken by a man. Presentation of baby-like doll figures to the initiates at one point during seclusion affirms the reproductive potential of this totally male world.

During seclusion, the boys are also fed large quantities of pig meat with the aim of instilling in them a craving for pork which is a male food. This identification with pork severs them once and for all from the food fed them by their mothers, and when they first return to their home village after seclusion the food they are fed makes them retch and vomit. The seclusion village is an image of a masculine world, with masculine unity as its basis. Meat and food are plentiful; there is no discord; life is good away from women (ibid.: 92–115).

The two highest grades (*nggwal bunafunei* and *nggwal walipeine*) are elaborate and time-consuming. They too involve revelations, and reflections on knowledge construction. *Nggwal bunafunei* celebrates the full social, intellectual and physical maturity of masculinity, and *nggwal walipeine* its decline into old age. Taken overall, the five stages of the Tambaran are much more than simply a matter of initiation: they are a long reflection and elaboration on the imaginative, practical and physical issue of what it is to be masculine. Over and above all this, the Tambaran cult presided over great works of art and architecture produced in its name, over war, peace and sorcery, over the social institutions and organizational forms of Ilahita society (clans, sub-clans, moieties, wards, villages and partnerships), over morality and over the most mundane and repetitive of daily activities. In short, it grounded masculinity in the power of ideology, and simultaneously embodied ideology in the paradox of masculinity. It worked over the conundrum that masculinity is a 'thing of ideology and ontology' (Tuzin, 1997: 181).

How is the cult of the Tambaran to be interpreted? The first point to make is that while the cult rigorously separates boys from their mothers, and institutes a view of healthy and productive masculinity that can only be achieved by the regular purging of feminine substances from the body, it also reveals that men are dependent on female fertility and that women once owned the Tambaran that men now claim for themselves.[3] Women's previous ownership of the Tambaran is attested to in myths which explicitly state that once men have been taught the secrets by women, they kill them so that no one will find out that the secrets were not theirs all along. The symbols and ritual sequences of the various Tambaran grades thus reveal to men that their secrets, far from being masculine, were once feminine, and that they arrogated them to themselves by force. In his discussion of the Tambaran cult, Tuzin makes it very clear that men experienced great anxiety about whether women would discover their secrets, in particular whether they would discover that the Tambaran was nothing more than a male drama, something produced by men, a deception, a lie, an illusion. The men discussed among themselves the problem of what they would do if women were to find out that they had once owned these ritual powers, and then claimed them back. If the secret got out, men would be revealed as foolish and ridiculous; they would lose all authority and social control. As Tuzin queries, given the levels of very real anxiety involved, why did men keep talking about this secret, continue to reveal it to new initiates at each performance of the Tambaran and persist in discussing the problem? Why didn't they just forget about it (Tuzin, 1997: 159–61)?

In the Tambaran the men had created a monstrous, phallic, greedy, woman-hating thing, and they were terrified that the women would find out that this was all an illusion, a male fantasy. The keeping of the secret had much to do with the levels of violence and aggression associated with the cult. Aggression against women was particularly marked because Nggwal was actually said to prey upon women to satisfy his lust for human blood, and in the past would have been held responsible for the ritual strangulation of any woman learning of cult secrets or transgressing the rules of the Tambaran cult. Ritual murder of various kinds was a feature of the cult until it was outlawed in the 1950s, but death by sorcery remained a genuine fear until the 1980s. Feeding Nggwal is the overt purpose of the rites connected with the highest grades. This feeding not only forestalls his wrath, but induces him to dispense fertility and general well-being (including war success) to his human protégés, as well as guaranteeing the reproductive success of natural species, especially pigs (Tuzin, 1980: 210–12). At one point in the rites, the novices are ritually killed or eaten by Nggwal, only to re-emerge later as unscathed. The purpose then of the Nggwal rites is to pacify the powers of the natural world and protect society from their worst effects, but it is also to come close to the Tambaran so that men may share in those powers.

Tuzin has recorded Ilahita men expressing guilt and anxiety regarding the exclusion of women from the cult and its feasts, but most especially concerning the deceptions they practise on women and the fact that their ritual superiority lacks legitimacy. One of Tuzin's informants expressed it in the following way: 'It is true that sometimes men feel ashamed and guilty over eating good food while their wives go hungry. But if we told them now that for all these generations they had been deceived, they would make life unbearable for us. There is nothing we can do' (Tuzin, 1982: 350). This moral unease apparently extends to the treatment of novices during the rites. In fact, the Tambaran structure is set up so that fathers do not directly assault their own sons; all acts of aggression are performed by the father's ritual partners whose own sons will then be initiated by them. In addition, in many contexts the mother's brother steps in to help and comfort the initiate. Tuzin does report, however, that fathers feel both anxious and guilty about the fact that the Nggwal rites reveal to initiates that not only have they been systematically deceived, but that their own fathers have been sharing in the spirit feasts, eating the food produced through their labour (Tuzin, 1980: 242; 1982: 349). On the basis of his ethnography, Tuzin suggests that the ritual brutality and the murderous aggression employed to make sure that cult secrets are maintained are connected to the guilt and moral ambivalence men feel, and their possible fear of castrative revenge (Tuzin, 1982: 350).

The Tambaran was a secret so important it was guarded with murder, and yet in September 1984, an historic event took place in Ilahita. During a Sunday church service, several senior men came forward and confessed to the women in the congregation that the secret men's cult of the Tambaran was a lie, that the whole thing was a series of illusions and deceptions perpetrated by men. The men asseverated that with Christian belief they now realized that the spirits they had venerated were manifestations of Satan, and, by unmasking Satan, they hoped to cleanse the community and to prepare it for Christ's second coming (Tuzin, 1997: 1–3). Why did the men do this? The Ilahita had been under the influence of Christian teaching for 32 years and the absolute control of the Tambaran over the affairs of society had already started to wane with the coming of a modern legal system, education and wage labour. The last major cult performance had been held in 1972, and in some ways the Tambaran was already dying (Tuzin, 1997: 178–81). However, as Tuzin makes clear, the converts did not just want the Tambaran to die: they wanted to kill it (ibid.: 65). But who or what did they want to kill? Tuzin likens the killing of the Tambaran to an act of collective parricide (ibid.: ix), and thus invokes Freud and the primal horde.

But what did the women do? When the women were told that the secrets of the Tambaran were a sham and that it was all a bag of tricks orchestrated by men, they apparently took very little interest in the revelation, except to say that they had pretty much guessed something of the sort all along (ibid.: 161). In his earlier fieldwork, women had refused to talk to Tuzin and his wife about the cult, but once the revelation took place they said that they had always assumed men were lying when they spoke of gigantic people-eating monsters, the transformation of adolescent initiates into flying foxes and other unlikely events. It was just that they did not know and did not care what was behind the men's antics. The women were, however, furious at having been misled, duped and excluded. Men's ritual was variously seen as 'irrelevant, hostile and fraudulent', but mostly the women were unimpressed (ibid.). What did happen was that they became much more assertive. Many took to going to long church meetings, leaving their husbands to care for the children, while others became community leaders. Responsibility for childcare became a major issue, particularly for younger husbands and wives. Women began to refuse to tend the family gardens and to refuse to have sex with their husbands, both apparently because of the demands of religious observance. Women had more frequent recourse to the village court, seeking satisfaction for wrongs imposed on them by male authority. Domestic disputes involving violence between spouses, based on claims of respect withheld and neglected duties by women, took increasing amounts of court time (ibid.: 44–54). Men, of course, were at a disadvantage, because everything they had done in relation to the Tambaran in the past was in the new scheme of things associated with Satan. The result was that in the context of Revivalist Christianity, women had moral and spiritual superiority on their side. What men did was to become much more aggressive towards women in a domestic context than they had been in the past. Now, without the ritual activities of the Tambaran, men are driven more into the domestic sphere, while women are taking a much larger role outside it. The result is hugely increased levels of conflict between women and men. Physical violence against wives and mothers is far more frequent and severe (ibid.: 55). Women no longer bend to male authority without question, believing that without the Tambaran men are powerless, and that these changes are somehow sanctioned by their new-found spiritual authority. Men react violently, a situation which is exacerbated by the declining control of older men over younger, and also a consequence of the removal of the Tambaran, but greatly accelerated by education, wage labour and improved communications. In the past, men feared women's power and dominated them ruthlessly, even murderously; now they no longer dominate them, they just hit them (ibid.: 175–6).

Clearly, this picture is a generalized one, based on trends and the observance of individual cases and events. There are obvious differences in the way these trends are experienced and interpreted by women and men, young and old, Christian converts and 'traditionalists'. There will also be a significant number of marriages, as well as intimate and social relations, which do not evince these trends. But we still have to answer two questions: why did the men reveal their secret? and what are we to make of these changes in gender relations?

The causes and consequences of social change

There could be many reasons why the men might have wanted to bring an end to the Tambaran cult. Perhaps, as Tuzin suggests, it was already on its way out, and many men felt it to be counter to the demands and rationalities of modern life, and its upkeep to be burdensome and pointless in the context of a world increasingly framed by global markets, communication and consumption (Tuzin, 1997: 178–80). However, as Tuzin points out, there might be deeper cultural logics at play here. To understand why the men felt they had to kill the Tambaran, it might be helpful to recall the story of Nambweapa'w recounted in the previous chapter. The story contains within it the possibility of revival and redemption because the youngest son is swept up on a wave to America from whence he will one day return. The creation myth – known to everyone – foretold the possibility of a second coming. The good life promised by Christianity is associated all over Papua New Guinea with the advent of and access to modern goods and consumption items. Hence the importance of the son's return from America.[4] The Tambaran, with its associations with anti-Christ, was widely understood as standing in the way of this return – and perhaps of modernity and prosperity more generally – and thus had to be killed rather than simply allowed to die. The Nambweapa'w story tells of the redemptive killing of masculinity, whose power has only been maintained through deception, and characterizes the world that follows as paradise-like, where the inhabitants want for nothing. In essence, the men killed the Tambaran hoping that a new world would come about, one characterized by plenitude. The irony was that in putting in place the conditions for the cassowary's revenge, they had apparently not foreseen that this would be, as the myth foretold, a turn to a world dominated by the power of the maternal, and the very evidence for this is, in their eyes, the new-found assertiveness of women (ibid.: 181–6).

In the demise of the Tambaran, we see myth folding itself over and around social and economic change. The Tambaran as a rigid, hierarchical, secret cult which took up large amounts of the time of adult men could never have survived the advent of education, wage labour and improved communications and transport. But its importance lay in the way it tied masculine subjectivity to the conditions for the social. The killing of the Tambaran caused a crisis in masculinity because it signalled not only the rejection of tradition, but the repudiation of the masculine self. Masculinity, as we have said, is a thing of ideology and ontology, thus the repudiation of the ideology necessarily brings a crisis in being. As Tuzin argues, the 'obsessive misogynistic secrecy of Tambaran activities served constantly to remind men of the *masculine* significance of what they were doing' (ibid.: 182, emphasis in the original). The Tambaran used to be 'what men do', but what does masculinity become when it is no longer a matter of doing Tambaran things? The old men, as Tuzin records, understood something that the young men did not, and that was that the details and paraphernalia of the cult mattered much less than the fact that the cult was concerned with male secrets (ibid.: 176). These secrets were openly acknowledged by older men to be concealed best by hiding them in plain view (Taussig, 1999: part II). For example, when the boys are taken to the forest to purge them of maternal essences by slashing their genitals, the women were told that they were forced to slide down a thorny sago palm, thus ripping their parts against an object that for the Ilahita is a quintessentially maternal symbol. Men took pleasure in the fact that women were being told the truth, but did not know how to see it, how to interpret it (Tuzin, 1997: 185). Deception was itself part of the ritual efficacy of the Tambaran cult. The exposure of the secret was thus a double killing, since it not only revealed that the cult was an illusion, but it destroyed its efficacy.

The efficacy of illusion was key to the cult in more ways than one, but its most important function was what it revealed about masculinity to men themselves. In their constant preoccupation with stories of how men stole the Tambarans from women, with how this secret might get out, men reveal that masculinity is an illusion, that it is founded on something that is not so, that it has at its core an absence, and that this absence is constitutive of all that can be deemed phallic. The men, especially the older ones, were in no doubt that they were promulgating an illusion, and they were anxious about it because male power was sustained by this deception. The Tambaran was the privileged signifier of the symbolic order; to become male one had to be eaten by the Tambaran and survive, one's body had to be marked by one's accession to its power. But the Tambaran was an illusion, it did not exist. What defined femininity, in contrast, was that one had not been marked by the Tambaran, one did not know that it was an illusion. Sustaining the illusion of the Tambaran was burdensome, and perhaps, in the context of the particular rationalities of modernity, might have seemed pointless, as we have said. Consequently, there would no doubt have been some men who would have been only too glad to give it up. But in actively and publicly repudiating it, two sets of logics and chains of association were simultaneously made. The first was the one that the old men knew and reflected on, the founding lack of the masculine subject, the illusion at the core of masculinity, the idea that men possessed the phallus and that it was rightfully theirs. This phallus was not, of course, a male organ, or rather it only became male by virtue of the fact that the Tambaran embodied it. This phallus representing symbolic power, the power to create through illusion, had originally belonged to women. What men stole from women was not the physical power to give birth, but their ability to create and control the Tambarans, their ability to create illusions, to give form to power, to inaugurate the social, as well as representation and language (Lattas, 1989: 455; Tuzin, 1972; 1992; 1995). This capacity to control the originary powers of the imagination, to make the social, is given form in the Tambarans, and in that form acts as the privileged signifier of the social order, the signifier that inaugurates and marks the limits of sexual difference. Repudiating the Tambaran meant not only relinquishing the ordering power of the social world; it was also tantamount to a declaration that men no longer possessed the phallus, that they were no longer masculine.

The second set of associations draws on an equally powerful metaphoric logic, but one which, although it emerges out of the first, is of a rather different nature. Men's possession of the Tambaran was an illusion in two ways: first, because they had acquired it through murderous deception and, second, because it is not possible to order the world as one wishes, to control representation and language completely, there is always something that will exceed the reach of power. This is made evident both in the fact that men only acquire this power through theft – it is an illegitimate power – and in their anxiety that this secret would be revealed. The act of unmasking the Tambaran, whether or not it had the consequences intended, was an act of bravery and of extreme optimism. Tuzin is right when he says that the Tambaran might have withered away in time, becoming obsolete in a modern world, but that only a competing ritual system could have killed it (Tuzin, 1997: 183). What Revivalist Christianity promised was a bright new future, one in which old wrongs would be righted, where gender relations would be equal with regard to ritual, where God would provide and protect, where modernity would prevail. In this world, there would be no need to fear the Tambaran, and no need to fear the revelation of the secret, no need to bear the guilt and anxiety of past deeds and misdeeds. In this world, masculinity would not be founded on a deception, on an absence; it would not be an illusion, it would be founded in God's grace, made whole, be at one with itself, and be guiltless. Masculinity would therefore no longer be divided against itself, no longer founded on lack.

Desire is something unrealizable, and must remain so as a condition for social existence. What the Tambaran reveals is the uncertainty of the relation of language and representation to the world, driven by a desire to make representation and the world coincide, to control their relation, to bring things into being. The whole edifice of masculinity and of the Tambaran was constructed in the oscillation of this desire, built upon its impossibility, its failure, revealing once again that sexual difference is a failure of signification. The old men knew that their success was built upon this failure and did not want it revealed. The young men thought that they could transcend it, block its functioning, base self and society on wholly stable foundations with no murderous pasts behind them. Those who revealed the Tambaran were certainly revolutionaries in some sense: they wanted to usher in a new age. They certainly did not want to obliterate or abolish sexual difference, but they did want to change society. All changes in ideology on this scale involve changes in ontology, in ways of being, and this makes gender relations the terrain of transformation. So has the destruction of the Tambaran brought about changes in the experience and understanding of masculinity and femininity?

From the data available, it seems to have brought about changes in the understandings of what it is to be a woman and of how women relate to men, and the kinds of lives they might expect to lead. Has it liberated them?[5] This is an altogether different question, for which one would have to turn first to them for an answer, but it is at least worth bearing in mind that the changes that had already begun to undermine the Tambaran gathered enormous speed and force with the collapse of its punitive ideology, and not always for the better. Without the control of adult sexuality provided by the cult, women are having more children and they are subject to more domestic violence; the declining control of older men over younger and the increasing wealth of the latter has led to increased polygyny; and women are now subject to more violence from their sons, who are often unemployed, frustrated and furious. On the other hand, women are receiving primary education, some are community leaders, others are involved in church activities and are employed. Women are less subject to the authority of men, and the shape of patriarchy has shifted. These changes do not affect all women equally: they are not necessarily linear or permanent. The future is all ahead.

What has happened to the men? Some, of course, are bemoaning the passing of better times and saying, 'I told you so'; others are finding new opportunities in employment outside the area and in involvement in education, politics and commerce. Yet others are struggling with the changes to their domestic relations, with the pressures of declining incomes, population growth and pressure on resources. Young men seem particularly badly affected, dislocated, disappointed and feel increasingly dispensable in a world shaped as much by the changing patterns of consumption, aspiration, knowledge and markets as by local cultural and social values.[6] Both masculinity and femininity are experienced, interpreted and lived through other axes of difference: class, ethnicity, nationality and religion. The relationship between ontology and ideology is shifting in concert with these other forms of difference, multiply over-determined by all of them. In the absence of a further study, it is impossible to say what is happening to masculinity in any detail. What is clear is that huge changes have come about. Will it make a difference not to think of masculinity in terms of the fictions and demands of the Tambaran? Most certainly, it already has. Will it make a difference to post-oedipal understandings of masculinity (and femininity) not to be preoccupied for large amounts of your adult life with masculine secrets, not to have had your body slashed by adult men, not to have been subjected to certain traumas and ordeals that seek to rearrange your ontological relation to your body and to those of others? How could it not? Will all this make a difference to the imaginary relations that women and men have to their bodies and to those of others, and which they carry over into their parenting and into their social values and cultural productions? Will all these changes have an impact on concepts of the gendered self, on ideas about the maternal and the paternal, and on the way the masculine and the feminine are attached to objects and part objects? It would be very difficult to argue the counter case.

The images in which a subject finds itself come to it from outside. As discussed in previous chapters, the self body ego forms as a result of an engagement with a lived world of objects – including parents and significant others – and develops through the interface between physical embodiment and representation. The subject recognizes itself and its desires within certain representations, images, sounds and narratives. What happens when all these change? The relation of the subject to the symbolic order is itself an imaginary relation, and one which is informed by the imaginary relations of others. As we have seen in this book, myth, ritual and symbolism often emphasize the relational aspects of masculinity and femininity, their doubled-over, mutually determining relations. They bring such images and representations into a relation with the oedipal binary, oppositional categories of gender. These post-oedipal understandings of masculinity and femininity are concerned with preserving tensions and ambiguity, providing the basis for cultural production and intellectual reflection. When these cultural productions disappear, what are the contexts or domains for reflection on the vexed question of sexual difference and how it relates to women and men?

There are presumably many possibilities – art, religion, psychoanalysis, anthropology. Yet, the nature, extent and content of such locations/domains matter because they are some of the major contexts in which humans work over the relationship of the imaginary to the symbolic, in which they set up their imaginary relation to the symbolic and through which they are constituted as subjects. This process of working over is both conscious and unconscious, and cultures clearly vary with regard to the degree that such matters are brought into conscious reflection; so too do different kinds of ideologies. These matters were of primary concern in the Tambaran, at least for men. They were also there in myths, art and other cultural productions that women would have been party to (Tuzin, 1972;

1992; 1995). In the context of Revivalist Christianity, the forum(s) for reflecting on these matters has shifted because we know that, in addition to the Tambaran, magic, spells, art forms, traditional oratory, competitive yam exchanges, funeral celebrations and memorial meetings were all banned. Many of these things may come back, and anthropological accounts are full of the demise and subsequent revival of cultural forms and activities.[7] It seems likely that new contexts – prayer meetings, sermons, etc. – will have emerged, and while we know nothing about the content of these new domains, it is possible that the way they imagine the nature of masculinity and femininity and their relations to male and female bodies, as well as how they work over the relationship of the imaginary to the symbolic, are quite different from before. Indeed, Christianity in its revivalist forms has a history of adhering quite directly to binary and essentialist models of gender linked to very particular understandings of sexuality, the family and morality.

The future of sexual difference

Sexuality and gender are the terrain of social transformation, the location of intense struggles over power, symbols, meanings, values and resources. They are the major means through which a society represents itself to itself, and through which individuals and collectivities engage with the problem of history, and its relationship to agency and structure. There is a certain contradiction which has historically fractured the relationship between anthropology and psychoanalysis, as well as that between psychoanalysis and feminism. The vanishing point around which this contradiction moves is sexual difference, and one of the modalities in which it is expressed is the question of the relation of the social to the symbolic. At the moment, when the men stand up in church and declare the Tambaran dead, that question becomes urgent. The particular value of psychoanalysis is its insistence on the fact that the subject does not coincide with herself or with her consciousness. Rosi Braidotti puts it elegantly when she says the unconscious is the 'guarantee of non-closure in the practice of subjectivity' (2002: 39). The subject is processually constituted out of the dynamic interactions of power and desire, agency and structure. In a straightforward sense, this means that when the men make their declaration, we cannot simply gloss this as a will to power. There are two dimensions here. First, the men may have intended to change gender relations, but were the changes that arose merely confined to the form of their social manifestations, leaving the structure of the symbolic order intact? Second, given that entrance into the symbolic order, accession to the limits of sexual difference, is a condition for subjectivity, is it possible to will or achieve a change in the structure of the symbolic order?

We certainly know that it is possible to desire a change in the symbolic order, in the way that the female and the male are marked by sexual difference. This is, after all, one definition of the project of feminism. But, feminists are divided on precisely what this project entails and on whether or not it is realizable. Can changes in gender relations (the social) bring about changes in the symbolic order? Do alternative figurations of subjectivity actually bring about changes in the way subjects are formed or are they just ways of reordering existing structures? Are the structures of the symbolic universal and if so do they ignore the differences between and within women (and men)? The usual charge is that the concept of sexual difference is essentialist, universalistic and heterosexist, and thus ignores cultural diversity, social change, the differences between women and the existence of non-heterosexual desires/ subjects (e.g. Felski, 1997). In short the symbolic order is utterly indifferent to the social, its determinations, multiplicities and transformations (Butler, 2004: 48).

This seems a strange kind of assertion to make, and it is certainly deeply puzzling in relation to the ethnographic material because understanding the relation between the imaginary and the symbolic immediately raises the question of the relation of the body to history. Human sexuality is a consequence of a particular configuration of desire and representation which places the sexed subject firmly within history. The constitutive nature both of desire and representation (see chapters 5 and 8) means that we cannot begin with the idea of an already given or formed subject who encounters history and the social order. Indeed, both psychoanalysis and modern neurological science make it clear that the subject/self is formed only in and through the representation of the sensate engagement with space, time and others that is both individual and collective history. But, the human subject is always other to itself, it does not coincide with its consciousness, signs come to it from outside, and it is constituted through the desires of others. The symbolic order, therefore, produces subjects, but is itself other to them, and cannot be construed as the product of autonomous subjects. Shepherdson develops this point and argues that while it is the symbolic order that makes history possible, it cannot be reduced to the historical conditions external to the subject or to the specific institutions of patriarchy that arise at a particular time (2000: 34–6). For Shepherdson, it is the symbolic that lifts the sexed subject out of nature and into history, but paradoxically this history would appear to be contentless and definitively non-social.

Silverman struggles with the same problem, but suggests an alternative. She proposes that we should distinguish between the symbolic order and the forms of its conventional cultural representation. She claims that it is unfortunate that 'the phallus often emerges within the Lacanian text as a universal signifier of desire, rather than as the variable metaphor of an irreducible lack' (1992: 38). The dominant fiction of western society, as Silverman sees it, conceptualizes 'the lack installed through language as the absence of the male sexual organ' (ibid.: 37). She argues that the dominant fiction and the symbolic order exist in a relation of mutual determination, and that when belief in the dominant fiction is withheld then the symbolic order is jeopardized (ibid.: 41). A particular ideology of masculinity is crucial in constructing the dominant fiction, and thus Silverman would appear to offer us a model for understanding what happened on that day in September 1984. The dominant ideology of masculinity, constituted through the metaphor of lack (the Tambaran), was undermined and consequently the symbolic order was put into jeopardy. However, Silverman is careful to say that there are 'irreducible' and 'provisional' aspects of the symbolic order, and it is only the latter that are put into jeopardy. If I have read her correctly, she distinguishes between the 'law of language', a discursive order that pre-exists, constructs and exceeds the subject, and the 'law of kinship structure', the culturally and historically variable elaboration of a universal dictate, the incest prohibition (ibid.: 35). Thus, what is universal about the symbolic order is that, through language, it divides and splits the subject, and does so through the incest taboo. What is variable are the cultural and historical forms of the incest taboo. Consequently there can be subjectivities which have established a different relation to the family from the one depicted in the classic formulation of the Oedipus complex, and theoretically there could be subjectivities that have a different relation to the law of language and the law of kinship structure (ibid.: 41). Silverman does not provide examples of what these latter subjectivities and their variable relations are or might be. This is not surprising, because to do so would,

I think, be tantamount to saying that the symbolic order always takes a social form.

Why should this be such a problem? To claim that the symbolic always takes a social form is not necessarily the same thing as reducing the symbolic to the social. We can push this argument further by returning to the question of the relationship of sexual difference to gender. Where ethnographic material is useful is in demonstrating that sexual difference is a conundrum for all human societies, that because human sexuality is set up in language and representation, there is a genuine puzzle about how masculinity and femininity relate to the male and the female – appearance does not coincide with being. The sexed subject is founded on this non-coincidence and is always a very particular kind of response to the problem of sexual difference. This particular response is always both social or cultural, and individual. The cultural response is, as we have seen, very often concerned with the relation of the imaginary to the symbolic, and thus works over the engagement of the body and desire with the history of representations and imaginary identifications with others. The individual response is one set within that cultural/social context, but not wholly determined by it. The unconscious is characterized by contradictions, paradoxes and inconsistencies; its workings both guarantee social subjectivity and create a space in which the specific forms of that subjectivity can be resisted, disavowed and distanced (Braidotti, 2002: 39–40). In other words, it provides the possibility for refusing – either consciously or unconsciously, in language or in practice – the kind of sexed subject the symbolic order requires. It is for this reason that the social and the psychic cannot be neatly mapped onto each other, and cannot be said to determine each other.

From this perspective, it is not difficult to imagine how sexed subjects – gay, lesbian, trans – can emerge who do not coincide with the binary model of sexual difference, and whose desires are mapped in circulating and cross-cutting ways across bodies, identifications and representations. Sexual difference is in fact the enabling condition for the emergence of new forms of sexed subjectivity. This is perhaps easier to see in the ethnographic material because of the way the imaginary is much more closely linked to the symbolic, and because of the way that post-oedipal models of gender make such explicit use of the tensions and ambiguities between the pre-oedipal and the oedipal. In this context, the so-called determinations of the symbolic order, and their heterosexual matrix, look rather different. If masculinity and femininity are compromise positions, then so too are other sexed subjectivities. It is important to reiterate here that the relation of the subject to the symbolic order is an imaginary one, set up in representation, and the fundamental incompleteness of meaning undermines any ultimate claim that the sexed subject is fully determined by the symbolic. This is the case, even in the kinds of societies I have been describing, where gender ideologies are frequently binary, exclusionary and hierarchical.

However, making this point does not address the question of whether or not alternative sexed subjectivities are linked to changes in the symbolic order. It would seem logical, at least to me, that changes in the structures of desiring subjects do have the potential to bring about changes in the content of the symbolic order, and in the imaginary relation of sexed subjects to the symbolic order, and in the way the symbolic order signifies the difference between masculinity and femininity. The ethnographic material moves us away from a model that ties our understanding of sexual difference too closely to object choice. A focus on object choice (see chapter 7) rather hinders our understanding of how others in different contexts deal with the puzzle of sexual difference. What is particularly striking is how much of what might be considered to be in the realm of the unconscious in western understandings of sexed subjectivity is part of collective and critical reflection and elaboration in these contexts: what an issue these communities have made of sexual difference, how imaginative they have been in linking the problem of what masculinity and femininity means and entails to sexuality, fertility, power, social continuity and politics. How little we understood of this when we simply categorized these societies as patriarchal and, all too often, as fixed by tradition. We could do worse, as anthropologists, feminists and psychoanalysts, than to use their imaginations to empower our own and think a little less about the determinations of the symbolic and a little more about the powers of the imaginary.

Notes

Chapter 1   Body, Mind and World

1   Psychoanalytic thinking has influenced the development of theoretical models in anthropology far more than is generally recognized. See Birth (1994) for an account of this in the context of British anthropology. The history of the relationship in the USA has been, however, very different from that of Europe, and within Europe different trajectories have been followed in the French as compared to the British contexts.

2   In the USA in the first part of the twentieth century, the culture and personality school dominated debates on the relationship between the individual and culture (e.g. Benedict, 1934; 1946; Kardiner, 1945; Wallace, 1961; Whiting and Child, 1953). The legacy of this school has been crucial for the development of anthropology as a discipline. While this work was not predominantly inspired by psychoanalysis, it later attracted the label neo-Freudian as a consequence of its emphasis on parenting and socialization (e.g. Mead, 1942[1930]; Whiting, 1941). See Shweder (1979a; 1979b; 1980) for a reassessment of the main arguments of the culture and personality school and a discussion of current and future research deriving from it.

3   For overviews of psychoanalytic anthropology, see Boyer, 1978; Devereux, 1978; Gehrie, 1977; Hiatt, 1987; Huxley, 1985; Kakar, 1985; Juillerat, 2001: ch. 1; Paul, 1989.

4   For exceptions see Ewing, 1998; Pandolfo, 1997; Pradelles de la Tour, 1991; Trawick, 1990; 1992; Weiner, 1995.

5   I am thinking here of Bernard Juillerat's work with André Green (Juillerat, 1992b), Maurice Godelier's work with Jacques Hassoun (Godelier and Hassoun, 1996) and René Devisch's work with Claude Brodeur (Devisch and Brodeur, 1999).

6   For discussions of the intellectual issues which continue to divide anthropology and psychoanalysis in the contemporary moment, see Bidou et al., 1999; Green, 1999; Heald et al., 1994; Juillerat, 2001: ch. 1; Pulman, 1984.

7   Lévi-Strauss's structuralism is famous for its bracketing – some would say rejection – of the individual and individual agency. Thus, his comments in *The Jealous Potter* and elsewhere should be more accurately viewed as part of a determination to keep psychoanalysis and anthropology separate, to distinguish them from each other, rather than to bring them together (Bidou et al., 1999: 13).

8   Recent work on kinship has shown us that kinship can no longer be grounded – if it ever could – in a fixed and singular idea of a 'natural' relation. Kinship is no longer considered as providing the basis for culture in the way that it once was in anthropology, but it does continue to function on the interface, naturalizing cultural relationships and transforming natural relations into cultural forms (e.g. Strathern, 1992a; 1992b; 2005; Franklin and McKinnon, 2002). In fact, in this context the terms 'nature' and 'culture' are both rather misleading. I develop my argument against the self-evident and naturalized category of the mother in psychoanalytic thinking in the following chapters.

9   This idea is implicit in Freud's notion of libido, but other examples would include Merleau-Ponty (1962) in his account of the phenomenology of perception, the neurologist Antonio Damasio (2000) in his claim that consciousness is what allows us to know life and to seek it, and Rosi Braidotti (2002) in her account of Spinoza's conatus as a striving to engage. See also Paul (1990) for a discussion relating to anthropology.

10 'The inescapable and remarkable fact about these three phenomena – emotion, feeling, consciousness – is their body relatedness. We begin with an organism made up of body proper and brain, equipped with certain forms of brain response to certain stimuli and with the ability to represent the internal states caused by reacting to stimuli and engaging repertoires of present response. As the representations of the body grow in complexity and coordination, they come to constitute an integrated representation of the organism, a proto-self. Once that happens, it becomes possible to engender representations of the proto-self as it is affected by interactions with a given environment. It is only then that consciousness begins, and only thereafter that an organism that is responding beautifully to its environment begins to discover that *it* is responding beautifully to its environment. But all of these processes – emotion, feeling, and consciousness – depend for their execution on representations of the organism. Their shared essence is the body' (Damasio, 2000: 284); see also Damasio, 1995: ch. 10.

11 This argument is analogous to the one that cognitive anthropologists make about language (Bloch, 1998). Language is not the condition of thought, but thought is the condition of language.

12 Strictly speaking, from a psychoanalytic point of view there can be no such thing, since the phallus as signifier is not the male penis. For a discussion of this debate, see chapter 5. However, I use this mixed term intentionally because the ethnographic material provides plenty of examples of phalli that are not the male organ, and also questions our habitual tendency to think that we know in advance the gender of particular body parts. I am therefore signalling my disagreements in advance.

13 My argument here should not be confused with theories of resistance in anthropology that emphasize the practical, non-conscious nature of resistance (e.g. Scott, 1985), although they are perfectly compatible with my argument and a general theory of resistance, should one ever be thought desirable or possible, would have to take account of both.

14 There are, of course, societies in the world which reveal the opposite through exegesis and performance, which present their cultural representations and social arrangements as timeless, fixed and unchanging, but they too are preoccupied with the same matters, but are handling them in a different way. See Barth, 1975 and 1990 for an analogous discussion of why and how different societies handle knowledge in different ways.

Chapter 2   A Genealogy of the Anthropological Subject

1 For example: 'The Dinka have no conception which at all closely corresponds to our popular modern conception of the "mind" as mediating and, as it were, storing up the experiences of the self. There is no such interior entity to appear, on reflection, to stand between the experiencing self at any given moment and what is or has been an exterior influence upon the self' (Lienhardt, 1961: 149).

2 See also Fogelson, 1982; Lock, 1981.

3 Mead took a sophisticated view of the self/object relation, arguing that its symbolic representation must be at the basis both of self and of society. However, the distinction between self and object is not fixed or singular; rather, the relationship is one of mutual constitution: 'What we term the meaning of the object is found . . . in the organised attitude of response on the part of the organism' (Mead, 1934: 131). Mead's concern is with the way humans symbolize the world of objects, give value to those objects and convey those values to others. Key to this process is language as a means both of symbolic representation and of communication. For Mead, mind arises as a consequence of the ability to symbolize an environment and to establish control over it, thus any individual's psychological nature is a product of this process.

4 Many anthropologists were critical of this dichotomous view and preferred to follow Mauss. Mauss was more willing to explore

psychological issues than his uncle, and made a distinction between a sense of self (self-awareness) and the cultural or social concept of self/person. He argued that a sense of self must be found in all societies in the world, but that concepts of self/person had evolved over time and through history. He thus portrayed earlier societies as more socio-centric, while avoiding crude evolutionism, and described notions of the individuated, autonomous self as evolving over time, but as characteristic of modern societies (Mauss 1985[1938]).

5 See also Rapport, 1997 and Sökefeld, 1999.

6 For example, Kenneth Read's famous essay on the Gahuku-Gama of New Guinea argued that their concept of the human individual did not 'allow for any clearly recognised distinction between the individual and the status which he occupies' (Read, 1955: 225). Read's contention was that the Gahuku-Gama failed to separate the individual from the social context in which they operated and thus there was no notion of an individuated self endowed with moral worth (ibid.: 257). However, while Read characterized the Gahuku-Gama as primarily socio-centric, he did not thereby imply that they had no sense of individuality, of self-awareness, of the idiosyncratic self, of ego or of the psyche (ibid.: 191).

7 Cohen (1994: 14) rightly points out that the treatment of the relationship between individual and society was problematic in British structural-functionalism because individuals were considered as members of collectivities: lineages, villages, castes.

8 Both Strathern (1992) and Reisman (1977) show in different ways that 'western' persons/selves are both conceived of and actually experienced as individual and as based on social relationships. Strathern's discussion of English kinship demonstrates that ideas about kinship are connected to complex sets of ideas about individuality and social relationships that interpenetrate, thus providing evidence that individuals are recognized as the product of relationships: 'Individuality would thus be both a fact of and "after" kinship' (Strathern, 1992: 15). Reisman argues that the notion and the experience that western selves are made up of the selves they live with clashes with dominant ideas of individualism and autonomy, so that the theory of western individuality is actually an ideology. An ideology that explains many of the views we hold about how selves are formed (Riesman, 1977: 219–23).

9 However, a number of psycho-dynamically oriented anthropologists, some of them with theoretical interests in post-structuralism and postmodernism, have at different times discussed the relationships between the anthropological self and the selves of their informants, and analysed the self-reflective, hermeneutic nature of cross-cultural understanding, as well as issues of transference, identification and projection (Crapanzano, 1980; Devereux, 1967; Kracke, 1987a; 1987b; Mageo, 1998; Rabinow, 1977; Riesman, 1977).

10   For example, Marilyn Strathern argues one very important difference concerns the way relationships between society and the individual, persons and things, subjects and objects affect ideas about actions and transactions (Strathern, 1988; cf. Wagner, 1991; Battaglia, 1995). Strathern shows that Melanesians do not recognize an opposition between the individual and society. The western discourse of selves, individuals, property and society do not make sense in terms of Melanesian idioms. Strathern is, of course, writing here about cultural concepts and categories, and not about actual selves or individuals or persons in Melanesia and how they frame experience, self-awareness and self-continuity. But, the problem of cultural difference still has to be faced, theorized and analysed.

11   Persons and selves are not always seen as bounded or as delimited by embodiment or as defined in contradistinction to society. Maurice Leenhardt argued that the Canaque of New Caledonia regard the person as being connected to other persons, both human and non-human, and that the body is conceived of as a temporary locus, and not the source of individual identity. Anne Strauss argued for the Cheyenne that the concept of the person extends beyond human beings to include other non-human persons, and that relationships with such persons are crucial for the development of the self (both cited in Moore, 1994: 31–4).

12   Paul Riesman makes the same kind of argument in his study of the Fulani – perhaps not surprisingly given that Dorothy Lee was his mentor – pointing out that local psychologies only make sense in relation to local ideas about human nature, human growth and parental roles (Riesman, 1977: 179).

13   'In assessing the reality of inner states in alien cultures, it is possible hypothetically to distinguish those which have a natural basis from those which are ideological inventions; but no inner state can be expressed socially in a purely natural way, and in consequence there are strictly speaking no inner states, as collectively recognized conditions of consciousness, that are universal' (Needham, 1981: 76).

14   What Shweder's discussion illustrates is how much our understanding of the relationship between society and individual, and culture and psyche is bound up with the 'ideological inventions' of anthropology and indeed other disciplines. Cultural psychology, ethnopsychology and psychological anthropology are differentiated – if not always completely separate – theoretical positions that deploy particular notions of the self, allow for different degrees of universalism in psychological functioning and give differential weight to arguments based on cultural construction and cultural relativism. In short, they define self and culture, and theorize their relations, in different ways.

15   There is a strong emphasis in much of the anthropological literature on narratives of self and on the role of narratives in self-awareness, self-creation and self-identification (cf. Ewing, 1998; Jean-Klein, 2000;

Mageo, 1998). However, the notion of narratives of self can be confusing since it is applied variously to internal narratives of self with self; social narratives of events or actions told in public situations which bear on aspects of the self; and historical, textual or performative narratives that provide discursive formations within which aspects of the self can be reinterpreted. These are all clearly types of narrative which bear in some way or another on individual and/or group understandings of self/person, but they should not be analytically collapsed together.

16   Lienhardt, for example, shows that the Dinka do not base their sense of self on a mind–body dichotomy, and demonstrates that they 'integrate the moral and physical attributes of persons together within the physical matrix of the human body' (1985: 150). Moral and mental conditions are not thought of as abstract states, nor are their embodied characteristics to be thought of as purely metaphorical: anthropologists frequently mistake metaphors for mere representations. The importance of the bodily matrix for the Dinka is shown in the use of the word *gwop* (body) as the synonym for self: the self is always embodied in the sense that it takes a particular material form.

17   Feminist work on gender identity has emphasized that it must be understood as a lived set of embodied potentialities rather than as the result of an externally imposed categorization or ideology (cf. Braidotti, 1994; Butler, 1993; Diprose, 1994; Grosz, 1994).

18   For further critiques of Bourdieu on this point, see de Certeau, 1984; Ortner, 1984; and Quinn and Strauss, 1997.

19   It is in his discussion of masculine domination that Bourdieu comes closest to a theory of subjectivity, and he does acknowledge the importance of fantasy, desire and self-image in his discussion of gender differences. However, he remains critical of psychoanalysis and psychology (Bourdieu, 1990: 77; 2001).

20   Anthropology has long demonstrated that binary biological sex does not provide a universal basis for the cultural categories of gender. Much of the early work in anthropology and elsewhere discussed the 'third sex', hermaphrodism and transsexualism as a way of making this point (Herdt, 1994; Nanda, 1990; Whitehead, 1981; Wikan, 1977; Williams, 1986).

21   See for example Bornstein, 1994; Prosser, 1998; Sampson, 1993; Warner, 1993; 1999.

22   A growing body of work exists in anthropology on the relationship between power structures/discourses and emotions. This sees emotion 'talk' as political and traces the links between emotions, gender politics and socio-economic structures (see, for example, Abu-Lughod, 1986; Lutz, 1988; Lutz and Abu-Lughod, 1990b).

23   Mageo questions 'whether there is any part of the self uncontaminated and unconstructed by culture', thus her theory would not allow for views of the self to arise ex nihilo (Mageo, 1998: 11).

24   'This form of power applies itself to immediate everyday life which
     categorizes the individual, marks him by his own individuality. . . . It
     is a form of power which makes individual subjects. There are two
     meanings of the word *subject*: subject to someone else by control and
     dependence, and tied to his own identity by a conscience or self-
     knowledge. Both meanings suggest a form of power which subjugates
     and makes subject to' (Foucault, 1982: 212). Foucault's original critique
     of the Cartesian subject had emphasized that the subject cannot be
     understood as the foundation and source of knowledge of the world,
     but should be seen rather as a product or effect of power and discourse
     (Foucault, 1982). This view of the subject was heavily criticized, espe-
     cially by feminists, for its passive, over-determined nature, its func-
     tionalist and monolithic account of power and its lack of attention
     to issues of difference, particularly gender and race (cf. Diamond
     and Quinby, 1988; McNay 1992; Ramazonoglu, 1993). Foucault
     responded to these critiques and others, by introducing the notion of
     techniques or practices of the self; the phrase refers to the processes
     through which an individual comes to recognize him- or herself as
     a subject.

25   Cohen's critique of earlier anthropological views of person/self
     focused on the way culture was seen as determining, and anthropo-
     logical notions of person and selves were derived from the theoretical
     construction of culture (Cohen, 1994: 128). This analysis is a sound one,
     but it is worth pointing out that interactive and creative views of the
     self and selfhood are equally bound to contemporary notions of
     culture. If earlier views of culture were bounded and based on a notion
     of self-conscious differentiation that underpinned the cross-cultural
     project of anthropology, contemporary views of culture are quite
     different. Cultures are no longer theorized as bounded units – if they
     ever truly were – but are seen as contested and contradictory fields of
     social and symbolic significations connected to flows of people, ideas,
     images and goods (cf. Marcus, 1998; Appadurai, 1996; Comaroff and
     Comaroff, 2000). The emphasis on the commodification of cultural dif-
     ference in this theoretical perspective, and on the partiality of per-
     spectives and voices – even fragmentation – underscores the partiality
     of analytical models. It also, however, raises questions about the frag-
     mented, plural and multiplex nature of the identities of individuals
     inhabiting such cultures: 'It is the burden of the modernist ethnogra-
     phy to capture distinctive identity formations in all their migrations
     and dispersions' (Marcus, 1998: 63). Difference both in terms of culture
     and identity is understood as inherently plural. This is the context in
     which the notion of the creative and interactive self has taken root.
     While it is true that a relational view of self had existed earlier in an
     anthropology concerned with kinship and social structures, its present
     manifestations are strongly connected to changes in disciplinary
     understandings of the concept of culture.

26 However, Cohen's work is a notable exception here (Cohen, 1994).

27 Jean-Klein (2000: 101) notes the relationship between her work and that of Suad Joseph on Beirut which speaks of subjects enmeshed by kinship, and of 'relational selves' and 'connected identities' (Joseph, 1994: 55, 58).

28 Ewing (1998: 5) also argues that personal narratives and interpersonal arguments are contexts in which the functioning of the complex subject can be seen at work. Through these interactions it is possible to demonstrate the ways in which the experiencing subject moves among and through discourses.

Chapter 3   Culture, Power and Desire

1 Notable and very welcome exceptions include Trawick, 1990; 1992; Ewing, 1998.

2 '[I]t is impossible to overlook the extent to which civilization is built upon a renunciation of instinct, how much it presupposes precisely the non-satisfaction (by suppression, repression or some other means?) of powerful instincts. This "cultural frustration" dominates the large field of social relationships between human beings' (Freud 1985a[1929/1930]: 286–7).

3 This is clearly seen in Freud's account of the relationship between sexuality and knowledge which he based on what he called the 'sexual researches of children' (Moore, 2004). What children seek is knowledge of the origins of babies, the nature of the parental relationship and the difference between the sexes. Freud viewed children's sexual theories as false, but saw them as paradigmatic of a quest to understand the mystery of being human: 'Although they go astray in a grotesque fashion, yet each one of them contains a fragment of real truth; and in this they are analogous to the attempts of adults, which are looked at as strokes of genius, at solving the problems of the universe which are too hard for human comprehension' (Freud, 1977a[1908]: 193).

4 'On the one hand love comes into opposition to the interests of civilization; on the other, civilization threatens love with substantial restrictions' (Freud, 1985a[1929/1930]: 292). Freud drew extensively on early anthropologists in his writing on religion, including Fraser, Spencer, Morgan, Bachofen, Tyler and McLennan (Wallace, 1983: ch. 1).

5 However, it is important to recall here that, for Freud, external reality is also psychically constituted.

6 Freud does actually note several times in this essay that the identification may be with either parent (Freud, 1984b[1923]: 370–3).

7 In fact the definition of all these terms is a complex matter, and they all have a history within Freud's writings as he refined and changed

his ideas. What is more, the boundaries or distinctions between them are very unclear and the more so because they are dynamically related. One relevant debate is that on the question of whether, and indeed what parts of, the ego are unconscious.

8 'The ego ideal is therefore the heir of the Oedipus complex, and thus it is also the expression of the most powerful impulses and most important libidinal vicissitudes of the id. By setting up this ego ideal, the ego has mastered the Oedipus complex and at the same time placed itself in subjection to the id' (Freud, 1984b[1923]: 376). Freud emphasizes that although subjectivity is the product of a relation to culture, there is a fundamental dissonance between the self and the world, and their relations are characterized much more by ambivalence than by harmony.

9 'Demand in itself bears on something other than the satisfactions it calls for. It is demand of a presence or of an absence – which is what is manifested in the primordial relation to the mother, pregnant with that Other to be situated *within* the needs that it can satisfy. Demand constitutes the Other as already possessing the "privilege" of satisfying needs, that is to say, the power of depriving them of that alone by which they are satisfied. This privilege of the Other thus outlines the radical form of the gift of that which the Other does not have, namely, its love' (Lacan, 1977: 286).

10 'The subject originally locates and recognises desire through the intermediary, not only of his own image, but of the body of his fellow being. It's exactly at that moment that the human being's consciousness, in the form of consciousness of self, distinguishes itself. It is in so far as he recognises his desire in the body of the other that the exchange takes place. It is in so far as his desire has gone over to the other side that he assimilates himself to the body of the other and recognises himself as body' (Lacan, 1988a: 147).

11 'The Oedipus complex means that the imaginary, in itself an incestuous and conflictual relation, is doomed to conflict and ruin. In order for the human being to be able to establish the most natural of relations, that between male and female, a third party has to intervene, one that is the image of something successful, the model of some harmony . . . there has to be a law, a chain, a symbolic order, the intervention of the order of speech, that is, of the father. Not the natural father, but what is called the father' (Lacan, 1993: 96). As Jane Gallop argues: 'Castration for Lacan is not only sexual, it is also linguistic: we are inevitably bereft of any masterful understanding of language; and can only signify ourselves in a symbolic system that we do not command, that, rather commands us' (Gallop, 1985: 20).

12 '[T]he law of man has been the law of language since the first words of recognition presided over the first gifts . . . these gifts, their act and their objects, their erection into signs, and even their fabrication, were

so much a part of speech that they were designated by its name' (Lacan: 1977: 61).

13 Lacan is clear that the world of language is not created by the child, but rather the child is inserted into it, and that it is also the world of the 'Law of the Father', of culture and of wider social and family networks. Thus the human subject is the product of, rather than the producer of, this social world. Many critics see Lacan's notion of the symbolic order as very over-determining and as leaving no room for the creative imaginary capacities of the self, or for critical self-reflection and autonomy, or indeed for resistance to domination. In short, Lacan's subject does not seem to be a full social agent. However, as Paul Smith says: 'In Lacan's re-reading of Freud's metapsychological theory, the "subject" appears as a complicated articulation of different moments or instances and is conceived as a kind of process of production in the symbolic order, rather than as that order's direct and fixed effect' (Smith, 1988: 21).

14 '[M]an's desire is the *désir de l'Autre* (the desire of the Other) in which the *de* provides what grammarians call the "subjective determination", namely that it is *qua* Other that he desires (which is what provides the true compass of human passion)' (Lacan, 1977: 312).

15 Since the *objet a* is minimally defined as 'the cause of desire', that which interrupts the law and acts as the cause or object of desire, Lacan provides numerous understandings of glosses for this complex notion. The concept under went extensive revision by him, and has been commented on exhaustively by others since (see Lacan, 1977; 1978; 1994).

16 For Lacan, unconscious fantasy can be minimally defined as 'an image set to work in the signifying structure' (Lacan, 1977: 272).

17 Lacan gives a different account of the importance of identification in the formation of the subject from that of Freud. While Freud sees the oedipal identifications as primary, Lacan sees the subject's primary identification as being with itself. The subject has only one object of desire and that is itself: 'It is in this erotic relation, in which the human individual fixes upon himself an image that alienates him from himself, that are to be found the energy and the form on which this organization of the passions that he will call his ego is based' (Lacan, 1977: 19).

18 The term 'real' as used by Lacan is to be distinguished from 'reality', and is that which logically precedes and structures the symbolic order. 'The paradox of the Lacanian Real, then, is that it is an entity which, although it does not exist (in the sense of "really existing", taking place in reality), has a series of properties – it exercises a certain structural causality, it can produce a series of effects in the symbolic reality of subjects' (Žižek, 1989: 163).

19 Enjoyment or *jouissance* is a pleasure that is excessive, and while it is fascinating, it can also be overwhelming and lead to a sense of disgust.

20 The child wants to be recognized by the parents as worthy of their desire, but their desire is also potentially too much, compulsive and possibly lethal. It is through fantasy that the subject manages to keep desire at the right distance and in circulation: 'the desire structured through fantasy is a defence against the desire of the Other' (Žižek, 1989: 118).

21 'Fantasy conceals the fact that the Other, the symbolic order, is structured around some traumatic impossibility, around something which cannot be symbolized' (Žižek, 1989: 123).

22 Castoriadis is extremely critical of Lacan and of his use of structural linguistics, linking his position on language to an attempt 'to persuade the subject of his non-existence or his lack of responsibility, and to render him passive in the face of "structures"' (Castoriadis, 1984: 100).

Chapter 4   Objects and Relations with (M)others

1 For overviews of these developments see Elliott, 1992; Frosh, 1997.

2 This is also true of self psychology and ego psychology, albeit in different ways. Self psychologists, primarily Heinz Kohut and his followers, explore how early relationships form the self and its structures, and they give more emphasis to the self than to the ego. Ego psychologists, such as Anna Freud and Heinz Hartmann, examine how an autonomous ego that can adapt to social life is formed and maintained.

3 Castoriadis's theories have several similarities with those of Klein and Winnicott, despite his criticisms of Klein (e.g. Castoriadis, 1987: 275). See also Castoriadis (1987: 101–7) on the ego and the id.

4 This, of course, differentiates Winnicott from Fairbairn because the latter insists on the primary unity of the ego from the start: see above.

5 There is some debate about Winnicott's views on the id. He certainly used the term and held to the importance of conventional Freudian thinking. However, he also suggests that there is no id before ego, the start is where the ego starts (Winnicott, 1965: 56). Adam Phillips takes the view that the mediating role of the mother in Winnicott's theory assumes that the mother manages instinctual satisfaction for the child: 'Where the Id of the infant is, the mother's Ego must also be' (Phillips, 1988: 100).

6 'The relatively secure internalization of the good breast is characteristic of some innate strength of the ego. A strong ego is less liable to fragmentation and therefore more capable of achieving a measure of integration and a good early relation to the primal object' (Klein, 1997f[1963]: 309).

7 Benjamin argues that this figure could be the mother, but is most likely to be a 'third' figure associated with independence from the mother.

8 Benjamin distinguishes the intersubjective view from more conventional ego psychology separation-individuation theory. Instead of focusing on how the object is internalized, assimilated into the self, intersubjective theory emphasizes the recognition of other subjects as separate from the self (Benjamin, 1988: 42–3).

9 There is always a balance to be struck, according to Benjamin, between the recognition of the other and the assertion of self (Benjamin, 1988: 46).

10 Benjamin's theorizing is optimistic and could be considered utopian, not just because of its focus on the self as an active, enjoying agent, but also because of her characterization of the external world as a condition of freedom rather than domination for the self (Benjamin, 1988: 48).

11 For collections which do address these issues, see Dimen and Goldner, 2002; Domenici and Lesser, 1995; Fairfield et al., 2002.

12 While Lacan and others may emphasize the separation of 'woman' from actual women, these forms of exclusion produce particular kinds of problems. On the one hand, they make 'woman' non-representable, and on the other they exclude and/or repress the imaginary, and these two manoeuvres are connected.

13 This was a point emphasized by both Freud and Lacan, and I discuss this further in chapter 5.

14 As Jane Flax says, 'Men have always "written from the body" – the "phallus" role as primary signifier is not accidental or arbitrary. Juxtaposing feminine writing against and within phallocentric discourse allows the system of signification and its "signified" – the subject and its modes of consciousness – to be transformed' (Flax, 1990: 174).

15 See Oliver (1993: 9–10) for a discussion of Kristeva's use of the term 'symbolic'.

16 There is a certain ambivalence in Kristeva's theory on this point which is difficult to interpret. She asserts that the semiotic is the basis for potential subversion and social change within the symbolic order, but she also appears to accept the idea that the symbolic is subject to the law of the father, and thus although the semiotic can disrupt and escape the paternal law, it always remains within the domain of that law (Butler, 1990: 88). This makes it difficult to understand how social change could affect psychic processes, and vice versa. As a result, detractors argue that there is no basis for social change in the theory (for example, Fraser, 1990; Jones, 1984; Leland, 1989). Supporters on the other hand argue that the semiotic must always be within the law to some degree, that there is no possibility of living outside the law or even of describing a position outside the law because for either to be possible the law must be instantiated.

17 In object relations theory, an object is anything to which a subject relates. The term 'object' has a particular meaning and objects are usually people (mother, fathers, others), parts of significant others

(mother's breast) or things such as transitional objects to which we form attachments (blankets, toys, animals). The child's developing relationships with these objects are incorporated into the self and the term – object relations – refers to a self structure which internalizes in early childhood and which functions as a template for establishing and maintaining future relationships. I use the term object much more broadly here to encompass objects in the material world – including body parts, tools and spaces – that form part of a lived relationship to a gendered self and the multiple models of gender and gender identification on which it is based. This is particularly relevant in contexts where the western subject–object distinction does not have the same purchase (see chapter 2).

18   Obeyesekere argued that the relationship of primary process material to cultural fantasy provides the basis for understanding the relationship between personal and cultural symbols, but he also suggested that the evident and explicit use of imaginary material in cultural production demonstrates that there is no hard and fast barrier between the id and the ego. Thus, a serious consideration of cross-cultural material would entail a reformulation of Freud's typology of mind (Obeyesekere, 1990: 51–68). I have shown earlier that Freud himself saw the different structures of the mind less as entities in relation than as a dynamic set of processes, and that, in any event, object relations theorists and relational theorists, from Klein onwards, have argued that there can be no rigid barrier between the conscious and the unconscious mind.

19   This theme is more directly explored in chapter 8, where I discuss the relationship between the emergence of subjectivity and the origins of the social.

20   See, for example, Strathern, 1988: Jackson, 1996.

21   This is discussed further in chapter 8, where I take up Marilyn Strathern's notion of sex as a limiting aesthetic (Strathern, 1988).

Chapter 5   The Problem of the Phallus

1   It begins with his account of infantile sexual instincts and the oral phase where the child suckles from the need for nourishment, but finding the satisfaction of the need pleasurable, moves to sucking the thumb where pleasure can be experienced in itself, as separate from need. The anal phase provides a context where pleasurable sensations, through toilet training, begin to come under the sway of social dictates. 'The contents of the bowels, which act as a stimulating mass upon a sexually sensitive portion of mucous membrane, behave like forerunners of another organ, which is destined to come into action after the phase of childhood. But they have other important meanings for the infant. They are clearly treated as a part of the infant's own

body and represent his first "gift": by producing them he can express his active compliance with his environment and, by withholding them, his disobedience' (Freud, 1977b[1905]: 103–4).

2 Many feminists have accused Freud of biological determinism. Juliet Mitchell is one who has strongly defended Freud against phallocentric and biologistic readings: 'Sexual difference can only be the consequence of a division; without this division it would cease to exist. But, it must exist because no human being can become a subject outside the division into two sexes. One must take up a position as either a man or a woman. Such a position is by no means identical with one's biological sexual characteristics, nor is it a position of which one can be very confident' (Mitchell, 1985: 6).

3 These arise because of the masculinist and phallocentric nature of Freud's account of castration and of female sexuality in general (see, for example, Chodorow, 1994). While the oral and the anal phases are the same for both sexes, the phallic phase, which links to the Oedipus complex and the threat of castration, is not (Freud [1924] 1977d). From this point on female sexuality becomes a conundrum: '... we can describe this state of things only as it affects the male child; the corresponding processes in the little girl are not known to us' (Freud 1977e[1923]: 308–9).

4 In his first article on phallocentric theory, Jones argued that castration cannot be the concept for understanding female sexuality, and that it is merely one form of a more general fear of loss of libido, aphanisis, that both sexes may experience (Jones, 1927).

5 'I object to all of you (Horney, Jones, Rado, etc.), to the extent that you do not distinguish more clearly and cleanly between what is psychic and what is biological, that you try to establish a neat parallelism between the two' (Freud, 1935, cited in Mitchell and Rose, 1985: 1).

6 'Castration may derive support from privation, that is to say, from the apprehension in the Real of the absence of the penis in women – but even this implies a symbolization of the object, since the Real is full and "lacks" nothing. In so far as one finds castration in the genesis of the neuroses, it is never real but symbolic and aimed at an imaginary object' (Lacan, 1966: 512, quoted in Grosz, 1990: 71).

7 '[T]he signifier "phallus" functions in distinction from "penis", but it must also always refer to "penis"' (Gallop, 1982: 96). 'The phallus *symbolizes* the penis; and insofar as it symbolizes the penis, retains the penis as that which it symbolizes; it *is* not the penis' (Butler, 1993: 83).

8 Close readings and reinterpretations of Lacan's texts have provided detractors and defenders with a variety of evidence for their positions. For an overview, see Bowie, 1991: ch. 5; Butler, 1993: ch. 2; Flax, 1990; Gallop, 1982; 1985; Grosz, 1990: chs. 5 and 6; Mitchell, 1974; Mitchell and Rose, 1985; Moi, 2004; Ragland-Sullivan, 1986).

9 'The symbolic function of the phallus envelops the penis as the tangible sign of a privileged masculinity, thus in effect naturalizing male dominance' (Grosz, 1990: 123).

10 For an argument that Lacan's formulation of the symbolic is not to be seen as invariant and ahistorical, see Brennan, 1993.

11 The Chagga are a group of people living on the slopes of Mount Kilimanjaro in Tanzania. A number of anthropological studies have been written on the Chagga, and this discussion is based on a reinterpretation of the data offered in the following sources (Dundas, 1924; Emanatian, 1996; Falk Moore, 1976; 1977; 1986; Gutmann, 1926; 1932; 1935; 1938; Raum, 1939; 1940; Setel, 1996; 1999).

12 The last full initiation camp for boys in Old Moshi was held around 1850, but shortened versions survived until 1927 (Gutmann, 1926; 1932). Raum records the last camps in Machame to have been held in the 1890s (Raum, 1940: 320). There are obvious questions about the reliability of the anthropological data on the male initiation rituals, which was all collected through recollection. However, the crucial role of faecal material in Chagga symbolism and ritual is well attested to by more recent data. Even if we assume that some of the accounts of the initiation rituals are fabrications, we should remember Freud's injunction that all lies contain elements of the truth. The correctness of the data is therefore perhaps less important than the fact that the stories take the particular form they do.

13 Setel notes that in some areas *mregho* were still being used for teaching in 1998 (Setel, 1999: 256).

14 In many contexts in the world, biology and culture do not map easily and unproblematically onto reproduction and sexuality. This argument requires careful elaboration, but it is one of the reasons why the debate between feminist philosophers and psychoanalytic theorists regarding the margins of negotiation with regard to sexed identities in the context of the 'de-naturalization' of reproduction and multiple sexualities (e.g. Butler, 2004) are sometimes misconceived.

15 I develop this argument further in chapter 7.

Chapter 6 Being and Having

1 These kinds of issues were a problem from the earliest days of psychoanalysis and required constant specification of analytical level: '[W]e have two kinds of unconscious – the one which is latent but capable of becoming conscious, and the one which is repressed and which is not, in itself and without more ado, capable of becoming conscious. The latent, which is unconscious only descriptively, not in the dynamic sense, we call *preconscious*; we restrict the term *unconscious* to the dynamically unconscious repressed' (Freud, 1984b[1923]: 353).

2   Anthropological data make it clear that none of these terms consistently defines stable entities, and that distinctions between sex and gender, for example, are not necessarily cross-culturally applicable, in that they do not necessarily map easily onto the theories and metaphysics of other societies and cultures.

3   Both Grosz (1994: ch. 2) and Butler (1993: ch. 2) discuss Freud's work on the body ego and narcissism brilliantly, and make a clear case for a reformulated understanding of the sexed body.

4   Women eat ferns as part of the mourning rites (Gillison, 1993: 142–3).

5   This is a heavily condensed telling of a myth provided in Gillison, 1993.

Chapter 7   Kinship and Sexuality

1   Excerpted from W. H. Auden's 'Heavy Date', ©1945, in Auden's *Collected Poems*, London: Faber and Faber. Used by permission of Random House, Inc.

2   The debate in anthropology has always been about the male Oedipus complex for the most part; anthropologists, like Freud, have little to say about girls and the female Oedipus complex (cf. Kurtz, 1991; 1993; Lidz and Lidz, 1989; Spiro, 1982a; 1992; Stephens, 1962); see also below.

3   Ernst Jones strongly disagreed with Freud on this point and argued that both sexes have a positive Oedipus complex (Jones, 1927; 1933; 1935).

4   Negative in the sense that instead of relinquishing desire for the mother and identifying with the father, the boy identifies with the mother and has a submissive feminine relation to the father.

5   'Now let our fantasy transgress normal bounds and imagine Freud, not in Vienna, but in Delhi as an Indian doctor working with Hindu neurotics. . . . Is it likely that he would have independently formulated, and foisted on the Indians, the Greek model of the Oedipus complex in the face of a different body of data? I think not. He would have had little choice but to formulate the positive form of the Indian "Oedipus complex" in terms of the Indian clinical and mythological data, i.e., in terms of identification with the mother and submission to the father. He would also have noted that this situation would result in the male developing feminine characteristics – enhanced of course by constitutional bisexuality!' (Obeyesekere, 1990: 86–7).

6   Kurtz's argument here is explicitly developed contra Sudhir Kakar (Kakar, 1978: 87–103; 1982). Kakar's view is that the early relationship to the mother is extremely close and that the move into the world of men is abrupt and bewildering. However, at other points, Kurtz's and Kakar's views emerge along parallel lines. Kakar actually argues that fatherhood must be understood contextually, that the 'western' father cannot stand as the model for India, and that it is not the individual

biological father, but the whole assembly of elder males in the family who demand that the boy relinquish his close tie to the mother.

7   Despite the fact that Kurtz frames his arguments contra Kakar, the latter makes a similar point with regard to the boy's relation to the father, which is mediated by the demands of group attachment: 'For the strength and cohesion of the extended family depend on a certain emotional diffusion; it is essential that nuclear cells do not build up within the family, or at the very least, that these cells do not involve intense emotional loyalties that potentially exclude other family members and their interests' (Kakar, 1982: 422).

8   See Ingham (1996) and Spiro (1992) for a critique of Kurtz; and see Kurtz (1992: ch. 8; 1993) for rejoinders to Spiro.

9   This is exactly the argument that Ottenberg (1989) makes with regard to boys' secret societies in West Africa.

10 Once again, it is men who are the subject of interest here, despite the existence of initiation rituals for women (cf. Allen, 1967; Brown, 1963; La Fontaine, 1985a; Lutkehaus and Roscoe, 1995; Young, 1965). The link between initiation rituals and sexed identity has been almost exclusively explored in relation to male subjects. There is very little work on girls and what there is tends to focus on their relations to their mothers and other significant females. This situation parallels the difficulties in psychoanalysis in theorizing the female Oedipus complex and the relation of girls to their fathers. In anthropology, this situation has arisen because of the history of the way questions have been framed. The influence of Freud on anthropology in Europe and the United States in the 1940s and 1950s, and particularly on the culture and personality school, established a series of questions about boys, their relations to their mothers, and aggressiveness that gave rise to a very specific approach to initiation as an aspect of socialization. As Margaret Mead argued from the 1930s onwards, sex has something to do with temperament, and both are linked to questions of child-rearing and socialization (cf. Mead, 1935). Mead's discussion in *Male and Female* (1977[1949]) of how Iatmul boys first identified with their mothers and subsequently had to be resocialized as men was an early example of a set of discussions conjoining childrearing practices with initiation, sexed identities, male dominance and male envy of women's reproductive functions.

11 'Circumcision is the symbolic substitute for the castration which the primal father once inflicted upon his sons in the plenitude of his absolute power, and whoever accepted that symbol was showing by it that he was prepared to submit to the father's will, even if it imposed the most painful sacrifice on him' (Freud, 1985e[1939(1934–8)]: 369–70); see also Freud, 1985d[1913].

12 For an overview, see Allen, 1967: 1–27.

13 But, see Nunberg (1949) for a fascinating discussion of bisexual fantasies and circumcision.

14 'Societies which have sleeping arrangements in which the mother and baby share the same bed for at least a year to the exclusion of the father and societies which have a taboo restricting the mother's sexual behavior for at least a year after childbirth will be more likely to have a ceremony of transition from boyhood to manhood than those societies where these conditions do not occur (or occur for briefer periods)' (Whiting et al., 1958: 364).

15 In subsequent articles, this theory was further developed to elaborate the notion of status envy whereby, since the mother controls the boy's access to resources – food, water, love, comfort, etc. – the boy envies her status and thus identifies with her and her role in the first years of his life (Burton and Whiting, 1961; d'Andrade, 1973; Whiting, 1960). Mere love and attention are not enough to bring about identification. A stronger imperative – status envy – has to be posited to account for the boy's wish to be like the mother, to identify with her.

16 These studies in anthropology were influenced by – and in turn influenced – a series of studies in psychology and child development on father absence and paternal behaviour, and the masculinity and behaviour, including sex role identification, of young boys (see Biller, 1971; 1976; Green, 1974; Leichty, 1960; Santrock, 1970), as well as by a series of psychoanalytic and psychological studies of transsexuals and differentiation from the mother (e.g. Greenson, 1966; 1968; Loewald, 1951; Socarides, 1973; Stoller, 1966; 1968; 1974).

17 It should be noted, however, that in Africa in the 1960s and 1970s, there were a large number of studies of mother–child interaction and infant care, but these did not normally draw on psychoanalytic theory (cf. Ainsworth, 1967; Kilbride and Kilbride, 1975; Lusk and Lewis, 1972), as well as a series of studies on the cognitive development and mental functioning of children (see Evans, 1970 for an overview).

18 The notion that the result of differentiation from the mother should be an autonomous self is an ethnocentric one, as noted earlier. However, Lidz and Lidz do acknowledge that: 'The processes by which boys gain a firm male identity in Papua New Guinea are obviously very different from the psychoanalytic concepts based primarily on analyses and observations in western societies' (1989: 187). In general, they want to focus more on the pre-oedipal period and less on the oedipal transition, and this is in keeping, as chapter 4 shows, with recent thinking in psychoanalytic theory. What they also stress however is that the way a boy deals with the loss of his mother will depend not just on the individual or on how the parents relate to each other, but on the nature of family transactions as a whole (ibid.: 185; 1977: 28). In other words, differentiation is not accomplished either by the mother or the father acting alone, but by larger kinship and group structures.

19 There are a number of problems with analyses of this kind, and many involve the use of ordinary language terms to designate psychological processes (see chapter 2). Terms like 'envy', 'engulfment', 'fear' and

even 'anxiety' are often used to describe such processes, but are often little more than interpretations of putative responses to observed sociological or ethnographic facts. Langness, for example, has been very critical of the idea that Bena Bena men can in anyway be said to 'envy' women's procreative functions on the basis that they once practised initiation rituals essentially similar to their neighbours the Gahuku-Gama involving blood-letting and cane-swallowing. He argues that men are in no doubt about their role in reproduction and that they are in a commanding and controlling position in a society that is dominated by an aggressive male cult. However, this is not to say 'that males do not emulate procreation or that they do not attempt to control it', just that it cannot be said that they 'envy' women's powers (Langness, 1974: 202).

20 Following Freud, it has long been suggested in the psychology, psychoanalytic and child development literature that boys who have absent or ineffectual fathers and a close relationship with their mothers are more likely to develop homosexual patterns of behaviour (cf. Bieber et al., 1962; Green, 1987; Saghir and Robbins, 1973; West, 1967). This work suffers from the same problems as the more general arguments about father absence or paternal deprivation, namely that absence and deprivation are context-dependent and interpretive terms rather than analytic concepts, as are such notions as maternal dominance, maternal identification and devaluation of the male role. There have been a number of studies that have suggested that father absence is not a good predictor of sex role behaviour in boys precisely because key variables and/or analytic concepts are too broadly or ethnocentrically defined to make the studies reliable (cf. Biller, 1971; Harrington, 1970; Herzog and Sudia, 1971). Consistent conflation of homosexuality with the non-masculine, and of variation in sex role identification with psychopathology is a common feature of much of the literature (cf. Stoller, 1985). There are also methodological problems such as a failure to adequately compare so-called father-absent families with father-present ones, and the fact that individuals with parental problems are over-represented in any set of individuals with psychological problems. However, in terms of cross-cultural analysis, these methodological problems are compounded by the necessity of extrapolating from families in western societies to society-level socialization practices and social structures in non-western ones (cf. Rabain, 1979). Such extrapolation frequently takes little account of cultural variation in kinship practices and roles, in local understandings of parental behaviour and roles and/or of the cultural desirability of certain outcomes in terms of sexuality and gender roles (cf. Kakar, 1978; 1982; Schurmans, 1972). In consequence, much of the work on father absence in anthropology suffers from the fact that psychological assumptions are made about other cultures that are often not adequately validated by independent psychological evidence, and which are based on

further assumptions about cross-cultural continuities that are not verified by anthropological work on indigenous psychology (cf. Levine,
1973; 1981; Obeyesekere, 1981; 1990). This is surprising given that
scholars (psychologists, anthropologists and psychiatrists) working on
Africa in the 1960s and 1970s, particularly those associated with the
Fann Hospital in Dakar, Senegal, were using indigenous concepts and
ideas to make sense of personality structures and developmental
processes, as well as illness and healing (cf. Ortigues and Ortigues,
1966; Zempleni and Rabain, 1965; Field, 1960; Forssen, 1979).

21 In the thirty years since Herdt began studying the Sambia, there have
been enormous changes in the nature and extent of the rites described
here, and in the social, economic and political life of the Sambia. Many
Sambia are now Christians and would want to disassociate themselves
from the rites described here and the whole corpus of beliefs and practices surrounding them. I use the present tense throughout my account
of the Sambia material as a device to convey the status of this material as a form of exegesis or 'theory', and not as a means to imply
that these rites and/or beliefs are upheld in the present day in an
unchanged form.

22 Male cults involving secrecy and segregation, traumatic initiations,
imitation of women's procreative powers, theories of male-controlled
growth and anxieties about women's bodily fluids and their effects on
male bodies are well documented from other parts of the world (cf.
Crocker, 1985; Chapman, 1982; Gregor, 1985; Hiatt, 1971; Murphy,
1959; Welmers, 1949).

23 Nose-bleeding is likened to female menstruation in a number of New
Guinea contexts (Hogbin, 1970; Lewis, 1980; Lidz and Lidz, 1977;
Read, 1965). However, the Sambia believe that while nose-bleeding is
not the same as menstruation, it is its equivalent (Herdt, 1999: 157).

24 It has been suggested that the purpose of ritual homosexuality and
indeed traumatic initiation rites is to put a brake on heterosexual
development, to control the sexual impulses of young men and turn
them away from the wives of older men. This last is said to be more
important in societies where the age gap between husband and wife
is large. Institutionalized homosexual sex, female avoidance taboos,
fear of menstrual blood and semen depletion all work to turn boys
away from heterosexual sex. However, as Stoller and Herdt (1982:
43–4) point out, this is only relevant to actual heterosexual sex, it does
not apply to heterosexuality in general.

25 Knauft (1986: 268) makes the same point for the Gebusi.

26 The role of kinship and marriage in structuring homoerotic relationships and their wider meanings has been noted for a wide range of
Melanesian societies (Herdt, 1999: ch. 9).

27 Herdt has long been cautious about the use of the term homosexuality in his work, first preferring the phrase 'boy-inseminating rites'
(Herdt, 1991; 1993a), and later the term 'homoerotics' (Herdt, 1999).

28 See Aron (1995: 204) for a related argument.
29 Langness makes the same point for the Bena Bena (Langness, 1990: 396).
30 Knauft (1986: 271) argues for the Gebusi that homosexual relations develop between unrelated boys and young men through spontaneous homoeroticism.
31 There are a significant number of societies in Melanesia that practise ritual homosexuality, but it makes little sense to treat them as a single category for comparative purposes, since the fact that they all practise homosexuality says as little and as much about them as the fact that all also practise heterosexuality (cf. Herdt 1991; 1993a; Elliston, 1995: 862–3; Allen, 1998; Knauft, 1993).

Chapter 8   Mothers and Men

1 This point is reinforced in the account in the myth of the initial sexual encounter between the women and the young hero which does not privilege the penis as the site of sexual exchange or pleasure.
2 Weiner makes a similar point in this Lacanian-inspired analysis of myth in Papua New Guinea, demonstrating that the very contingency of language is a guarantee of its incompleteness (Weiner, 1995: xx–xxi, 10).
3 The MacGuffin is a device employed by Hitchcock in order to create motivation and drive for the characters in a given film. Hitchcock used a MacGuffin in most of his films. In itself it was never important, but the fact that it got the plot moving and spurred characters to action was. One of the best MacGuffins ever – in the film *North by Northwest* – was a person who did not exist, but was obsessively pursued by the main character throughout the film.
4 Juillerat actually speaks more precisely of the rite as reworking the loss of both the mother and the father incarnated in the totemic coconut and sago palms. His argument is that these totems are 'sacralized absences' (Juillerat, 2001: 187).
5 Weiner (1995) makes an analogous argument in his analysis of ritual and myth in New Guinea which he analyses as seeking to make things – including interpretations – incomplete rather than complete.
6 Juillerat notes that this part of the rite is not performed if the Naven is for a young woman (Juillerat, 2001: 218, n7). Silverman states that most Naven are occasioned by male rather than female achievements, and that the uncle is prohibited from performing *nggariik* on his nieces (Silverman, 2001: 140). Bateson, however, noted this gesture as being performed on nieces (Bateson, 1936: 17–18; see also Houseman and Severi, 1998: 50).
7 The various approaches have been carefully analysed and summarized by both Juillerat (2001) and Silverman (2001) and do not bear repeating here.

8   The eastern Iatmul also practise sister exchange and elective marriage (Silverman, 2001: 105).
9   According to the kinship system of the eastern Iatmul, the male term for daughter-in-law is *nyame*, and this applies to all categories of women regardless of prior kinship links to the groom and his father. However, only in the case of *iai* marriage is a woman conceptualized as mother and called as such by her father-in-law before the marriage takes place. Thus, in such instances the maternal associations of the bride not only precede the marriage, but motivate it. Other daughters-in-law only acquire the terminological status of mother after marriage, and unlike the *iai* brides who are seen as genuinely nurturing, are often seen as greedy and failing to support the groom's parents (Silverman, 2001: 108–9).
10 In conventional psychoanalytic thinking, this tension is resolved through the Oedipus complex, which forces the child to make a choice, to identify on one side and to love on the other. My view is that the Melanesian material demonstrates that this choice, if it is ever made, does not produce a clear-cut outcome and remains a fundamental tension which finds cultural elaboration. See also chapter 6.

Chapter 9   Social Transformations

1   This is presumably what Tuzin means when he writes of the Tambaran initiation cycle that it was 'the personified mystique of a total way of life' (1980: 325).
2   My account of the Tambaran and associated myths is entirely based on the work of Donald Tuzin, and makes extensive use of his insightful interpretations (Tuzin, 1976; 1980; 1982; 1991; 1997).
3   With the exception of one, *maolimu*, which was owned by dogs (Tuzin, 1980: 79–80).
4   As Tuzin makes clear, this interpretation was given particular force and moment by his own return from America after a long period of absence, in the context of a series of importance connections and associations linking him to the Nambweapa'w myth and its origins (Tuzin, 1997: ch. 6).
5   I am asking this question rhetorically here and I am more than mindful of the recent critiques of feminist theories of agency and self determination advanced so powerfully by Saba Mahmood (2005).
6   A number of anthropologists have discussed the impact of colonialism and missionization on gender identity, self-worth and ideas about the qualities necessary to be a moral person, and indeed to be a modern person in Melanesia, noting the damaging effects of long-run inequality on local identities and commenting that masculinity is under particular strain. There are also reports of villagers equating poverty with aggression and lack of co-operation (e.g. Brison,

1995; Gewertz and Errington, 1993a; 1993b; Kulick, 1992; Lattas, 1991; White, 1991).

7   A number of anthropologists have noted that male cults in Melanesia have gone through cycles of abandonment and revival (Brison, 1995). In some cases, the men have exposed their secrets to women and children, and in others missionaries or colonial officials have entered men's houses, exposed and destroyed ritual objects (Gillison, 1993; Bateson, 1936). In some cases the cults later revived, a fascinating situation that would bear further study.

References

E. Abel, B. Christian and H. Moglen (eds.) (1997) *Female Subjects in Black and White: Race, Psychoanalysis and Feminism*. Berkeley: University of California Press.

L. Abu-Lughod (1986) *Veiled Sentiments: Honor and Poetry in a Bedouin Society*. Berkeley: University of California Press.

P. Adams (1989) 'Of female bondage', in T. Brennan (ed.), *Between Feminism and Psychoanalysis*. London: Routledge.

M. Ainsworth (1967) *Infancy in Uganda: Infant Care and the Growth of Love*. Baltimore: Johns Hopkins University Press.

M. Allen (1967) *Male Cults and Secret Initiations in Melanesia*. Melbourne: Melbourne University Press.

M. Allen (1998) 'Male cults revisited: the politics of blood versus semen', *Oceania* 68: 189–99.

L. Althusser (1971) *Lenin and Philosophy*. New York: Monthly Review Press.

A. Appadurai (1996) *Modernity at Large: Cultural Dimensions of Globalization*. Minneapolis: University of Minnesota Press.

L. Aron (1995) 'The internalized primal scene', *Psychoanalytic Dialogues* 5(2): 195–237.

H. Barry and A. Schlegel (1980) 'Early childhood precursors of adolescent initiation ceremonies', *Ethos* 8: 132–45.

F. Barth (1975) *Ritual and Knowledge among the Baktaman of New Guinea*. New Haven: Yale University Press.

F. Barth (1990) 'The guru and the conjurer: transactions in knowledge and the shaping of culture in southeast Asia and Melanesia', *Man* 25(4): 640–53.

D. Bassin (2002) 'Beyond the he and the she: toward the reconciliation of masculinity and femininity in the postoedipal female mind', in M.

Dimen and V. Goldner (eds.), *Gender in Psychoanalytic Space: Between Clinic and Culture*. New York: Other Press, 2002.

G. Bateson (1936) *Naven: A Survey of the Problems Suggested by a Composite Picture of the Culture of a New Guinea Tribe Drawn from Three Points of View*. Cambridge: Cambridge University Press.

D. Battaglia (ed.) (1995) *Rhetorics of Self-Making*. Berkeley: University of California Press.

T. Beidelman (1964) 'Pig (Guluwe): an essay on Ngulu sexual symbolism and ceremony', *Southwestern Journal of Anthropology* 20: 359–92.

T. Beidelman (1997) *The Cool Knife: Imagery of Gender, Sexuality, and Moral Education in Kaguru Initiation Ritual*. Washington, DC: Smithsonian Institution Press.

A. Bell and M. Weinberg (1978) *Homosexualities: A Study of Diversity among Men and Women*. New York: Harper and Row.

R. Benedict (1934) *Patterns of Culture*. Boston: Houghton Mifflin.

R. Benedict (1946) *The Chrysanthemum and the Sword*. Boston: Houghton Mifflin.

J. Benjamin (1986) 'A desire of one's own: psychoanalytic feminism and intersubjective space', in T. de Lauretis (ed.), *Feminist Studies/Critical Studies*. Bloomington: Indiana University Press.

J. Benjamin (1988) *The Bonds of Love*. New York: Pantheon.

J. Benjamin (1995) *Like Subjects, Like Objects: Essays on Recognition and Sexual Difference*. New Haven: Yale University Press.

J. Benjamin (1998) *Shadow of the Other: Intersubjectivity and Gender in Psychoanalysis*. London: Routledge.

J. Benjamin (2004) 'Revisiting the riddle of sex: an intersubjective view of masculinity and femininity', in I. Matthis (ed.), *Dialogues on Sexuality, Gender and Psychoanalysis*. London: Karnac.

B. Bettelheim (1954) *Symbolic Wounds: Puberty Rites and the Envious Male*. Glencoe, Ill.: The Free Press.

P. Bidou, J. Galinier and B. Juillerat (1999) 'Arguments', *L'Homme* 149: 7–23.

I. Bieber et al. (1962) *Homosexuality: A Psychoanalytic Study*. New York: Basic Books.

H. Biller (1971) *Father, Child, and Sex Role*. Lexington, Mass.: Heath and Co.

H. Biller (1976) 'The father and personality development', in M. Lamb (ed.), *Role of the Father in Child Development*. New York: Wiley.

K. Birth (1994) 'British anthropology and psychoanalysis before World War II: the evolution of asserted irrelevance', *Canberra Anthropology* 17(1): 53–69.

M. Bloch (1989) *Ritual, History and Power: Selected Papers in Anthropology*. London: Athlone Press.

M. Bloch (1998) *How We Think They Think: Anthropological Approaches to Cognition, Memory and Literacy*. Boulder, Colo.: Westview Press.

H. Blum et al. (1988) *Fantasy, Myth and Reality: Essays in Honor of Jacob A. Arlow, M.D.* Madison Conn.: International University Press.

K. Bornstein (1994) *Gender Outlaw*. London: Routledge.

P. Bourdieu (1977) *Outline of a Theory of Practice*. Cambridge: Cambridge University Press.

P. Bourdieu (1990) *The Logic of Practice*. Cambridge: Polity.

P. Bourdieu (2001) *Masculine Domination*. Cambridge: Polity.

M. Bowie (1991) *Lacan*. London: Fontana Press.

L. B. Boyer (1978) 'On the mutual influences of anthropology and psychoanalysis', *Journal of Psychological Anthropology* 1: 265–96.

J. Bowlby (1969) *Attachment and Loss*. Vol I: *Attachment*. New York: Basic Books.

J. Bowlby (1973) *Attachment and Loss*. Vol II: *Separation and Anxiety*. New York: Basic Books.

R. Braidotti (1994) *Nomadic Subjects: Embodiment and Sexual Difference in Contemporary Feminist Theory*. New York: Columbia University Press.

R. Braidotti (1997) 'Comments on Felski's "The Doxa of Difference": working through sexual difference', *Signs* 23(1): 23–40.

R. Braidotti (2002) *Metamorphoses: Towards a Materialist Theory of Becoming*. Cambridge: Polity Press.

R. Braidotti and J. Butler (1994) 'Feminism by any other name', *Differences* 6(2–3): 27–61.

J. Brain (1977) 'Sex, incest and death: initiation rites reconsidered', *Current Anthropology* 18: 191–208.

T. Brennan (1993) *History after Lacan*. London: Routledge.

K. Brison (1995) 'Changing constructions of masculinity in a Sepik society', *Ethnology* 34(3): 155–75.

J. Brown (1963) 'A cross-cultural study of female initiation rites', *American Anthropologist* 65: 837–53.

R. Burton (1972) 'Cross-sex identity in Barbados', *Developmental Psychology* 6: 365–74.

R. Burton and J. Whiting (1961) 'The absent father and cross sex identity', *Merrill-Palmer Quarterly of Behavior and Development* 7: 85–95.

J. Butler (1990) *Gender Trouble: Feminism and the Subversion of Identity*. London: Routledge.

J. Butler (1993) *Bodies that Matter: On the Discursive Limits of Sex*. London: Routledge.

J. Butler (1994) 'Against proper objects', *Differences* 6(2–3): 1–26.

J. Butler (1995a) 'For a careful reading', in S. Benhabib, J. Butler, D. Cornell and N. Fraser (eds.), *Feminist Contentions: A Philosophical Exchange*. London: Routledge.

J. Butler (1995b) 'Melancholy gender – refused identification', *Psychoanalytic Dialogues* 5(2): 165–80.

J. Butler (2004) *Undoing Gender*. London: Routledge.

S. Caldwell (1999) 'The bloodthirsty tongue and the self-feeding breast: homosexual fellatio fantasy in a South Indian ritual tradition', in T. G Vaidyanathan and J. Kripal (eds.), *Vishnu on Freud's Desk: A Reader in Psychoanalysis and Hinduism*. New Delhi: Oxford University Press.

M. Carstairs (1967) *The Twice Born: A Study of a Community of High Caste Hindus*. Bloomington: University of Indiana Press.

C. Castoriadis (1984) *Crossroads in the Labyrinth*. Brighton: Harvester Press.

C. Castoriadis (1987) *The Imaginary Institution of Society*. Cambridge: Polity.

C. Castoriadis (1994) 'Radical imagination and the social instituting imaginary', in G. Robinson and J. Rundell (eds.), *Rethinking Imagination: Culture and Creativity*. London: Routledge.

C. Castoriadis (1997) 'The crisis of the identification process', *Thesis Eleven* 49: 85–98.

S. C. Chang (1988) 'The nature of the self: a transcultural view', *Transcultural Psychiatric Research Review* 25: 169–203.

A. Chapman (1982) *Drama and Power in a Hunting Society: The Selk'nam of Tierra del Fuego*. Cambridge: Cambridge University Press.

J. Chasseguet-Smirgel (1970) 'Feminine guilt and the Oedipus complex', in J Chasseguet-Smirgel (ed.), *Female Sexuality: New Psychoanalytic Views*. London: Karnac Books.

N. Chodorow (1978) *The Reproduction of Mothering*. Berkeley: University of California Press.

N. Chodorow (1989) *Feminism and Psychoanalytic Theory*. New Haven: Yale University Press.

N. Chodorow (1994) *Femininities, Masculinities, Sexualities: Freud and Beyond*. London: Free Association Books.

H. Cixous (1980a) 'Sorties', in E. Marks and I. de Courtivron (eds.), *New French Feminisms*. Amherst: University of Massachusetts Press.

H. Cixous (1980b) 'The laugh of the Medusa', in E. Marks and I. de Courtivron (eds.), *New French Feminisms*. Amherst: University of Massachusetts Press.

H. Cixous (1994a) 'Extreme fidelity', in S. Sellers (ed.), *The Hélène Cixous Reader*. London: Routledge.

H. Cixous (1994b) 'First names of no one', in S. Sellers (ed.), *The Hélène Cixous Reader*. London: Routledge.

S. Coates (1997) 'Is it time to jettison the concept of developmental lines?', *Gender and Psychoanalysis* 2(1): 35–54.

A. Cohen (1994) *Self-Consciousness: An Alternative Anthropology of Identity*. London: Routledge.

R. Collignon (1978) 'Vingt ans de travaux à la clinique psychia-trique de Fann-Dakar', *Psychopathologie Africaine* 14(2–3): 133–324.

J. Comaroff and J. L. Comaroff (2000) 'Millennial capitalism: first thoughts on a second coming', *Public Culture* 12(2): 291–343.

J. Copjec (1994) *Read My Desire: Lacan Against the Historicists*. Boston, Mass.: MIT Press.

T. Csordas (1990) 'Embodiment as a paradigm for anthropology', *Ethos* 18: 5–47.

T. Csordas (1994) *The Sacred Self: A Cultural Phenomenology of Charismatic Healing*. Berkeley: University of California Press.

D. Cornell (1997) "Comment on Felski's "The Doxa of Difference": diverging differences', *Signs* 23(1): 41–56.

V. Crapanzano (1980) *Tuhami: Portrait of a Moroccan.* Chicago: Chicago University Press.

J. C. Crocker (1985) *Vital Souls: Bororo Cosmology, Natural Symbolism and Shamanism.* Tucson: University of Arizona Press.

A. Damasio (1995) *Descartes' Error: Emotion, Reason, and the Human Brain.* New York: Avon Books.

A. Damasio (2000) *The Feeling of What Happens: Body, Emotion and the Making of Consciousness.* London: Vintage.

R. d'Andrade (1973) 'Father absence, identification and identity', *Ethos* 1: 440–55.

R. d'Andrade (1992) 'Schemas and motivation', in R. d'Andrade and C. Strauss (eds.), *Human Motives and Cultural Models.* Cambridge: Cambridge University Press.

J. de Boeck (1991) 'Of bushbucks without horns: male and female initiation among the Aluund of Southwest Zaire', *Journal des Africanistes* 61(1): 37–71.

M. de Certeau (1984) *The Practice of Everyday Life.* Berkeley: University of California Press.

G. Devereux (1967) *From Anxiety to Method in the Behavioral Sciences.* The Hague: Mouton.

G. Devereux (1978) *Ethnopsychoanalysis: Psychoanalysis and Anthropology as Complementary Frames of Reference.* Berkeley: University of California Press.

G. Devereux (1980) *Basic Problems of Ethnopsychiatry.* Chicago: Chicago University Press.

R. Devisch and C. Brodeur (1999) *The Law of Lifegivers: The Domestication of Desire.* Amsterdam: Harwood Academic Publishers.

I. Diamond and L. Quinby (eds.) (1988) *Feminism and Foucault: Reflections on Resistance.* Boston: Northeastern University Press.

M. Dimen (1991) 'Deconstructing difference: gender, splitting, and transitional space', *Psychoanalytic Dialogues* 1: 335–52.

M. Dimen (1995) 'The third step: Freud, the feminists, and postmodernism', *American Journal of Psychoanalysis* 55(4): 303–19.

M. Dimen and V. Goldner (eds.) (2002) *Gender in Psychoanalytic Space: Between Clinic and Culture.* New York: Other Press.

R. Diprose (1994) *The Bodies of Women: Ethics, Embodiment and Sexual Difference.* London: Routledge.

T. Domenici (1995) 'Exploding the myth of sexual psychopathology: a deconstruction of Fairbairn's anti-homosexual theory', in T. Domenici and R. Lesser (eds.), *Disorienting Sexuality: Psychoanalytic Reappraisals of Sexual Identities.* London: Routledge.

T. Domenici and R. Lesser (eds.) (1995) *Disorienting Sexuality: Psychoanalytic Reappraisals of Sexual Identities.* London: Routledge.

L. Dumont (1970) *Homo Hierarchicus.* Chicago: University of Chicago Press.

C. Dundas (1924) *Kilimanjaro and its People.* London: Witherby.

E. Durkheim (1971[1912]) *The Elementary Forms of the Religious Life*. London: George Allen and Unwin.

A. Elliott (1992) *Social Theory and Psychoanalysis in Transition: Self and Society from Freud to Kristeva*. Oxford: Basil Blackwell.

D. Elliston (1995) 'Erotic anthropology: "ritualized homosexuality" in Melanesia and beyond', *American Ethnologist* 22(4): 848–67.

M. Emanatian (1996) 'Everyday metaphors of lust and sex in Chagga', *Ethos* 24(2): 195–236.

A. L. Epstein (1999) *Gunantuna: Aspects of the Person, The Self and The Individual Among the Tolai*. London: C. Hurst and Co.

J. Evans (1970) *Children in Africa: A Review of Psychological Research*. New York: Teachers College Press.

K. Ewing (1990) 'The illusion of wholeness: "culture", "self", and the experience of inconsistency', *Ethos* 18(3): 251–78.

K. Ewing (1991) 'Can psychoanalytic theories explain the Pakistani Muslim woman? Intrapsychic autonomy and interpersonal engagement in the extended family', *Ethos* 19: 131–60.

K. Ewing (1998) *Arguing Sainthood*. Durham, NC: Duke University Press.

W. R. D. Fairbairn (1952) *Psychoanalytic Studies of the Personality*. London: Routledge.

S. Fairfield, L. Layton and C. Stack (eds.) (2002) *Bringing the Plague: Toward a Postmodern Psychoanalysis*. New York: Other Press.

S. Falk Moore (1976) 'The secret of the men: a fiction of Chagga initiation and its relation to the logic of Chagga symbolism', *Africa* 46: 357–70.

S. Falk Moore (1977) 'The Chagga', in S. F. Moore and P. Pruritt (eds.), *The Chagga and Meru of Tanzania*. London: International African Institute.

S. Falk Moore (1986) *Social Facts and Fabrications: "Customary" Law on Kilimanjaro, 1880–1980*. Cambridge: Cambridge University Press.

I. Fast (1984) *Gender Identity: A Differentiation Model*. Hillsdale, NJ: The Analytic Press.

I. Fast (1990) 'Aspects of early gender development: toward a reformulation', *Psychoanalytic Psychology* 7: 105–17.

D. Fel (1993) 'The "Real" since Freud: Castoriadis and Lacan on socialization and language', *American Imago* 50(2): 161–95.

R. Felski (1997) 'The doxa of difference', *Signs* 23(1): 1–22.

M. Field (1960) *Search for Security: An Ethno-Psychiatric Study of Rural Ghana*. Evanston: Northwestern University Press.

B. Fink (1995) *The Lacanian Subject: Between Language and Jouissance*. Princeton: Princeton University Press.

J. Flax (1990) *Thinking Fragments: Psychoanalysis, Feminism, and Postmodernism in the Contemporary West*. Berkeley: University of California Press.

R. Fogelson (1982) 'Person, self and identity: some anthropological retrospects, circumspects, and prospects', in B. Lee (ed.), *Psychosocial Theories of the Self*. New York: Plenum Press.

A. Forssen (1979) *Roots of Traditional Personality Development among the Zaramo in Coastal Tanzania*. Helsinki: Scandinavian Institute of Africa Studies.

M. Fortes (1987) 'Religion, morality and the person', in J. Goody (ed.), *Religion, Morality and the Person*. Cambridge: Cambridge University Press.

M. Foucault (1982) 'The subject and power', in H. Dreyfus and P. Rabinow (eds.), *Michel Foucault: Beyond Structuralism and Hermeneutics*. Brighton: Harvester Press.

M. Foucault (1985a) 'Sexuality and solitude', in M. Blonsky (ed.), *On Signs: A Semiotic Reader*. Oxford: Basil Blackwell.

M. Foucault (1985b) *The Use of Pleasure*. Harmondsworth: Penguin.

M. Foucault (1986) *The Care of the Self*. Harmondsworth: Penguin.

S. Franklin and S. McKinnon (eds.) (2002) *Relative Values: Reconfiguring Kinship Studies*. Durham, NC: Duke University Press.

N. Fraser (1990) 'The uses and abuses of French discourse theories for feminist politics', *Boundary 2* 17(2): 82–101.

S. Freud (1977a[1908]) 'On the sexual theories of children', in *On Sexuality*, vol. 7. Harmondsworth: Pelican.

S. Freud (1977b[1905]) 'Three essays on the theory of sexuality', in *On Sexuality*, vol. 7. Harmondsworth: Pelican.

S. Freud (1977c[1925]) 'Some psychical consequences of the anatomical distinction between the sexes', in *On Sexuality*, vol. 7. Harmondsworth: Pelican.

S. Freud (1977d[1924]) 'The dissolution of the Oedipus Complex', in *On Sexuality*, vol. 7. Harmondsworth: Pelican.

S. Freud (1977e[1923]) 'The infantile genital organization', in *On Sexuality*, vol. 7. Harmondsworth: Pelican.

S. Freud (1977f[1931]) 'Female sexuality', in *On Sexuality*, vol. 7. Harmondsworth: Pelican.

S. Freud (1982[1930]) *Civilisation and its Discontents*. London: The Hogarth Press.

S. Freud (1984a[1915]) 'The unconscious', in *On Metapsychology*, vol. 11. Harmondsworth: Penguin.

S. Freud (1984b[1923]) 'The Ego and the Id', in *On Metapsychology*, vol. 11. Harmondsworth: Penguin.

S. Freud (1984c[1920]) 'Beyond the pleasure principle', in *On Metapsychology*, vol. 11. Harmondsworth: Penguin.

S. Freud (1984d[1914]) 'On narcissism: an Introduction', in *On Metapsychology*, vol. 11. Harmondsworth: Penguin.

S. Freud (1985a[1929/1930]) 'Civilization and its discontents', in *Civilization, Society and Religion*, vol. 12. Harmondsworth: Penguin.

S. Freud (1985b[1927]) 'The future of an illusion', in *Civilization, Society and Religion*, vol. 12. Harmondsworth: Penguin.

S. Freud (1985c[1908]) '"Civilised" sexual morality and modern nervous illness', in *Civilization, Society and Religion*, vol. 12. Harmondsworth: Penguin.

S. Freud (1985d[1913]) 'Totem and taboo', in *The Origins of Religion*, vol. 13. Harmondsworth: Pelican.

S. Freud (1985e[1939(1934–8)]) 'Moses and monotheism', in *The Origins of Religion*, vol. 13. Harmondsworth: Pelican.

S. Frosh (1997) *For and Against Psychoanalysis*. London: Routledge.

M. Frye (1996) 'The necessity of differences: constructing a positive category of women', *Signs* 21(4): 991–1010.

J. Gallop (1982) *Feminism and Psychoanalysis: The Daughter's Seduction*. London: Macmillan.

J. Gallop (1985) *Reading Lacan*. Ithaca: Cornell University Press.

M. J. Gehrie (1977) 'Psychoanalytic anthropology: a brief review of the state of the art', *American Behavioral Sciences* 20: 721–32.

E. Gerber (1985) 'Rage and obligation: Samoan emotion in conflict', in G. M. White and J. Kirkpatrick (eds.), *Person, Self and Experience: Exploring Pacific Ethnopsychologies*. Berkeley: University of California Press.

D. Gewertz and F. Errington (1993a) 'First contact with God: individualism, agency, and revivalism in the Duke of York Islands', *Cultural Anthropology* 8: 279–305.

D. Gewertz and F. Errington (1993b) 'The triumph of capitalism in East New Britain? A contemporary Papua New Guinea rhetoric of motives', *Oceania* 64: 1–17.

G. Gillison (1991) 'The flute myth and the law of equivalence: origins of a principle of exchange', in M. Godelier and M. Strathern (eds.), *Big Men and Great Men: Personifications of Power in Melanesia*. Cambridge: Cambridge University Press.

G. Gillison (1993) *Between Culture and Fantasy: A New Guinea Highlands Mythology*. Chicago: Chicago University Press.

M. Godelier and J. Hassoun (1996) *Meurtre du Père, Sacrifice de la Sexualité. Approches Psychanalytique*. Paris: Éditions Arcanes.

V. Goldner (1991) 'Toward a critical relational theory of gender', *Psychoanalytic Dialogues* 1(3): 249–72.

A. Green (1999) 'Le psychisme entre anthropologies et psychanalystes: une difference d'intreprétation', *L'Homme* 149: 25–42.

R. Green (1974) *Sexual Identity Conflict in Children and Adults*. New York: Basic Books.

R. Green (1987) *The 'Sissy Boy Syndrome' and the Development of Homosexuality*. New Haven: Yale University Press.

D. Greenberg (1988) *The Construction of Homosexuality*. Chicago: Chicago University Press.

J. R. Greenberg and S. A. Mitchell (1983) *Object Relations in Psychoanalytic Theory*. Cambridge, Mass.: Harvard University Press.

R. Greenson (1966) 'A transvestite boy and a hypothesis', *International Journal of Psychoanalysis* 47: 396–403.

R. Greenson (1968) 'Dis-identifying from mother', *International Journal of Psychoanalysis* 49: 370–4.

T. Gregor (1985) *Anxious Pleasures: The Sexual Lives of an Amazonian People.* Chicago: Chicago University Press.

E. Grosz (1989) *Sexual Subversions: Three French Feminists.* Sydney: Allen and Unwin.

E. Grosz (1990) *Jacques Lacan: A Feminist Introduction.* London: Routledge.

E. Grosz (1994) *Volatile Bodies: Towards a Corporeal Feminism.* Bloomington: Indiana University Press.

H. Guntrip (1968) *Schizoid Phenomena, Object Relations and the Self.* London: Hogarth Press.

H. Guntrip (1973) *Psychoanalytic Theory, Therapy and the Self.* New York: Basic Books.

B. Gutmann (1926) *Das Recht der Dschagga.* Munchen: C. H. Beck.

B. Gutmann (1932) *Die Stammeslehren der Dschagga*, vol. I. Munchen: C. H. Beck.

B. Gutmann (1935) *Die Stammeslehren der Dschagga*, vol. II. Munchen: C. H. Beck.

B. Gutmann (1938) *Die Stammeslehren der Dschagga*, vol. III. Munchen: C. H. Beck.

A. I. Hallowell (1971) *Culture and Experience.* New York: Schocken Books.

A. I. Hallowell (1976) *Contributions to Anthropology.* Chicago: Chicago University Press.

D. Handelman (1979) 'Is Naven ludic? Paradox and the communication of identity', *Social Analysis* 1: 177–91.

R. Harré (1983) *Personal Being: A Theory for Individual Psychology.* Oxford: Basil Blackwell.

C. Harrington (1970) *Errors in Sex Role Behavior in Teenage Boys.* New York: Teachers College Press.

A. Harris (1991) 'Gender as contradiction: a discussion of Freud's "The psychogenesis of a case of homosexuality in a woman"', *Psychoanalytic Dialogues* 2: 197–224.

G. Harris (1989) 'Concepts of individual, self and person in description and analysis', *American Anthropologist* 91: 599–612.

S. Heald, A. Deluz and P.-Y. Jacopin (1994) 'Introduction', in S. Heald and A. Deluz (eds.), *Anthropology and Psychoanalysis: An Encounter Through Culture.* London: Routledge.

P. Heelas (1981) 'Introduction: indigenous psychologies', in P. Heelas and A. Lock (eds.), *Indigenous Psychologies: The Anthropology of the Self.* London: Academic Press.

G. Herdt (1981) *Guardians of the Flutes.* New York: McGraw-Hill.

G. Herdt (1982) 'Sambia nosebleeding rites and male proximity to women', *Ethos* 10: 189–231.

G. Herdt (1987) *The Sambia: Ritual and Gender in New Guinea.* New York: Holt, Reinhart and Winston.

G. Herdt (1989) 'Father presence and ritual homosexuality: paternal deprivation and masculine development in Melanesia reconsidered', *Ethos* 18: 326–70.

G. Herdt (1991) 'Representations of homosexuality: an essay on cultural ontology and historical comparison. Part II', *Journal of the History of Sexuality* 1(4): 603–32.

G. Herdt (1993a) *Ritualized Homosexuality in Melanesia*. Berkeley: University of California Press.

G. Herdt (1993b) 'Introduction to the paperback edition', in *Ritualized Homosexuality in Melanesia*. Berkeley: University of California Press.

G. Herdt (1994) 'Introduction: third sexes and third genders', in G. Herdt (ed.), *Third Sex, Third Gender: Beyond Sexual Dimorphism in Culture and History*. New York: Zone.

G. Herdt (1997) *Same Sex, Different Cultures: Perspectives on Gay and Lesbian Lives*. New York: Westview Press.

G. Herdt (1999) *Sambia Sexual Culture: Essays from the Field*. Chicago: University of Chicago Press.

G. Herdt and R. Stoller (1990) *Intimate Communications: Erotics and the Study of Culture*. New York: Columbia University Press.

E. Herzog and C. Sudia (1971) *Boys in Fatherless Families*. Washington, DC: US Department of Health, Education and Welfare.

L. Hiatt (1971) 'Secret pseudo-procreation rites among the Australian aborigines', in L. Hiatt and C. Jayawardena (eds.), *Anthropology in Oceania*. Sydney: Angus and Robertson.

L. Hiatt (1987) 'Freud and anthropology', in D. Austin-Broos (ed.), *Creating Culture: Profiles in the Study of Cultures*. London: Allen and Unwin.

I. Hogbin (1970) *The Island of Menstruating Men*. Scranton, Penn.: Chandler.

D. Holland and A. Kipnis (1994) 'Metaphors for embarrassment and stories of exposure: the not-so-egocentric self in American culture', *Ethos* 22: 316–42.

R. H. Hook (ed.) (1979a) *Fantasy and Symbol: Studies in Anthropological Interpretation*. London: Academic Press.

R. H. Hook (1979b) 'Phantasy and symbol: a psychoanalytic point of view', in R. H. Hook (ed.), *Fantasy and Symbol: Studies in Anthropological Interpretation*. London: Academic Press.

B. Hooks (1984) *Feminist Theory from Margin to Centre*. Boston: Southend Press.

M. Houseman and C. Severi (1998) *Naven or the Other Self: A Relational Approach to Ritual Action*. Leiden: Brill.

F. Huxley (1985) 'Psychoanalysis and anthropology', in P. Horden (ed.), *Freud and the Humanities*. New York: St Martin's Press.

J. Ingham (1963) 'Malinowski: epistemology and Oedipus', *Kroeber Anthropological Society Papers* 29: 1–14.

J. Ingham (1992) 'Freud in a forest of symbols: the religious background of psychoanalytic anthropology', in D. Spain (ed.), *Psychoanalytic Anthropology after Freud*. New York: Psyche Press.

J. Ingham (1996) 'Oedipality in pragmatic discourse: the Trobriands and Hindu India', *Ethos* 24(4): 559–87.

T. Ingold (1991) 'Becoming persons: consciousness and sociality in human evolution', *Cultural Dynamics* 4(3): 355–78.

L. Irigaray (1985) *This Sex Which Is Not One*. Ithaca: Cornell University Press.

M. Jackson (1996) *Things as They Are: New Directions in Phenomenological Anthropology*. Bloomington: Indiana University Press.

D. Jaffe (1968) 'The masculine envy of woman's procreative function', *Journal of the American Psychoanalytic Association* 16: 521–48.

W. James (1988) *The Listening Ebony: Moral Knowledge, Religion and Power among the Uduk of Sudan*. Oxford: Clarendon Press.

I. Jean-Klein (2000) 'Mothercraft, statecraft, and subjectivity in the Palestinian intifada', *American Ethnologist* 27(1): 100–27.

F. Johnson (1985) 'The western concept of the self', in A. Marsella, G. de Vos and F. Hsu (eds.), *Culture and Self: Asian and Western Perspectives*. London: Tavistock.

A. Jones (1984) 'Julia Kristeva on femininity: the limits of a semiotic politics', *Feminist Review* 18: 56–73.

E. Jones (1925) 'Mother-right and the sexual ignorance of savages', *International Journal of Psychoanalysis* 6: 109–30.

E. Jones (1927) 'The early development of female sexuality', *International Journal of Psychoanalysis* 8: 459–72.

E. Jones (1933) 'The phallic phase', *International Journal of Psychoanalysis* 14: 1–33.

E. Jones (1935) 'Early female sexuality', *International Journal of Psychoanalysis* 16: 263–73.

S. Joseph (1994) 'Brother–sister relationships: connectivity, love, and power in the reproduction of patriarchy in Lebanon', *American Ethnologist* 21(1): 50–73.

B. Juillerat (1991) *Oedipe Chasseur: Une Mythologie du Sujet en Nouvelle-Guinée*. Paris: Presses Universitaires de France.

B. Juillerat (1992a) '"The mother's brother is the breast": incest and its prohibition in the Yafar Yangis', in B. Juillerat (ed.), *Shooting the Sun: Ritual and Meaning in West Sepik*. Washington, DC: Smithsonian Press.

B. Juillerat (1992b) *Shooting the Sun: Ritual and Meaning in West Sepik*. Washington, DC: Smithsonian Press.

B. Juillerat (1995) *L'Avènement du Père: Rite, Représentation, Fantasme dans un Culte Mélanésien*. Paris: Éditions de la Maison des Sciences de L'Homme.

B. Juillerat (1996) 'Anthropologie/psychanalyse: les handicaps d'un dialogue', *Journal des Anthropologues* 64–5: 19–31.

B. Juillerat (2001) *Penser l'Imaginaire: Essais d'Anthropologie Psychanalytique*. Lausanne: Éditions Payot.

S. Kakar (1978) *The Inner World: A Psychoanalytic Study of Childhood and Society in India*. New Delhi: Oxford University Press.

S. Kakar (1982) 'Fathers and sons: an Indian experience', in S. H. Cath et al. (eds.), *Father and Child*. Boston: Little, Brown.

S. Kakar (1985) 'Psychoanalysis and non-western cultures', *International Review of Psychoanalysis* 12: 441–8.

A. Kardiner (1945) *Psychological Frontiers of Society*. New York: Columbia University Press.

R. Keesing (1982) 'Introduction', in G. Herdt (ed.), *Rituals of Manhood: Male Initiation in Papua New Guinea*. Berkeley: University of California Press.

B. Kilborne (1981) 'Dream interpretation and culturally constituted defense mechanisms', *Ethos* 9: 294–312.

J. Kilbride and P. Kilbride (1975) 'Sitting and smiling behavior of Baganda infants: the influence of culturally constituted experience', *Journal of Cross-Cultural Psychology* 6: 88–107.

S. Kirschner (1992) 'Anglo-American values in post-Freudian psychoanalysis', in D. Spain (ed.), *Psychoanalytic Anthropology after Freud*. New York: Psyche Press.

M. Kitahara (1974) 'Living quarter arrangements in polygyny and circumcision and segregation of males at puberty', *Ethnology* 13(4): 401–13.

M. Kitahara (1976) 'A cross cultural test of the Freudian theory of circumcision', *International Journal of Psychoanalytic Psychotherapy* 5: 535–46.

M. Klein (1997a[1952a]) 'The origins of transference', in *Envy and Gratitude and Other Works*. London: Vintage.

M. Klein (1997b[1952b]) 'The mutual influences in the development of ego and id', in *Envy and Gratitude and Other Works*. London: Vintage.

M. Klein (1997c[1946]) 'Notes on some schizoid mechanisms', in *Envy and Gratitude and Other Works*. London: Vintage.

M. Klein (1997d[1948]) 'On the theory of anxiety and guilt', in *Envy and Gratitude and Other Works*. London: Vintage.

M. Klein (1997e[1959]) 'Our adult world and its roots in infancy', in *Envy and Gratitude and Other Works*. London: Vintage.

M. Klein (1997f[1963]) 'On the sense of loneliness', in *Envy and Gratitude and Other Works*. London: Vintage.

M. Klein (1997g[1958]) 'On the development of mental functioning', in *Envy and Gratitude and Other Works*. London: Vintage.

M. Klein (1998a[1928]) 'Early stages of the Oedipus conflict', in *Love, Guilt and Reparation*. London: Vintage.

M. Klein (1998b[1930]) 'The importance of symbol-formation in the development of the ego', in *Love, Guilt and Reparation*. London: Vintage.

C. Kluckhohn (1943) 'Bronislaw Malinowski 1884–1942', *Journal of American Folklore* 56: 208–19.

B. Knauft (1986) 'Text and social practice: narrative "longing" and bisexuality among the Gebusi of New Guinea', *Ethos* 14: 252–81.

B. Knauft (1993) *South Coast New Guinea Cultures*. Cambridge: Cambridge University Press.

B. Knauft (1996) *Genealogies for the Present in Cultural Anthropology*. London: Routledge.

D. Kondo (1990) *Crafting Selves: Power, Gender, and Discourses of Identity in a Japanese Workplace*. Chicago: Chicago University Press.

W. Kracke (1987a) 'Encounter with other cultures: psychological and epistemological aspects', *Ethos* 15: 58–81.

W. Kracke (1987b) 'Myth in dreams, thought in images: an Amazonian contribution to the psychoanalytic theory of the primary process', in B. Tedlock (ed.), *Dreaming: Anthropological and Psychological Interpretations.* Cambridge: Cambridge University Press.

J. Kristeva (1974) *La Révolution du Langage Poétique.* Paris: Seuil.

J. Kristeva (1980) *Desire in Language: A Semiotic Approach to Literature and Art.* Oxford; Basil Blackwell.

J. Kristeva (1984) *Revolution in Poetic Language.* New York: Columbia University Press.

J. Kristeva (1986) 'Revolution in poetic language', in T. Moi (ed.), *The Kristeva Reader.* Oxford: Basil Blackwell.

D. Kulick (1992) *Language Shift and Cultural Reproduction.* Cambridge: Cambridge University Press.

S. Kurtz (1991) 'Polysexualization: a new approach to Oedipus in the Trobriands', *Ethos* 19(1): 68–101.

S. Kurtz (1992) *All the Mothers are One: Hindu India and the Cultural Reshaping of Psychoanalysis.* New York: Columbia University Press.

S. Kurtz (1993) 'A Trobriand complex', *Ethos* 21(1): 79–103.

W. La Barre (1954) *The Human Animal.* Chicago: Chicago University Press.

W. La Barre (1958) 'The influence of Freud on anthropology', *American Imago* 15: 275–328.

W. La Barre (1978) 'Psychoanalysis and the biology of religion', *Journal of Psychological Anthropology* 1: 57–64.

J. Lacan (1966) *Ecrits.* Paris: Seuil.

J. Lacan (1977) *Ecrits: A Selection.* London: Routledge.

J. Lacan (1978) *The Four Fundamental Concepts of Psychoanalysis.* New York: Norton.

J. Lacan (1985) 'God and the *jouissance* of the woman', in J. Mitchell and J. Rose (eds.), *Feminine Sexuality: Jacques Lacan and the Ecole Freudienne.* London: Macmillan.

J. Lacan (1988a) *The Seminar.* Book I: *Freud's Papers on Technique 1953–1954.* Cambridge: Cambridge University Press.

J. Lacan (1988b) *The Seminar.* Book II: *The Ego in Freud's Theory and in the Technique of Psychoanalysis 1954–1955.* Cambridge: Cambridge University Press.

J. Lacan (1993) *The Seminar.* Book III: *The Psychoses 1955–1956.* London: Routledge.

J. Lacan (1994) *Seminar IV: La Relation d'Objet.* Paris: Seuil.

J. La Fontaine (1985a) *Initiation.* London: Penguin.

J. La Fontaine (1985b) 'Person and individual: some anthropological reflections', in M Carrithers et al. (eds.), *The Category of the Person: Anthropology, Philosophy, History.* Cambridge: Cambridge University Press.

L. Langness (1967) 'Sexual antagonism in the New Guinea Highlands: a Bena Bena example', *Oceania* 37: 161–77.

L. Langness (1974) 'Ritual power and male dominance in the New Guinea Highlands', *Ethos* 2: 189–212.

L. Langness (1990) 'Oedipus in the New Guinea Highlands?', *Ethos* 387–406.

J. Laplanche and J.-B. Pontalis (1968) 'Fantasy and the origins of sexuality', *International Journal of Psychoanalysis* 49(1): 1–18.

A. Lattas (1989) 'Trickery and sacrifice: Tambarans and the appropriation of female reproductive powers in male initiation ceremonies in West New Britain', *Man* 24: 451–69.

A. Lattas (1991) 'Sexuality and cargo cults: the politics of gender and procreation in West New Britain', *Oceania* 6: 230–56.

J. Lave (1990) 'The culture of acquisition and the practice of understanding', in J. Stigler et al. (eds.), *Cultural Psychology*. Cambridge: Cambridge University Press.

D. Leader (1996) *Why Women Write More Letters Than They Post*. London: Faber and Faber.

K. Leary (1997) 'Race in psychoanalytic space', *Gender and Psychoanalysis* 2: 157–72.

D. Lee (1959) *Freedom and Culture*. New York: Prentice-Hall.

M. Leichty (1960) 'The effect of father-absence during early childhood upon the oedipal situation as reflected in young adults', *Merrill-Palmer Quarterly of Behavior and Development* 6: 212–17.

D. Leland (1989) 'Lacanian psychoanalysis and French feminism: toward an adequate political psychology', *Hypatia* 3(3): 81–103.

C. Lévi-Strauss (1988) *The Jealous Potter*. Chicago: Chicago University Press.

R. Levine (1973) *Culture, Behavior and Personality*. Chicago: Aldine.

R. Levine (1981) 'Psychoanalytic theory and the comparative study of human development', in R. Munroe et al. (eds.), *Handbook of Cross-cultural Human Development*. New York: Garland.

R. Levine (1992) 'The self in an African culture', in D. Spain (ed.), *Psychoanalytic Anthropology After Freud*. New York: Psyche Press.

R. Levy (1973) *Tahitians: Mind and Experience in the Society Islands*. Chicago: University of Chicago Press.

R. Levy (1983) 'Introduction: self and emotion', *Ethos* 11: 128–34.

G. Lewis (1980) *Day of Shining Red: An Essay on Understanding Ritual*. Cambridge: Cambridge University Press.

R. Lidz and T. Lidz (1977) 'Male menstruation: a ritual alternative to the oedipal transition', *International Journal of Psychoanalysis* 58: 17–31.

T. Lidz and R. Lidz (1989) *Oedipus in the Stone Age: A Psychoanalytic Study of Masculinization in Papua New Guinea*. Madison, Conn.: International Universities Press.

G. Lienhardt (1961) *Divinity and Experience*. Oxford: Clarendon Press.

G. Lienhardt (1985) 'Self: public, private. Some African representations', in M. Carrithers et al. (eds.), *The Category of the Person: Anthropology, Philosophy, History*. Cambridge: Cambridge University Press.

D. Lipset (1997) *Mangrove Man: Dialogics of Culture in the Sepik Estuary.* Cambridge: Cambridge University Press.

A. Lock (1981) 'Universal in human cognition', in P. Heelas and A. Lock (eds.), *Indigenous Psychologies: The Anthropology of the Self.* London: Academic Press.

H. Loewald (1951) 'Ego and reality', *International Journal of Psychoanalysis* 32: 10–18.

H. Loewald (1980) 'The waning of the Oedipus complex', in *Papers on Psychoanalysis.* New Haven: Yale University Press.

D. Lusk and M. Lewis (1972) 'Mother–infant interaction and infant development among the Wolof of Senegal', *Human Development* 15(1): 558–69.

N. Lutkehaus and P. Roscoe (eds.) (1995) *Gender Rituals: Female Initiation in Melanesia.* London: Routledge.

C. Lutz (1988) *Unnatural Emotions: Everyday Sentiments on a Micronesian Atoll and their Challenge to Western Theory.* Chicago: University of Chicago Press.

C. Lutz and L. Abu-Lughod (1990a) 'Engendered emotions', in C. Lutz and L. Abu-Lughod (eds.), *Language and the Politics of Emotion.* Cambridge: Cambridge University Press.

C. Lutz and L. Abu-Lughod (eds.) (1990b) *Language and the Politics of Emotion.* Cambridge: Cambridge University Press.

L. McDougall (1975) 'The quest of the Argonauts', in T. Williams (ed.), *Psychological Anthropology.* The Hague: Mouton.

L. McNay (1992) *Foucault and Feminism: Power, Gender and the Self.* Cambridge: Polity.

L. McNay (2000) *Gender and Agency: Reconfiguring the Subject in Feminist and Social Theory.* Cambridge: Polity.

G. Marcus (1998) *Ethnography Through Thick and Thin.* Princeton, NJ: Princeton University Press.

J. Mageo (1998) *Theorizing Self in Samoa: Emotions, Gender, and Sexualities.* Ann Arbor: University of Michigan Press.

J. Mageo (ed.) (2000) *Power and the Self.* Cambridge: Cambridge University Press.

J. Mageo and B. Knauft (2000) 'Introduction: theorizing power and the self', in J Mageo (ed.), *Power and the Self.* Cambridge: Cambridge University Press.

S. Mahmood (2005) *Politics of Piety: The Islamic Revival and the Feminist Subject.* Princeton: Princeton University Press.

B. Malinowski (1939) 'The group and the individual in functional analysis', *American Journal of Sociology* 44(6): 938–64.

B. Malinowski (1955[1927]) *Sex and Repression in Savage Society.* New York: Meridian Books.

I. Matthis (ed.) (2004) *Dialogues on Sexuality, Gender and Psychoanalysis.* London: Karnac.

M. Mauss (1985[1938]) 'A category of the human mind: the notion of person; the notion of self', in M. Carrithers et al. (eds.), *The Category of the Person: Anthropology, Philosophy, History*. Cambridge: Cambridge University Press.

R. May (1986) 'Concerning a psychoanalytic view of maleness', *Psychoanalytic Review* 73: 179–94.

G. H. Mead (1934) *Mind, Self and Society*. Chicago: University of Chicago Press.

M. Mead (1935) *Sex and Temperament in Three Primitive Societies*. London: Routledge and Kegan Paul.

M. Mead (1942[1930]) *Growing Up in New Guinea: A Study of Adolescence and Sex in Primitive Societies*. Harmondsworth: Penguin.

M. Mead (1977[1949]) *Male and Female: A Study of the Sexes in a Changing World*. Westport, Conn.: Greenwood Press.

M. Merleau-Ponty (1962) *The Phenomenology of Perception*. London: Routledge & Kegan Paul.

M. Mines (1988) 'Conceptualizing the person: hierarchical society and individual autonomy in India', *American Anthropologist* 90: 568–79.

M. Mines (1994) *Public Faces, Private Voices: Community and Individuality in South India*. Berkeley: University of California Press.

T. Mischel (1977) 'Conceptual issues in the psychology of the self', in T. Mischel (ed.), *The Self*. Oxford: Basil Blackwell.

J. Mitchell (1974) *Psychoanalysis and Feminism*. Harmondsworth: Penguin.

J. Mitchell (1985) 'Introduction – I', in J. Mitchell and J. Rose (eds.), *Feminine Sexuality: Jacques Lacan and the Ecole Freudienne*. London: W. Norton.

J. Mitchell (1991) 'Commentary on "Deconstructing difference: gender, splitting, and transitional space"' *Psychoanalytic Dialogues* 1(3): 353–59.

J. Mitchell and J. Rose (eds.) (1985) *Feminine Sexuality: Jacques Lacan and the Ecole Freudienne*. London: W. Norton.

C. Mohanty (2003) *Feminism Without Borders: Decolonizing Theory, Practicing Solidarity*. Durham, NC: Duke University Press.

T. Moi (1986) *The Kristeva Reader*. Oxford: Basil Blackwell.

T. Moi (2004) 'From femininity to finitude: Freud, Lacan, and feminism again', in I. Matthis (ed.), *Dialogues on Sexuality, Gender, and Psychoanalysis*. London: Karnac.

H. L. Moore (1986) *Space, Text and Gender: An Anthropological Study of the Marakwet of Kenya*. Cambridge: Cambridge University Press.

H. L. Moore (1988) *Feminism and Anthropology*. Cambridge: Cambridge University Press.

H. L. Moore (1994) *A Passion for Difference: Essays in Anthropology and Gender*. Cambridge: Polity Press.

H. L. Moore (1997a) 'Sex, symbolism and psychoanalysis', *Differences* 9(1): 68–94.

H. L. Moore (1997b) 'Interior landscapes and external worlds: the return of grand theory in anthropology', *The Australian Journal of Anthropology* 8(2): 125–44.

H. L. Moore (1999a) 'Gender, symbolism and praxis: theoretical approaches', in H. L. Moore, T. Sanders and B. Kaare (eds.), *Those Who Play with Fire: Gender, Fertility, and Transformation in East and Southern Africa*. London: Athlone Press.

H. L. Moore (1999b) 'Whatever happened to women and men? Gender and other crises in anthropology', in H. L. Moore (ed.), *Anthropological Theory Today*. Cambridge: Polity.

H. L. Moore (2004) 'On being young', *Anthropological Quarterly* 77(4): 735–45.

H. L. Moore (ed.) (1996) *The Future of Anthropological Knowledge*. London: Routledge.

H. L. Moore, T. Sanders and B. Kaare (eds.) (1999) *Those Who Play with Fire: Gender, Fertility, and Transformation in East and Southern Africa*. London: Athlone Press.

C. Morin and S. Thibierge (2004) 'L'image du corps en neurologie: de la cénesthésie à l'image spéculaire. Apports cliniques et théoriques de la psychanalyse', *L'Évolution Psychiatrique* 69: 417–30.

B. Morris (1978) 'Are there any individuals in India? A critique of Dumont's theory of the individual', *Eastern Anthropologist* 31: 365–77.

B. Morris (1991) *Western Conceptions of the Individual*. Oxford: Berg.

B. Morris (1994) *Anthropology of the Self: The Individual in Cultural Perspective*. London: Pluto Press.

R. Munroe (1980) 'Male transvestism and the couvade', *Ethos* 8: 449–59.

R. Munroe, R. H. Munroe and J. Whiting (1973) 'The couvade: a psychological analysis', *Ethos* 1: 30–74.

R. Munroe, J. Whiting and D. Hally (1969) 'Institutionalized male transvestism and sex distinction', *American Anthropologist* 71: 87–91.

R. Murphy (1959) 'Social structure and sex antagonism', *Southwestern Journal of Anthropology* 15(2): 89–98.

D. Murray (1993) 'What is the Western concept of the self? On forgetting David Hume', *Ethos* 21: 3–23.

S. Nanda (1990) *Neither Man nor Woman: The Hijras of India*. Belmont, Calif.: Wadsworth Publishing Company.

R. Needham (1981) 'Inner states as universals', in P. Heelas and A. Lock (eds.), *Indigenous Psychologies: The Anthropology of the Self*. London: Academic Press.

E. Norbeck, D. Walker and M. Cohen (1962) 'The interpretation of data: puberty rites', *American Anthropologist* 64: 463–85.

H. Nunberg (1949) *Problems of Bisexuality as Reflected in Circumcision*. London: Imago.

G. Obeyesekere (1981) *Medusa's Hair: An Essay on personal Symbols and Religious Experience*. Chicago: University of Chicago Press.

G. Obeyesekere (1990) *The Work of Culture: Symbolic Transformation in Psychoanalysis and Anthropology*. Cambridge: Cambridge University Press.

T. Ogden (1986) *The Matrix of the Mind*. Northvale, NJ: Aronson.

K. Oliver (1993) *Reading Kristeva: Unraveling the Double-Bind*. Bloomington: Indiana University Press.

M.-C. Ortigues and E. Ortigues (1966) *Œdipe Africaine*. Paris: Plon.

S. Ortner (1984) 'Theory in anthropology since the sixties', *Journal of Comparative Society and History* 26(2): 126–47.

S. Ottenberg (1989) *Boyhood Rituals in an African Society: An Interpretation*. Seattle: University of Washington Press.

A. Ouroussoff (1993) 'Illusions of rationality: false premises of the liberal tradition', *Man* 28: 281–98.

S. Pandolfo (1997) *Impasse of the Angels: Scenes from a Moroccan Space of Memory*. Chicago: Chicago University Press.

P. Parin, F. Morgenthaler and G. Parin-Matthey (1980) *Fear Thy Neighbor as Thyself: Psychoanalysis and Society Among the Anyi of West Africa*. Chicago: University of Chicago Press.

S. Parker, J. Smith and J. Ginat (1975) 'Father absence and cross-sex identity: the puberty rites controversy revisited', *American Ethnologist* 2: 687–705.

A. Parsons (1969) *Belief, Magic and Anomie: Essays in Psychosocial Anthropology*. New York: Free Press.

T. Parsons (1957) 'Malinowski and the theory of social systems', in R. Firth (ed.), *Man and Culture: An Evaluation of the Work of Bronislaw Malinowski*. London: Routledge & Kegan Paul.

R. Paul (1976) 'Did the primal crime take place?', *Ethos* 4(3): 311–52.

R. Paul (1982) *The Tibetan Symbolic World: Psychoanalytic Explorations*. Chicago: Chicago University Press.

R. Paul (1989) 'Psychoanalytic anthropology', *Annual Review of Anthropology* 18: 177–202.

R. Paul (1990) 'What does anybody want? Desire, purpose, and the acting subject in the study of culture', *Cultural Anthropology* 5(4): 431–51.

A. Phillips (1988) *Winnicott*. London: Fontana.

C.-H. Pradelles de la Tour (1991) *Ethnopsychanalyse en Pays Bamliléké*. Paris: EPEL.

J. Prosser (1998) *Second Skins: The Body Narratives of Transsexuality*. New York: Columbia University Press.

B. Pulman (1984) 'Anthropologie et psychanalyse: "paix et guerre" entre les herméneutiques', *Connexions* 44: 81–97.

N. Quinn and C. Strauss (1997) *A Cognitive Theory of Cultural Meanings*. Cambridge: Cambridge University Press.

J. Rabain (1979) *L'Enfant du Lignage. Du Sevrage à la Classse d'Âge chez les Wolof du Senegal*. Paris: Payot.

P. Rabinow (1977) *Reflections on Fieldwork in Morocco*. Berkeley: University of California Press.

E. Ragland-Sullivan (1986) *Jacques Lacan and the Philosophy of Psychoanalysis*. Urbana: University of Illinois Press.

A. K. Ramanujan (1999) 'The Indian Oedipus', in T. G. Vaidyanathan and J. Kripal (eds.), *Vishnu on Freud's Desk: A Reader in Psychoanalysis and Hinduism*. New Delhi: Oxford University Press.

C. Ramazonoglu (1993) *Up Against Foucault: Explorations of Some Tensions Between Foucault and Feminism*. London: Routledge.

N. Rapport (1993) *Diverse Worldviews in an English Village*. Edinburgh: Edinburgh University Press.

N. Rapport (1997) *Transcendent Individual: Towards a Literary and Liberal Anthropology*. London: Routledge.

O. Raum (1939) 'Female initiation among the Chaga', *American Anthropologist* 41(4): 554–65.

O. Raum (1940) *Chaga Childhood: A Description of Indigenous Education in an East African Tribe*. London: Oxford University Press.

K. Read (1955) 'Morality and the concept of the person among the Gahuku-Gama', *Oceania* 25: 233–82.

K. Read (1965) *The High Valley*. New York: Scribner.

T. Reik (1962[1946]) *Ritual: Four Psychoanalytic Studies*. New York: Grove Press.

P. Riesman (1977) *Freedom in Fulani Social Life: An Introspective Ethnography*. Chicago: University of Chicago Press.

P. Riesman (1983) 'On the irrelevance of childrearing methods for the formation of personality: an analysis of childhood, personality, and values in two African communities', *Culture, Medicine and Psychiatry* 7: 103–29.

M. Rivera (1989) 'Linking the psychological and the social: feminism, post-structuralism, and multiple personality', *Dissociation* 2(1): 24–31.

A. F. Robertson (1996) 'The development of meaning: ontogeny and culture', *Journal of the Royal Anthropological Institute* 2(4): 591–610.

W. Rogers and J. Long (1968) 'Male models and sexual identification: a case from the out Island Bahamas', *Human Organization* 27: 326–31.

G. Roheim (1942) 'The transition rites', *Psychoanalytic Quarterly* 11: 336–74.

G. Roheim (1950a) *Psychoanalysis and Anthropology: Culture, Personality, and the Unconscious*. New York: International University Press.

G. Roheim (1950b) 'The Oedipus complex, magic and culture', in G. Roheim (ed.), *Psychoanalysis and the Social Sciences*. New York: International Universities Press.

G. Roheim (1971) *The Origin and Function of Culture*. New York: Doubleday Anchor.

M. Rosaldo (1984) 'Towards an understanding of self and feeling', in R. Shweder and R. Levine (eds.), *Culture Theory*. Cambridge: Cambridge University Press.

G. Rosolato (1992) 'Les fantasmes originaires et leurs mythes correspondants', *Nouvelle Revue de Psychanalyse* 46: 223–45.

G. Rubin (1975) 'The traffic in women: notes on the 'political economy of sex', in R. Rapp Reiter (ed.), *Toward an Anthropology of Women*. New York: Monthly Review.

M. Saghir and F. Robbins (1973) *Male and Female Homosexuality*. Baltimore: Williams and Wilkins.

E. Sampson (1993) *Celebrating the Other: A Dialogic Account of Human Nature*. Boulder, Colo.: Westview Press.

J. Santrock (1970) 'Paternal absence, sex-typing, and identification', *Developmental Psychology* 2: 264–72.

D. Schurmans (1972) 'Le problème de l'oedipe en Afrique', *Psychopathologie Africaine* 8(3): 325–53.

J. Scott (1985) *Weapons of the Weak: Everyday Forms of Peasant Resistance*. New Haven: Yale University Press.

K. Seshadri-Crooks (2000) *Desiring Whiteness: A Lacanian Analysis of Race*. London: Routledge.

P. Setel (1996) 'Aids as a paradox of manhood and development in Kilimanjaro, Tanzania', *Social Science and Medicine* 43(8): 1169–78.

P. Setel (1999) *A Plague of Paradoxes: Aids, Culture and Demography in Northern Tanzania*. Chicago: University of Chicago Press.

C. Shepherdson (2000) *Vital Signs: Nature, Culture, Psychoanalysis*. London: Routledge.

R. Shweder (1979a) 'Rethinking culture and personality theory part I: a critical examination of two classical postulates', *Ethos* 7(3): 255–78.

R. Shweder (1979b) 'Rethinking culture and personality theory part II: a critical examination of two more classical postulates', *Ethos* 7(4): 279–311.

R. Shweder (1980) 'Rethinking culture and personality theory part III: from genesis and typology to hermeneutics and dynamics', *Ethos* 8(1): 60–94.

R. Shweder (1991) *Thinking Through Cultures*. Harvard: Harvard University Press.

R. Shweder and E. Bourne (1984) 'Does the concept of the person vary cross-culturally?', in R. Shweder and R. Levine (eds.), *Culture Theory*. Cambridge: Cambridge University Press.

E. Silverman (2001) *Masculinity, Motherhood and Mockery: Psychoanalyzing Culture and the Iatmul Naven Rite in New Guinea*. Ann Arbor: University of Michigan Press.

K. Silverman (1992) *Male Subjectivity at the Margins*. London: Routledge.

P. Smith (1988) *Discerning the Subject*. Minneapolis: University of Minnesota Press.

C. Socarides (1973) 'Sexual perversion and the fear of engulfment', *International Journal of Psychoanalysis and Psychotherapy* 2: 433–49.

M. Sökefeld (1999) 'Debating self, identity and culture in anthropology', *Current Anthropology* 40(4): 417–47.

D. Spain (1992) 'Oedipus rex or edifice wrecked? Some comments on the universality of oedipality and on the cultural limitations of Freud's thought', in D. Spain (ed.), *Psychoanalytic Anthropology after Freud*. New York: Psyche Press.

M. Spiro (1982a) *Oedipus in the Trobriands*. Chicago: University of Chicago Press.

M. Spiro (1982b) 'Collective representations and mental representations in religious symbol systems', in J. Maquet (ed.), *On Symbols in Anthropology*. Malibu: Undena Publications.

M. Spiro (1987) *Culture and Human Nature*. Chicago: Chicago University Press.

M. Spiro (1992) 'Oedipus redux', *Ethos* 20(3): 358–76.

M. Spiro (1993) 'Is the Western concept of the self "peculiar" within the context of world cultures?', *Ethos* 21(2): 107–53.

M. Stanek (1983) 'Les travestis rituels des Iatmul', in F. Lupu (ed.), *Océanie: Le Masque au Long Cours*. Paris: Ouest-France.

D. Stanton (1989) 'Difference on trial: a critique of the maternal metaphor in Cixous, Irigaray, and Kristeva', in Allen and Young (eds.), *The Thinking Muse: Feminism and Modern French Philosophy*. Bloomington: Indiana University Press.

M. Stephen (1995) *A'isa's Gifts: A Study of Magic and the Self*. Berkeley: University of California Press.

W. Stephens (1962) *The Oedipus Complex: Cross-cultural Evidence*. New York: The Free Press of Glencoe.

P. Stephenson (1989) 'Going to McDonald's in Leiden: reflections on the concept of self and society in the Netherlands', *Ethos* 17: 226–47.

R. Stoller (1966) 'The mother's contribution to infantile transvestic behavior', *International Journal of Psychoanalysis* 47: 384–95.

R. Stoller (1968) 'A further contribution to the study of gender identity', *International Journal of Psychoanalysis* 49: 364–8.

R. Stoller (1974) 'Symbiosis anxiety and the development of masculinity', *Archives of General Psychiatry* 30: 164–72.

R. Stoller (1985) *Observing the Erotic Imagination*. New Haven: Yale University Press.

R. Stoller and G. Herdt (1982) 'The development of masculinity: a cross-cultural contribution', *Journal of the American Psychoanalytic Association* 30: 29–59.

M. Strathern (1988) *The Gender of the Gift: Problems with Women and Problems with Society in Melanesia*. Berkeley: University of California Press.

M. Strathern (1991) *Partial Connections*. Savage, Md.: Rowman and Littlefield.

M. Strathern (1992) *After Nature: English Kinship in the Late Twentieth Century*. Cambridge: Cambridge University Press.

M. Strathern (2005) *Kinship, Law and the Unexpected: Relatives are Always a Surprise*. Cambridge: Cambridge University Press.

M. Taussig (1999) *Defacement: Public Secrecy and the Labor of the Negative*. Stanford: Stanford University Press.

C. Toren (1983) 'Thinking symbols: a critique of Sperber', *Man* 19(2): 260–8.

C. Toren (1990) *Making Sense of Hierarchy*. London: Athlone Press.

C. Toren (1999) *Mind, Materiality and History: Explorations in Fijian Ethnography*. London: Routledge.

M. Trawick (1990) *Notes on Love in a Tamil Family*. Berkeley: University of California Press.

M. Trawick (1992) 'Desire in kinship: a Lacanian view of the South Indian familial self', in D. Spain (ed.), *Psychoanalytic Anthropology after Freud*. New York: Psyche Press.

V. Turner (1967) *The Forest of Symbols: Aspects of Ndembu Ritual*. Ithaca, NY: Cornell University Press.

V. Turner (1974) *Dramas, Fields and Metaphors: Symbolic Action in Human Society*. Ithaca: Cornell University Press.

D. Tuzin (1972) 'Yam symbolism in the Sepik: an interpretative account', *Southwestern Journal of Anthropology* 28(3): 230–54.

D. Tuzin (1976) *The Ilahita Arapesh: Dimensions of Unity*. Berkeley: University of California Press.

D. Tuzin (1980) *The Voice of the Tambaran: Truth and Illusion in Ilahita Arapesh Religion*. Berkeley: University of California Press.

D. Tuzin (1982) 'Ritual violence among the Ilahita Arapesh: the dynamics of moral and religious uncertainty', in G. Herdt and R. Keesing (eds.), *Rituals of Manhood: Male Initiation in Papua New Guinea*. Berkeley: University of California Press.

D. Tuzin (1991) 'The cryptic brotherhood of big men and great men in Ilahita', in M. Godelier and M. Strathern (eds.), *Big Man and Great Men: Personifications of Power in Melanesia*. Cambridge: Cambridge University Press.

D. Tuzin (1992) 'Sago subsistence and symbolism among the Ilahita Arapesh', *Ethnology* 31(2): 103–14.

D. Tuzin (1995) 'Art and procreative illusion in the Sepik: comparing the Abelam and the Arapesh', *Oceania* 65(4): 289–303.

D. Tuzin (1997) *The Cassowary's Revenge: The Life and Death of Masculinity in a New Guinea Society*. Chicago: University of Chicago Press.

R. Wagner (1991) 'The fractal person', in M. Godelier and M. Strathern (eds.), *Big Men and Great Men: Personifications of Power in Melanesia*. Cambridge: Cambridge University Press.

A. Wallace (1961) *Culture and Personality*. New York: Random House.

E. Wallace (1983) *Freud and Anthropology: A History and Reappraisal*. New York: International Universities Press.

J. Walton (1995) 'Re-placing race in (white) psychoanalytic discourse: founding narratives of feminism', *Critical Enquiry* 21(4): 775–804.

M. Warner (ed.) (1993) *Fear of a Queer Planet: Queer Politics and Social Theory*. Minnesota: University of Minnesota Press.

M. Warner (1999) *The Trouble with Normal: Sex, Politics, and the Ethics of Queer Life*. New York: Free Press.

J. Watson (1983) *Tairora Culture: Contingency and Pragmatism*. Seattle: University of Washington Press.

J. Weiner (1995) *The Lost Drum: The Myth of Sexuality in Papua New Guinea and Beyond*. Madison: University of Wisconsin Press.

F. Weiss (1987a) 'Kinembe', in F. Morgenthaler, F. Weiss and M. Morgenthaler (eds.), *Conversations au bord du Fleuve Mourant: Ethnopsychanalyse chez les Iatmul de Papouasie/Nouvelle Guinée*. Carouge-Genève: Éditions Zoé.

F. Weiss (1987b) 'Magendaua', in F. Morgenthaler, F. Weiss and M. Morgenthaler (eds.), *Conversations au bord du Fleuve Mourant: Ethnopsychanalyse chez les Iatmul de Papouasie/Nouvelle Guinée*. Carouge-Genève: Éditions Zoé.

W. Welmers (1949) 'Secret medicines, magic, and the rites of the Kpelle tribe in Liberia', *Southwestern Journal of Anthropology* 5: 208–43.

D. West (1967) *Homosexuality*. Chicago: Aldine.

G. M. White (1985) 'Premises and purposes in a Solomon Islands ethnopsychology', in G. M. White and J. Kirkpatrick (eds.), *Person, Self and Experience: Exploring Pacific Ethnopsychologies*. Berkeley: University of California Press.

G. M. White (1991) *Identity through History: Living Stories in a Solomon Islands Society*. Cambridge: Cambridge University Press.

G. M. White (1992) 'Ethnopsychology', in T. Schwartz, G. White and C. Lutz (eds.), *New Directions in Psychological Anthropology*. Cambridge: Cambridge University Press.

G. M. White and J. Kirkpatrick (eds.) (1985) *Person, Self and Experience: Exploring Pacific Ethnopsychologies*. Berkeley: University of California Press.

H. Whitehead (1981) 'The bow and the burden strap: a new look at institutionalized homosexuality in Native North America', in S. Ortner and H. Whitehead (eds.), *Sexual Meanings: The Cultural Construction of Gender and Sexuality*. Cambridge: Cambridge University Press.

J. Whiting (1941) *Becoming a Kwoma. Teaching and Learning in a New Guinea Tribe*. New Haven: Yale University Press.

J. Whiting (1960) 'Resource, mediation and learning by identification', in I. Iscoe and M. Stevenson (eds.), *Personality Development in Children*. Austin: University of Texas Press.

J. Whiting and I. Child (1953) *Child Training and Personality*. New Haven: Yale University Press.

J. Whiting and B. Whiting (1975) 'Aloofness and intimacy of husbands and wives', *Ethos* 3: 183–207.

J. Whiting, R. Kluckhohn and A. Anthony (1958) 'The function of male initiation ceremonies at puberty', in E. Maccoby, T. Newcomb and E. Hartley (eds.), *Readings in Social Psychology*. Third edition. New York: Holt, Rinehart and Winston.

U. Wikan (1977) 'Man becomes woman: transsexualism in Oman as a key to gender roles', *Man* 12(2): 304–19.

W. Williams (1986) *The Spirit and the Flesh: Sexual Diversity in American Indian Culture*. Boston: Beacon Press.

D. W. Winnicott (1965) *The Maturational Processes and the Facilitating Environment*. New York: International Universities Press.

S. Yanagisako and J. Collier (1987) 'Toward a unified analysis of gender and kinship', in J. Collier and S. Yanagisako (eds.), *Gender and Kinship: Essays Toward a Unified Analysis*. Stanford: Stanford University Press.

F. Young (1965) *Initiation Ceremonies: A Cross-Cultural Study of Status Dramatization*. Indianapolis, IN: Bobbs-Merrill.

A. Zempleni and J. Rabain (1965) 'L'enfant *nit ku bon*, un tableau psychopathologique traditionnel chez les Wolof et les Lebou du Senegal', *Psychopathologie Africaine* 1(3): 329–441.

M. Zinn and B. Dill (1996) 'Theorizing difference from multiracial feminism', *Feminist Studies* 22(2): 321–31.

S. Žižek (1989) *The Sublime Object of Ideology*. London: Verso.

Index